GREAT BASIN NATURALIST MEMOIRS

BIRDS OF UTAH

BURCH

Library of Congress Catalog Card Number: 76-55878
International Standard Book Number: 0-8425-0663-2
© 1976 by Brigham Young University Press. All rights reserved
Brigham Young University Press, Provo, Utah 84602
Printed in the United States of America
12-76 3M   19790

GREAT BASIN NATURALIST MEMOIRS

Number 1   Brigham Young University   1976

BIRDS OF UTAH

C. Lynn Hayward
Clarence Cottam
Angus M. Woodbury
Herbert H. Frost

Photographs by
Richard Porter and Robert J. Erwin

CONTENTS

Birds of Utah

No. 1   Brigham Young University, Provo, Utah   1976

C. Lynn Hayward,[1] Clarence Cottam,[2] Angus M. Woodbury,[3] and Herbert H. Frost[4]
Photographs by Richard D. Porter[5] and Robert J. Erwin[6]

PREFACE

Prior to 1926 very little intensified work on the birds of Utah had been done by local students of ornithology. Several lists of Utah birds had been published earlier, including those of Baird (1852), Merriam (1873), Henshaw (1874), and Ridgway (1877). Cottam (1927) for a master's thesis at Brigham Young University compiled a list of Utah birds based on a search of published records up to that time and on considerable fieldwork of his own. Behle (1944) produced a check-list of Utah birds.

Beginning about 1930 Angus M. Woodbury, of the University of Utah, Clarence Cottam, then of the U.S. Fish and Wildlife Service, and John W. Sugden undertook a comprehensive work on Utah birds. This included a search of the literature, a visit to most of the museums containing Utah birds, and considerable fieldwork. An extensive treatment of ornithological work in Utah and an account of the species including all collection records, nesting records, and sight records known to the writers constituted the major part of the manuscript. A brief description of each species, a treatment of the natural history of each species,

a key to the birds of the state, and an extensive bibliography were also included.

The result of this work was a massive manuscript of some 1,200 typewritten pages, some of it single-spaced. This manuscript was completed about 1948 or 1949, but it appears that there was little search of the literature after 1945. Means for publication were not forthcoming when the manuscript was completed, and, owing in part to the accidental death of Woodbury, the work was not published. When it became evident that there was no way of publishing the account after its completion, Woodbury, Cottam, and Sugden determined to produce a check-list based on the larger manuscript (Woodbury, Cottam, and Sugden 1949).

In 1968 Cottam, then director of the Welder Wildlife Foundation near Sinton, Texas, invited me to join him in an attempt to revive the manuscript and prepare it for publication under the authorship of Hayward, Cottam, and Woodbury. Herbert H. Frost was later added as one of the authors as a result of the considerable work he had done on a bibliography of Utah ornithology.

The question then arose as to how the

[1]Professor Emeritus of Zoology, Brigham Young University, Provo, Utah 84602.
[2]Former Director of the Rob and Bessy Welder Wildlife Foundation, Sinton, Texas. Deceased.
[3]Professor of Zoology, University of Utah, Salt Lake City, Utah. Deceased.
[4]Professor of Zoology, Brigham Young University, Provo, Utah 84602.
[5]Research Biologist, U.S. Fish and Wildlife Service, Provo, Utah 84601.
[6]892 East 3250 North, North Ogden, Utah 84404.

manuscript could be revised to make it of value and yet be reduced to reasonable size for publication. Since the completion date of the original work, a great amount of fieldwork has been done in the state, particularly by personnel of the University of Utah and Brigham Young University. A number of important works have also been published recently. Were all these new data to be added to the original format of the manuscript, the size would have been at least doubled. It was determined, therefore, that the following plan would be followed: (1) The section of the original paper dealing with the history of ornithology in Utah and other general matters has been retained complete with a few revisions and additions; (2) descriptions of the species and subspecies, as well as identification keys, have been omitted; (3) most of the references to the early collections and writings of Ridgway, Henshaw, and others were retained inasmuch as these older references are less accessible to many students; (4) the general status including relative abundance and habitat preference of each species is indicated; (5) in the case of unusual or rare species found in the state, all records pertaining to them known to us are included. In certain instances a few records of the more common species are included where it seems desirable to indicate their widespread occurrence in the state. Every effort has been made to consult all the literature on Utah birds to date, but only the references cited in the text are included in this work.

While the original manuscript was freely used and consulted, the present work is essentially an account of the history of ornithology in Utah, an up-to-date checklist and reference list, and a more extensive annotation of each species than usually appears in check-lists.

The unfortunate and untimely passing of Clarence Cottam, 30 March 1974, left a great void in the authorship of this publication. However, prior to his death he had critically examined and approved the entire manuscript except for the final revision.

C. Lynn Hayward

LIST OF FIGURES

19. Spotted Sandpiper. Pigeon Lake, Bayfield County, Wisconsin, no date. Photo by R. D. Porter.
20. Black-necked Stilt. Ogden Bay, Weber County, Utah, spring 1953. Photo by R. D. Porter and R. J. Erwin.
21. Black-necked Stilt. Ogden Bay, Weber County, Utah, spring 1953. Photo by R. D. Porter and R. J. Erwin.
22. Wilson's Phalarope. Ogden Bay, Weber County, Utah, 20 June 1961. Photo by R. J. Erwin.
23. Black Tern. Rochester, Monroe County, New York, 11 July 1967. Photo by R. J. Erwin.
24. American Kestrel. Ogden, Weber County, Utah, 27 February 1973. Photo by R. J. Erwin.
25. American Avocet. Willard Bay, Box Elder County, Utah, 6 May 1973. Photo by R. J. Erwin.
26. Mourning Dove. Tremonton, Box Elder County, Utah, 30 June 1974. Photo by R. J. Erwin.
27. Barn Owl. Ogden, Weber County, Utah, 8 August 1973. Photo by R. J. Erwin.
28. Barn Owl. Ogden, Weber County, Utah, 8 August 1973. Photo by R. J. Erwin.
29. Long-eared Owl. Promontory, Box Elder County, Utah, 30 June 1969. Photo by R. J. Erwin.
30. Long-eared Owl (young). Hogup Mountains, Box Elder County, Utah, 25 June 1974. Photo by R. J. Erwin.
31. Burrowing Owl. Ogden, Weber County, Utah, 8 August 1973. Photo by R. J. Erwin.
32. Short-eared Owl. Dugway, Tooele County, Utah, 23 March 1953. Photo by R. D. Porter.
33. Saw-whet Owl. Weber River bottoms, Weber County, Utah, 1948. Photo by R. D. Porter and R. J. Erwin.
34. Saw-whet Owl (young). Weber River bottoms, Weber County, Utah, April 1948. Photo by R. D. Porter.
35. Horned Lark. Hogup Mountains, Box Elder County, Utah, 11 June 1972. Photo by R. J. Erwin.
36. Willow Flycatcher. Blacksmith Fork, Cache County, Utah, 18 July 1954. Photo by R. D. Porter and R. J. Erwin.
37. Tree Swallow. Blacksmith Fork, Cache County, Utah, 17 July 1954. Photo by R. D. Porter and R. J. Erwin.
38. Cliff Swallow. West Weber, Weber County, Utah, 15 July 1954. Photo by R. J. Erwin.
39. Loggerhead Shrike. Dugway Valley, Tooele County, Utah, May 1953. Photo by R. D. Porter and R. J. Erwin.
40. Rock Wren. Big Bend National Park, Brewster County, Texas, May 1958. Photo by R. D. Porter and R. J. Erwin.
41. House Wren. North Fork Ogden River, Weber County, Utah, 11 June 1954. Photo by R. J. Erwin.
42. Mockingbird. Cedar Mountains, Tooele County, Utah, 19 June 1953. Photo by R. D. Porter and R. J. Erwin.
43. Hermit Thrush. Monte Cristo, Rich County, Utah, 15 June 1959. Photo by R. J. Erwin.
44. Mountain Bluebird. Blacksmith Fork, Cache County, Utah, 18 July 1954. Photo by R. D. Porter and R. J. Erwin.
45. Blue-gray Gnatcatcher. Cedar Mountains, Tooele County, Utah, 18 June 1953. Photo by R. D. Porter and R. J. Erwin.
46. Blue-gray Gnatcatcher. Cedar Mountains, Tooele County, Utah, 18 June 1953. Photo by R. D. Porter and R. J. Erwin.
47. Black-capped Chickadee. Rochester, Monroe County, New York, 16 October 1968. Photo by R. J. Erwin.
48. White-crowned Sparrow. Monte Cristo, Rich County, Utah, 14 July 1973. Photo by R. J. Erwin.
49. Brewer's Sparrow. Vernon, Tooele County, Utah, 2 June 1954. Photo by R. D. Porter and R. J. Erwin.
50. Black-throated Sparrow. Camel Back Mountain, Tooele County, Utah, no date. Photo by R. D. Porter.
51. Black-throated Sparrow. Camel Back Mountain, Tooele County, Utah, 12 June 1954. Photo by R. D. Porter.
52. Sage Sparrow. Rush Valley, Tooele County, Utah, 31 May 1954. Photo by R. D. Porter and R. J. Erwin.
53. Sage Sparrow. Rush Valley, Tooele County, Utah, 31 May 1954. Photo by R. D. Porter and R. J. Erwin.
54. Long-billed Marsh Wren. Ogden Bay, Weber County, Utah, 1 July 1969. Photo by R. J. Erwin.
55. Dark-eyed Junco. Monte Cristo, Rich County, Utah, 27 June 1973. Photo by R. J. Erwin.
56. Chipping Sparrow. North Fork Ogden River, Weber County, Utah, 30 June 1930. Photo by R. J. Erwin.

57. Yellow Warbler. Rochester, Monroe County, New York, 9 July 1967. Photo by R. J. Erwin.
58. Yellow-rumped Warbler. Monte Cristo, Rich County, Utah, 7 July 1973. Photo by R. J. Erwin.
59. Solitary Vireo. North Fork Ogden River, Weber County, Utah, 8 July 1956. Photo by R. J. Erwin.
60. Warbling Vireo. Snow Basin, Weber County, Utah, 30 June 1959. Photo by R. J. Erwin.
61. Northern Oriole. Ogden, Weber County, Utah, 18 June 1973. Photo by R. J. Erwin.
62. Brewer's Blackbird. Tremonton, Box Elder County, Utah, 9 June 1974. Photo by R. J. Erwin.
63. House Finch. Cedar Mountain, Tooele County, Utah, 30 June 1953. Photo by R. D. Porter and R. J. Erwin.
64. Gray Jay. Paradise Park, Uinta Mountains, Uintah County, Utah, 30 July 1953. Photo by R. J. Erwin.
65. Scrub Jay. Ogden, Weber County, Utah, 10 May 1959. Photo by R. J. Erwin.

INTRODUCTION

Because of their widespread popular as well as scientific interest throughout the world, birds are the best known group of animals. It is unlikely that there is any species living in North America that has not been identified and named, and there are few kinds even in the remote areas of the world that have not been discovered. With a few exceptions, the numerous species of birds are rather easily distinguished from one another; and one could assume that their classification might have long since become well stabilized. However, more recent taxonomic studies using some of the newer behavioral, physiological, ecological, genetical, and biochemical techniques, as well as the older morphological approach, have resulted in some rather drastic changes in classification of birds. On the subspecies level there has been a tendency by recent workers to eliminate or combine some of the named races in polytypic species, especially among the passerine birds. In the complex sparrowlike and finchlike species a number of the kinds formerly recognized as being in separate genera have been combined into fewer genera. The phylogenetic arrangement of the several families, particularly in the passerine birds, has been considerably altered by several workers.

The phylogenetic arrangement of the orders and families as an indication of their evolutionary relationships is still not well understood, due in part to the relative scarcity of fossil material. As a result, there appears to be no standard and universally accepted classification system for birds at the present time. In preparing this list of birds, we are, therefore, faced with the need of making some arbitrary decisions as to the phylogenetic arrangement and nomenclature to be used. Some of the more recent and comprehensive treatments of phylogeny and classification of birds are as follows: Peters, Check-list of Birds of the World, Vols. 9 (1960), 10 (1964), 12 (1967), 13 (1970), 14 (1968), 15 (1962); Wetmore (1960), A Classification for the Birds of the World, Smithsonian Misc. Coll., 139(11):1–37; Mayr and Short (1970), Species Taxa of North American Birds, Publ. of the Nuttall Ornith. Club, No. 9:1–322; Storer (1971), Classification of Birds *in* Avian Biology, Farner, King, and Parkes, eds., Academic Press, New York; Cracraft (1972), The Relationships of the Higher Taxa of Birds, Condor 74(4):379–392; AOU Committee on Classification and Nomenclature (1973), Thirty-second supplement of the AOU Check-list of North American Birds, Auk 90(2):411–419.

In the present treatment of Utah birds, the authors have followed, in the main, the arrangement of orders and families and nomenclature of the 1957 (5th) edition of the AOU Check-list of North American Birds and its thirty-second supplement (1973) for the orders up to and including the Piciformes, as well as certain families not yet treated in the series of Peters, Check-list of Birds of the World. For the remaining families (essentially the Passeriformes) Peters, Check-list of Birds of the World, Vols.

9(1960), 10(1964), 12(1967), 13(1970), 14 (1968), and 15(1962), is followed with a few exceptions.

In the discussion of each species the statement on status includes the relative abundance, general seasonal occurrence, and preferred habitat. Under the subtitle of records reference is made to some of the early records. In the case of uncommon species all acceptable references known to us are included. No attempt is made to include all the known records of the more common speices, although most of the early records are cited and a limited number of more recent records are included to indicate the extent of their occurrence in the state. In the case of polytypic species, where only one subspecies is known to occur in the state, the entire trinomen is given. Where two or more subspecies are known to occur in Utah, only the binomen is given in the heading, and the subspecific status is discussed in a separate paragraph.

For the most part, the list of species in the main body of the text is based on the actual collection of specimens within the boundaries of the state. A few species are included based on sight records that are, in the judgment of the authors, well authenticated by photographs or repeated observations by competent ornithologists.

Division of labor among the authors has been as follows: Woodbury wrote most of the original manuscript upon which the present paper is based. Cottam assisted materially through his own knowledge of Utah birds and through his search for specimens in several museums and records from the literature. Hayward searched the more recent literature and was responsible for writing most of the present text. Frost assisted with the literature search, revised the literature list, and checked the references to the literature.

ACKNOWLEDGMENTS

The writers wish to express appreciation to the numerous individuals and organizations that have assisted us over the many years of preparation of this work.

Financial support for the final typing and publication was obtained through the generosity of the following: Division of Research, Brigham Young University, Leo P. Vernon, Director; State of Utah Division of Wildlife Resources, John E. Phelps, Director; members of the family of the late Clarence Cottam: Mrs. Ivan L. (Glenna) Sanderson, Mrs. Margery Osborne, Mrs. Douglas (Josephine) Day, and Mrs. Dwayne (Caroline) Stevenson; College of Biological and Agricultural Sciences, Brigham Young University, A. Lester Allen, Dean; Mt. Timpanogos Chapter, National Audubon Society, Merrill Webb, President; Utah Audubon Society, National Audubon Society, Durrell H. McGarry, President.

We also extend our thanks to Dr. Wilmer W. Tanner, Director of the Life Sciences Museum, Brigham Young University, who has generously placed the facilities of the museum at our disposal and aided in obtaining financial support. Dr. William H. Behle of the University of Utah has been most liberal in furnishing information regarding certain records from his own experience and files.

HISTORICAL

Perhaps the first white persons to make observations on the birds of Utah were members of the Domínguez[7] and Vélez de Escalante party who visited Utah Valley and other parts of the state in September 1776. Members of the party were more interested in converting the resident Indians to Christianity than in studying birds but Fathers Domínguez and Vélez de Escalante did

---

[7]Fray Francisco Atanasio Domínguez was the leader of the party and the senior author of the report, but he fell into ecclesiastical disfavor and all credit for the expedition was given to his junior companion by the church and subsequent historians until recently (Warner 1975).

mention that Utah Lake abounded in geese and other waterfowl. In commenting on the situation Domínguez and Vélez de Escalante (Auerbach 1943:70) state: "The Timpanogotzis (Utah Lake) is teeming with several kinds of edible fish in addition to geese, beaver and other land and water animals which we did not see." They also speak of "wild hens" being abundant and being used as food by the Indians. Other writers have translated this to mean "sage-hens" (Philip Harry in Simpson 1876:492). Domínguez and Vélez de Escalante also mentioned seeing nests of Cliff Swallows in what is now Spanish Fork Canyon.

The next explorer to leave a record of Utah bird life was Captain John C. Fremont (1845) who visited the Great Salt Lake area on his second trip to the West in the summer of 1843. Fremont visited the lake at the mouth of Bear River and the mouth of Weber River and commented particularly on the abundance of waterfowl (p. 149):

> The water fowl made this morning a noise like thunder. A pelican (*Pelecanus onocrotalus*) was killed as he passed by, and many geese and ducks flew over the camp. . . . The whole morass was animated with multitudes of water fowl, which appeared to be very wild — rising for the space of a mile around about at the sound of a gun, with a noise like distant thunder. Several of the people waded out into the marshes, and we had tonight a delicious supper of ducks, geese, and plover.

The presence of gulls in the area is attested to by Fremont's statement, that on 12 September (p. 158) "we had tonight a supper of sea gulls, which Carson killed near the lake."

Captain Howard Stansbury (1852), under the direction of the War Department, conducted an expedition to Salt Lake Valley for the purpose of making explorations of the lake and surrounding areas. He arrived in the valley 28 August 1849 and remained exactly a year. His report (1852) contains a number of references to the birds. From Promontory Point on 22 October 1849 he made the following observation of the bird life of Bear River Bay (p.100):

> The Salt Lake, which lay about half a mile to the eastward, was covered by immense flocks of wild geese and ducks, among which many swans were seen, being distinguished by their size and the whiteness of their plumage. I had seen large flocks of these birds before, in various parts of our country, and especially on the Potomac, but never did I behold anything like the immense numbers here congregated together. Thousands of acres, as far as the eye could reach, seemed literally covered with them, presenting a scene of busy, animated cheerfulness, in most graceful contrast with the dreary, silent solitude by which we were immediately surrounded.

Visits were made by Stansbury and his party to several of the islands in Great Salt Lake in the spring of 1850. His accounts of some of these visits are as follows (p. 161):

> Rounding the northern point of Antelope Island, we came to a small rocky islet, about a mile west of it, which was destitute of vegetation of any kind, not even a blade of grass being found upon it. It was literally covered with wild waterfowl; ducks, white brandt, blue herons, cormorants, and innumerable flocks of gulls, which had congregated here to build their nests. We found great numbers of these, built of sticks and rushes, in the crevices of the rock, and supplied ourselves, without scruple, with as many eggs as we needed, principally those of the herons, it being too early in the season for most of the other waterfowl.

On 8 May Stansbury visited Gunnison Island and described the gull and the pelican colonies (p. 179):

> The whole neck and the shores on both of the little bays were occupied by immense flocks of pelicans and gulls, disturbed now for the first time, probably, by the intrusion of man. They literally darkened the air as they rose upon the wing, and, hovering over our heads, caused the surrounding rocks to re-echo with their discordant screams. The ground was thickly strewn with their nests, of which there must have been some thousands. Numerous young, unfledged pelicans, were found in the nests on the ground, and hundreds of half-grown, huddled together in groups near the water, while the old ones retired to a long line of sand-beach on the southern side of the bay, where they stood drawn up, like Prussian soldiers, in ranks three or four deep, for hours together, apparently without motion.

A full-grown one was surprised and captured by the men, just as he was rising from the ground, and hurried in triumph to the beach. He was very indignant at the unceremonious manner in which he was treated, and snapped furiously with his long bill to the right and left at everybody that came near him. On the top of his bill, about midway of its length, was a projection about an inch long and half an inch high, resembling the old-fashioned sight of a rifle; in the female this is wanting. We collected as many eggs as we could carry. That of the gull is of the size of a hen's egg, brown and spotted; that of the pelican is white, and about as large as a goose egg. The white of the latter, when cooked, is translucent,. and resembles clear *blancmange.*

During the year of their stay in the Salt Lake area, Stansbury's party obtained specimens of 31 species of birds. These specimens were later studied by Spencer F. Baird, and he reported upon them in Appendix C of Stansbury's report (1852).

The year after Stanbury's report appeared, Congress provided for a number of expeditions to discover practical routes for establishing a railroad across the United States. One of these routes crossed Utah and was explored during the summer and fall of 1853 by a party of 30 men commanded by Captain J. W. Gunnison. Mr. F. Kreuzfeldt was the naturalist of the party. In Utah the party entered the Grand River Valley and crossed Green River near the present town of Green River, Utah. They passed through Salina Canyon and arrived on the Sevier River 17 October 1853. A short time later Gunnison and Kreuzfeldt were killed by Indians. The remainder of the party, under the command of Lieutenant E. G. Beckwith, traveled to Salt Lake City where they spent the winter. Of some 25 species of birds collected by this expedition, 11 were probably taken in Utah. The birds of this and other railroad survey expeditions were examined and reported by S. F. Baird (1854, 1858).

Two French scientists, Jules Remy and Julius Brenchley, visited Utah in 1855 primarily to study the Mormons. They made observations on birds but apparently made no collections. Remy (1860) published in Paris a two-volume report of the trip, and the following year an English translation was published in London by Remy and Brenchley (1861). In both editions a list of 28 birds found in Utah is given.

The U.S. government's "Johnston's Army" (sent to Utah over a misunderstanding with the Mormons) entered Salt Lake Valley 26 June 1858 and later established Camp Floyd near the present town of Fairfield, Utah County. This camp was maintained until 1861 at the outbreak of the Civil War. During the Camp Floyd period Captain J. H. Simpson conducted several exploring trips into adjacent areas. During the most important of these expeditions (1859), he was accompanied by Henry Engelmann who served as geologist, meteorologist, and botanist, and Charles McCarthy, a taxidermist who collected birds and mammals. On one trip the party passed westward from Camp Floyd through Rush and Skull valleys, past Fish Springs and across Nevada to the foot of the Sierra Nevada Mountains. They returned over a more southerly route via the north end of Sevier Lake Valley. McCarthy's collections appear to have included not only those of this expedition (partly from Nevada) but also a good many specimens, mostly water birds from Utah Lake and from a pond near Camp Floyd formed by a large spring in the desert. His collections were identified and reported by S. F. Baird (1876). There were 258 specimens of 114 species included in the list. At that time the Territory of Utah extended further east and west than the present confines of Utah; thus some localities indicated as "Utah" are in present-day Wyoming and Nevada. Thirty-four species appear to have been collected in Utah, although some of the locations are not definitely given and cannot be accurately determined.

Little or no ornithological work was done during the Civil War, but during the reconstruction period following, Congress

(2 March 1867 and 3 March 1869) authorized the U.S. Army to make geological explorations of the West along the 40th parallel. This exploration party conducted by Clarence King included Robert Ridgway, zoologist, who, as a specialist trained in ornithology, made the first intensive collection of bird skins, nests, and eggs from the Great Basin. The expedition coming from the Pacific coast in 1867 crossed California and Nevada, reaching the Deep Creek Mountains in Utah in October 1868. After suspending activities for the winter, the expedition resumed collections in Utah 20 May 1869 and continued at Salt Lake City, Parley's Park, the west end of Uinta Mountains, Provo Canyon, and Utah Lake until 16 August. The collections of the expedition deposited in the U.S. National Museum of Natural History (formerly U.S. National Museum) included 769 skins and 753 nests and eggs, mainly from the Great Basin in Utah and Nevada. Ridgway (1873a) listed 107 species from near Salt Lake City, 116 species from Parley's Park, 6 from Deep Creek, 23 from Antelope Island, 3 from Carrington and Hat Islands, and 9 from Provo River. This report seems to be the first record of birds on Hat (Bird) Island. His total from the Great Basin reached 238 species.

In the East, the widespread interest in the specimens beginning to pour in about this time from the zoologically poorly known West stimulated an expedition from the Museum of Comparative Zoology, Harvard University, to investigate the Great Plains and the Rocky Mountains. This expedition, under the leadership of J. A. Allen, with C. W. Bennett as taxidermist and Richard Bliss as ichthyologist, crossed the plains in the spring of 1871, passed through the mountains, and reached the Great Salt Lake by fall. They collected along the east side of the lake, especially around Ogden from 1 September to 8 October 1871, covering the valley lands from Salt Lake to Ogden, Ogden Canyon, and the mountains to the northeast.

The list of birds collected or observed by the Allen party totaled 137 species and included 3 species reported to have been recently introduced: the English Sparrow, the California Quail, and the Eastern Bobwhite, the latter being the only one that failed to survive (Allen 1872a, 1872b). In the report the great variety of environmental conditions, such as marshes, flat valley lands, abruptly rising mountains, and alpine summits, was offered to account for the rich avian fauna. An increase in the small seed-eating, insectivorous, and fruit-eating birds was accounted for by the settlers' activity in transforming arid plains into farms with orchards and shade trees.

In the early 1870s the federal government paid considerable attention to explorations of the West. As early as 1867 Congress authorized the Interior Department to undertake a geological survey of the territories. Reports of the first two years' activities were made by the commissioner of the General Land Office, but thereafter they were directed by F. V. Hayden, United States geologist.

In 1870 the work was centered in Wyoming and northeastern Utah, and by 1872 it had moved westward to include northern Utah and portions of Idaho and Montana. It was the intention that "collections in all departments should be as complete as possible." Biologists accompanying the parties gathered specimens in several different fields.

The party in Wyoming in 1870 (August to November) was organized by Hayden and included James Stevenson as managing director, Henry D. Schmidt (Smith) as naturalist, and C. P. Carrington as zoologist, all of whom seem to have helped in the collection of specimens. The area covered by the work included Bear River, Muddy Creek, Black's Fork, Smith's Fork, and Henry's Fork on the north slope of the Uinta Mountains in Utah. In Hayden's report (1872) of work done in 1870, James Stevenson published a list of mammals and birds collected by the expedition. He remarked that it was a meeting ground between eastern and western forms and that it was too late in the season for nests and eggs. The list included 124 species, of which 31 are reported from the area within Utah on the north slope of the Uinta Mountains.

The work of 1872 was handled by two parties. One party, under Hayden's direction, worked southward from Bozeman, Montana, into Yellowstone National Park, which had been established that year. The other party, led by James Stevenson, started at Ogden, Utah, surveyed a route to Fort Hall, Idaho, and then proceeded to explore by pack train the headwaters of the Snake River in Idaho and Wyoming. This party included John M. Coulter as botanist, Campbell Carrington as naturalist, and C. Hart Merriam as ornithologist. During the work in Utah from 5 to 21 June, Merriam collected 120 bird skins and 52 nests with eggs. Merriam (1873) reported on the mammals and birds of the expedition and gave, in addition, a list of 176 species of birds then known from Utah, some of them contributed by Allen, Henshaw, and Ridgway.

Simultaneous with the geological surveys of the Interior Department, Congress authorized the War Department to undertake geographical and geological surveys of the West. This was a very extensive and elaborate scientific investigation under the direction of Captain George M. Wheeler of the U.S. Army. Developing from King's exploratory expedition of 1867–69, the investigation finally became a plan for a complete detailed topographic survey with associated natural history observations of the territory west of the one hundredth meridian. At a cost of $2.5 million, this was to have been the first great general survey during initial stages of settlement.

In 1872 the expedition concentrated on Utah. It was planned for two parties. Dr. H. C. Yarrow and H. W. Henshaw carried on the ornithological work. The parties were organized at Salt Lake City, and while they were assembling, the two ornithologists

moved 50 miles south to Provo on 22 July and plunged into their work during their two weeks' wait for plans to mature.

The routes followed by Yarrow and Henshaw after they left Provo have been described by Behle (1938:170). Yarrow accompanied a party led by Lieutenant Hoxie, who traveled a route westward from Provo through Fairfield and across the Great Basin as far as eastern Nevada. They then went southeastward to Fillmore, Utah, and thence eastward to Panguitch in the valley of the Sevier River. From there the course led southward to the Virgin River and eventually to the town of Toquerville, where they were to meet the other part of the expedition. Henshaw traveled with the party led by Lieutenant Wheeler, who went eastward to Strawberry Valley and then southward to Thistle and Sanpete Valley. The journey continued over Fremont Pass to Parowan and thence southward to Toquerville for a rendezvous with the Lieutenant Hoxie party. Yarrow and Henshaw later explored much of the Virgin River Valley in the vicinity of St. George before returning to Provo where they did additional collecting until the expedition disbanded in December.

Five months of field collecting netted the two collectors about 600 skins of 165 species of birds, including a skin from Iron City in Iron County destined to become the type for one of the races of the Plain Titmouse.

An annotated list of 214 species of birds of Utah, including data furnished by Allen and Ridgway, was read by Henshaw before the Lyceum of Natural History, New York, 6 April 1874 (Henshaw 1874). His list was reprinted the same year with minor modifications as a government publication (Yarrow and Henshaw 1874). This included, in addition, most of the material later incorporated in Henshaw's paper published in the Wheeler report of 1875, Geographical Surveys west of the 100th Meridian.

By a coincidence, while Yarrow and Henshaw were working at Provo in late July

1872, the youthful Edward W. Nelson was making a private collection some ten miles north of Salt Lake City. The enthusiastic youth and a companion, Will Wentworth, earlier in the season had come west from Illinois with Samuel Garman to join E. D. Cope in collecting fossils in Wyoming. While at Fort Bridger Nelson borrowed an old gun from Cope and made a collection of birds from that region (including some from the north slope of the Uinta Mountains in Utah). Owing to a disagreement, Garman parted company with Cope and went on west toward the Pacific coast taking the two boys with him. They stopped over at "Sessions' Settlement" (near Bountiful, Davis County) from 27 July to 8 August. Nelson obtained a second-hand shotgun and continued bird collecting. They covered the prolific area around the mouth of the Jordan River and the valley lands between there and the Wasatch Mountains, gathering specimens and data on 41 species (Nelson 1875).

With all this work concentrated on Utah between the Civil War and 1875, the main outlines of Utah ornithology were fairly well established and most of the national investigations were thereafter directed elsewhere. Only one other expedition of importance was to reach Utah in the period of exploration and that only incidentally as it spread from Death Valley in southwestern Utah, 19 years after Yarrow and Henshaw had been there.

In 1886 and subsequent years, Congress provided for studies of the geographical distribution of animals and later (1890) of plants under the direction of the Department of Agriculture. In 1891 these studies were concentrated in Death Valley and the surrounding region, including an extension into southwestern Utah. During the progress of the work, Dr. C. H. Merriam and Vernon Bailey left the main camp on 24 April 1891 and set out for a trip to southwestern Utah during May and June. They traversed the Virgin River up as far as St. George and Santa Clara, then northward

through the mountains via Diamond Valley, Mountain Meadows, and Shoal Creek to the southwestern end of the Escalante Desert. Mr. Bailey's previous trip through Utah during the winter of 1888–89 had taken him down the Virgin River. He spent the forepart of January at St. George and vicinity, following the Virgin down to the Colorado River in the latter parts of the month. The ornithological results of the Death Valley studies were reported by A. K. Fisher (1893) and covered a list of 290 species which included a large number that extended into Utah.

It seems that C. Hart Merriam and his assistant Vernon Bailey made sporadic collections of birds in Utah Valley on some of their travels through the area. Specimens now in the U.S. National Museum of Natural History were collected at Provo in the fall of 1888. These include the Mountain Chickadee (*Parus gambeli*), Plain Titmouse (*Parus inornatus*), and Winter Wren (*Troglodytes troglodytes*). Bailey also collected a few specimens at Cedar Fort west of Utah Lake in the summer of 1890. Specimens of the Lazuli Bunting (*Passerina amoena*) and the Rufous-sided Towhee (*Pipilo erythrophthalmus*) from that locality are in the U.S. National Museum of Natural History collection. It is entirely possible that Merriam and Bailey made other ornithological collections in Utah Valley, but these workers were more interested in mammals. Consequently, the collection of birds was somewhat incidental.

The arrival of the Mormon pioneers in Utah in the summer of 1847 led to the establishment of permanent white settlements and the eventual development of interests and institutions whereby ornithological work of a local nature could take place. The Mormons themselves, confronted with the grim necessity of obtaining a livelihood from a rather hostile environment, were mainly interested in the economic aspects of ornithology. Soon after their arrival they organized drives to exterminate all kinds of "vermin," both birds

Fig. 1. Double-crested Cormorant. Geneva Steel Plant Dike, Orem, Utah County, Utah, 20 May 1970. Photo courtesy United States Steel Corporation.

and mammals, an indication that these animals were present in noticeable numbers.

An example of one of these drives of extermination is as follows: "Articles of agreement between Captains John D. Lee and John Pack, made this 24th day of December 1848 to carry on a war of *extermination* against all the ravens, hawks, owls, wolves, foxes, etc., now alive in the valley of the Great Salt Lake" (Journal History 24 December 1848).

The agreement provided for a social dinner to be given by the losers and indicated that ". . . the game shall count as follows: the right wing of a raven counting one, a hawk or owl two, the wings of an eagle five, the skin of a mink or pole cat five, the skin of a wolf, fox, wild cat, or catamount ten, the pelt of a bear or panther, fifty" (Journal History 24 December 1848).

The episode of the so-called "sea" gulls and Mormon crickets is the best known of the ornithological events in the early history of the settlements. Judging from the frequent references in diaries and the press from 1848 to 1850, there was a spectacular saving of the crops by the California Gull.

Apparently crickets were numerous in Salt Lake Valley when the pioneers arrived 22–24 July 1847. Orson Pratt's Journal under date of 22 July stated: "We found the drier places swarming with very large crickets about the size of a man's thumb" (Pratt 1926:211).

And William Clayton recorded about the same time: "The ground seemed literally alive with large black crickets crawling around on grass and bushes. They look loathsome but are said to be excellent for fattening hogs which would feed on them voraciously" (Clayton 1921:311).

Presumably in 1847 there was little concern about the crickets and no damage to crops, since the crickets would be on the wane for winter before the first summer and fall plowings could be started into production. In 1848, however, the crops were growing when the crickets hatched in the spring and furnished enticing bait when the insects began to move. The earliest available reference in that year is in Eliza R. Snow's journal of 28 May: "This morning's frost in unison with the ravages of the crickets for a few days past produces many sighs" (Snow 1848).

Isaac C. Haight's diary, 4 June 1848, said: "The crickets have destroyed some crops and are eating the heads of the grain as soon as it heads out" (Haight 1936:56).

Again on 6 July he remarked: "The prospects for crops begin to brighten although some have lost their crops by insects" (Haight 1936:57).

From a letter to Brigham Young, who was in the East, written by John Smith, Charles C. Rich, and John Young in Utah, 9 June 1848, came the following: "The crickets have done considerable damage to both wheat and corn, which has discouraged some, but there is plenty left if we can save it for a few days. The sea gulls have come in large flocks from the lake and sweep the crickets as they go" (Journal History 9 June 1848).

Writing again on 21 June, they informed Brigham Young: "The crickets are still quite numerous and busy eating, but between the gulls, our efforts and the growth of our crops, we shall raise much grain in spite of them. Our vines, beans and peas are mostly destroyed by frost and the crickets; but . . . we will still raise many pumpkins, melons, beans, etc." (Journal History 21 June 1848).

Thomas Callister, writing in retrospect on 13 February 1869 and referring to the "cricket war" in 1848, said:

When the crickets descended upon everything green. [sic] All the nursery trees had been destroyed, and much of the grain, and the inevitable destruction of everything was apparent to all. . . . So dark were the circumstances that the hearts of the strongest Elders were faint. . . . In a very short time after this, the gulls from the Lake made their appearance and devoured the crickets (Journal History 9 June 1848).

Despite all the evidence to the contrary and the corrections in the literature (Goodwin 1904a; V. Bailey 1905), occasional references still indicate the Black-headed Franklin instead of the California Gull as the one involved in saving the Mormon crops. The evidence is clear and definite to the contrary. In response to a query of the origin of the mistaken idea, Vernon Bailey (1905) wrote:

Yes, I know the whole and the history of the report of Franklin's Gull in Utah and am in part responsible for it. In the first edition of Mrs. Bailey's Handbook of Birds, the name *franklini* was edited into the note I gave on the gulls that destroyed the crickets and I did not notice it until the book was out. It was corrected in a later edition, but has been copied and used over and over and will never be eliminated. It was just one of the many editorial blunders that occur and keep reappearing.

We knew Franklin's Gull perfectly at the time and knew that it did not occur in the Salt Lake Valley.[8] The California Gull was the common species there then as it is now.

As has been pointed out, the principal concern with respect to birds and other wildlife of Utah in the early days of settlement centered on the economic aspect of these animals. Local people exhibited little interest in studying them scientifically. Limited studies in natural history arose with the establishment of institutions of higher learning, and over the years these studies have resulted in continual progress.

The University of Deseret, which later became the University of Utah, after a brief prior existence was revived in 1869 with Dr. John R. Park as president. From 1869 to 1874 Park taught natural science work himself, and during this time he initiated some "cabinets" to hold specimens including some bird eggs and skins.

Following Park, Francis Marion Bishop was responsible for natural history work, but it was during the time of Orson Howard, who followed Bishop, that ornithology received considerable emphasis as a part of the natural history curriculum. Howard began his work as a student and by 1884 was teaching zoology and botany. The next year, he was professor of natural science and English literature as well as curator of the museum which had grown from the "cabinets." He left the University in 1890 to obtain an M.D. degree, returning in 1898, after which he was active, particularly in the museum, until his retirement in 1912.

Following the retirement of Howard, there was little interest in ornithology at the university for a period of time. A collection of some 1,500 bird skins and mounted specimens with scientific data were, in the main, lost, or at least they disappeared. At about this time J. H. Paul, who was teaching courses in nature study, had access to the specimens which he used in classwork. The tags containing the data were often removed for convenience in class use.

Ralph V. Chamberlin returned to the university in December 1924, after which biological work was rapidly expanded and specialized. At that time the bird skin collection had reached a low point of about 100 mounted specimens and even fewer study skins. In 1927 a special course in ornithology was initiated by Angus M. Woodbury and continued by him until 1940. In 1931 a research collection of vertebrate specimens was established with Woodbury responsible for the birds and reptiles, and Stephen D. Durrant the mammals. William H. Behle took over the ornithological work in 1940. He and his students have been active since then in building at the university a collection of birds now containing some 25,000 specimens.

Utah State University, formerly Utah State Agricultural College, began the development of a museum soon after its establishment in 1888. Display cases were provided and mounted specimens were installed from time to time. By 1895 the cases contained 25 species of birds and by 1899, 44 species. The president's biennial report for 1901–1902 contained the following statement: "For the zoological museum, a collection of Utah birds, male and female, their nests, eggs, and young, should be commenced at once. Such a collection would grow in value with the years" (Biennial Report 1903:45).

By 1917 the display collection at Utah State had grown to about 100 mounted birds as well as a collection of mammals. When J. Sedley Stanford joined the zoology staff in 1930, the collection contained ap-

---

[8]The Franklin Gull does, of course, occur in Salt Lake Valley and may have occurred then.

proximately 150 mounted birds and 50 study skins. As a result of Dr. Stanford's efforts and those of his students, the collection had increased by 1942 to include about 225 mounted birds and 1,300 study skins. At present (1976) the bird skin collection consists of about 2,000 specimens. Stanford introduced the study of ornithology as a separate course in the summer school of 1939 and instituted it in the regular school year in the spring of 1936. Following the retirement of Dr. Stanford, the work in ornithology at Utah State has been continued by Keith L. Dixon and Gene H. Linford.

In 1903 Brigham Young Academy became Brigham Young University. Prior to that time courses taught in the biological sciences were on a high school level. In 1904–1905 Chester G. Van Buren offered a course in ornithology on a college level. In 1906–1907 courses in ornithology and zoological collecting and taxidermy were taught presumably by Professor Van Buren. Before that time Van Buren had collected birds and other natural history objects in Central and South America and had had some training in taxidermy. Beginning in 1908 a department of biology was established with Dr. Ralph V. Chamberlin as teacher, assisted by Van Buren and others. The biological curriculum was enlarged, but the course in ornithology was apparently discontinued. Van Buren and Chamberlin left about 1911 and the interest in ornithology died.

When I (Hayward) came to Brigham Young University as a student in 1923, there was a small collection of bird skins that, presumably, had been prepared by Van Buren or his students. At that time Walter P. Cottam taught a course called Field Biology which covered local trees, shrubs, spring flowers, and birds. The above mentioned collection was used for teaching purposes. As I recall, the specimens bore little data.

With the arrival of Dr. Vasco M. Tanner on the campus in 1925, the Department of Zoology and Entomology was organized. Soon afterward the building of a bird skin collection was begun. Clarence Cottam was the first student of birds at the institution. He began his work toward a master's degree in 1926 and wrote his thesis on the birds of Utah (Cottam 1927). During the early part of the summer of 1926 a field party led by Dr. Tanner and including Clarence Cottam, Claudeus Brown, and myself, visited parts of northern Utah collecting various natural history objects but principally insects and birds. The following school year I worked considerably with Cottam while he was preparing his thesis; and I became interested in birds, although at that time my chief interest was in entomology. Clarence Cottam remained at the university as a teacher until 1929 when he left to take a position with the U.S. Fish and Wildlife Service in Washington. During his years at the university he continued to collect birds in Utah Valley as well as other parts of the state. However, his thesis was never published. His writings on the birds of the valley were confined to a few short papers.

When I returned to Brigham Young University as a teacher in 1930, my interests were at first primarily in entomology. They soon shifted more toward ornithology and mammalogy and resulted in the building of a collection. With the help of other members of the staff and numerous students, the collection of bird skins at Brigham Young University has grown continuously until at present it contains about 5,500 skins and some 300 mounted specimens. In addition, the university has obtained several large bird-egg collections, including those of R. G. Bee, Ashby Boyle, Merlin J. Killpack, Lloyd Gunther, J. Donald Daynes, and part of the John Hutchings collection.

Another institution of importance in the early history of Utah ornithology was the Deseret Museum, which had its origin in 1869. It was established by John W. Young and Guglielmo Giosue Rosetti Sangiovanni ("Sangio" for short). Following a trip to

Europe, these two men decided they would start a museum and menagerie that would present "Utah at a glance" as a means of showing "tourists what we are doing." John W. Young was proprietor, under the patronage of his father, Brigham Young, and Sangio became curator of the menagerie.

They published requests for specimens from the public, and Sangio was soon busy housing the relics in a two-room adobe house at about 43 East on South Temple in Salt Lake City and building cages and pens outside for the great variety of animals that came pouring in to him. Sangio was principally occupied with the menagerie and paid little attention to the museum.

In May 1871 the museum, shorn of the menagerie, was moved to an abandoned store building opposite the south gate of the Temple Block, and "Professor" Joseph L. Barfoot, a studious, self-educated Englishman, was made curator.

About 1878 ownership of the collection passed to the Mormon Church under the name of the Deseret Museum, made popular by common usage. Professor Barfoot died 23 April 1882, leaving the museum in the hands of "custodians" who merely attempted to hold it intact, making no pretense of progress in museum building. The degree to which Professor Barfoot had developed the museum seems to be indicated by a statement in the University of Deseret catalog of 1882 that students of the university would have access to the extensive and diversified collections of the Deseret Museum.

In 1885 ownership of the museum passed to the newly organized Salt Lake Literary and Scientific Association, which thereafter maintained the museum and directed its policies for several years. In 1890 the museum building was sold and it became necessary to move the materials. After several months part of the exhibits were set up in a small room, inadequate for the purpose, in the Templeton Building (southeast of Temple Block) and reopened to the public in January 1891.

At this time James E. Talmage was made curator and J. Reuben Clark, Jr., assistant curator. The museum was now to witness a renaissance and second growth similar to that made under Professor Barfoot. The collection could not expand at that location, so two years later it was moved to the top floor of a new building erected by the Association on the Ellerbeck property at First North between First and Second West. Here the museum expanded and grew for ten years.

In 1894 the Salt Lake Literary and Scientific Association endowed the chair of Deseret Professor of Geology at the University of Deseret, then located at the present site of West High School. A building housing the museum was a part of the endowment.

Seven years later, in July 1910, the exhibits were installed in the new Vermont Building erected on a site across the road from the south Temple gate (now the Beneficial Life Building). In this location James E. Talmage was director and his son, Sterling B. Talmage, curator. Here it remained for eight years.

In October and November of 1918 the collection was dismembered, the fossils, minerals, and animals being allocated to the LDS University across the road east from the Temple, and the balance, mainly relics, being assigned to the Bureau of Information of the Mormon Church. The specimens of birds and other animals from the LDS University later (June 1931) passed to Brigham Young University at Provo. The birds are all mounted specimens, and only part of them bear complete data.

Some of the other colleges in the state have been active at times in collecting birds and have accumulated a number of specimens. At Dixie Junior College in St. George, Utah, Vasco M. Tanner, Angus M. Woodbury, D Elden Beck, and C. Ross Hardy, along with some of their students, have been active in adding to the bird collection. Some papers resulting from these studies have been published. There is also a collection of some 300 skins at Weber State College at Ogden.

Much information on Utah birds was assembled, particularly during the first half of the present century, by nonprofessional naturalists or persons interested in birds as a hobby. Most of these workers were interested primarily in the collection of eggs and nests, but some of the collectors exercised great care in preserving data on nesting habits and on the birds themselves. Since the building of private collections is no longer permitted, most of these collections have gone to the institutional museums of the state or to museums elsewhere, and some, unfortunately, have apparently become lost.

One of the earliest egg collectors in Utah was Alberto Treganza, an architect by profession, who with his father and other members of the family began collecting in Utah in 1901. They eventually amassed a collection of about 30,000 eggs, although many of these were obtained by exchange from all over the world. The Treganza family remained active in Utah until about 1927, when financial reverses forced them to move to Florida and later to California. The Treganza collection has been scattered to a number of localities, most of it at the Western Foundation of Vertebrate Zoology at Los Angeles. A number of sets from the collection are to be found at the Royal Ontario Museum, Toronto, Canada; Field Museum of Natural History, Chicago; American Museum of Natural History, New York; Carnegie Museum, Pittsburgh; U.S. National Museum of Natural History, Washington, D.C.; and elsewhere.

Another of the early-day naturalists and egg collectors was Harry Aldous, whose collection was made principally in northern Utah. About 1924 he loaned a collection of birds and eggs to be displayed in the State Capitol. Following his death in 1929 most of his collection went to J. Donald Daynes of Salt Lake City. Parts of the Aldous col-

lection are to be found at the U.S National Museum of Natural History, American Museum; Cleveland (Ohio) Museum, Field Museum, and at other localities.

Mark Jackson, a building contractor who lived in Panguitch and Parowan, Utah, learned taxidermy from his father in England and later practiced this art as a hobby after coming to America. He prepared more than a hundred specimens of local birds and mammals which were later given to the University of Utah.

Claude T. Barnes, a prominent lawyer and legislator of Salt Lake City, was an ardent student of birds who did much to promote public interest by writing a series of illustrated articles in the magazines called the Improvement Era and Juvenile Instructor, published by the Mormon Church. He also collected a number of skins and kept extensive notes on birds based on his own observations. Mr. Barnes was well acquainted with other naturalists, particularly in the Salt Lake area, and with their help was instrumental in establishing a chapter of the Utah Audubon Society in 1913.

Another early-day oologist of Utah was George R. Walker, who became an active collector in the early 1900s, partly through the encouragement of A. O. Treganza. In addition to his own material, he obtained part of the collections of W. H. Parker. Many of these eggs went at first to the University of Utah but were later transferred to the Harrison collection at the Western Foundation of Vertebrate Zoology in Los Angeles, California. Parts of the Parker collection, however, are to be found at the Florida State Museum, Carnegie Museum, and Field Museum of Natural History. Smaller numbers of sets are located in other places.

John W. Sugden, who came to Utah in 1869, made a large collection of bird eggs and insects. Following his death in 1933 his son, John W. Sugden, Jr., inherited the collection and continued to add to it for many years. The bulk of the Sugden collection went to the University of Utah and eventually to the Western Foundation of Vertebrate Zoology, Los Angeles. Some 30 sets of eggs of the collection are to be found at the Field Museum of Natural History, while lesser numbers are located in six other institutions.

Ashby D. Boyle, a Salt Lake City lawyer, began a collection of bird eggs about 1915. Following his death, this collection was presented to Brigham Young University where it is now housed.

Around 1922 John H. Brandt made a collection of nearly 300 sets of eggs in Utah. These are presently located at the Carnegie Museum. About this time (1925–1930) Lieutenant (now Colonel) L. R. Wolf, an army officer stationed at Ft. Douglas, Utah, collected bird eggs in the state. Most of this material is to be found in the Harrison collection at the Western Foundation of Vertebrate Zoology.

Another active egg collector in the Salt Lake area in recent times is J. Donald Daynes. Mr. Daynes has accumulated a large and well-prepared collection which he donated recently to the Brigham Young University Life Sciences Museum.

The U.S. National Museum of Natural History collection of bird eggs contains a number of sets obtained in Utah by early ornithologists. About 61 sets of eggs and nests were collected by Robert Ridgway in 1869. Lesser numbers were obtained by C. Hart Merriam in 1872 and later by A. K. Fisher and Alexander Wetmore.

In the meantime a few amateur ornithologists, interested primarily in the collection of eggs as a hobby, were active in the Utah Valley area. H. C. Johnson of American Fork was developing an egg collection, but persons who knew him indicate that much material was brought to him by others. Most of the Johnson material eventually found its way to the Harrison collection at the Western Foundation of Vertebrate Zoology, the Cleveland Museum of Natural History, and the Field Museum of Natural History. Johnson published a num-

ber of short papers dealing with the breeding of Clarke's [sic] Nutcracker (1900, 1902b), Duck Hawk (1899b), Raven (1899c), Wilson's Snipe (1899a), Pigmy Owl (1903), Pinyon [sic] Jay (1902a). With W. H. Parker he also privately published a pamphlet on the nesting of birds in Utah (1899?).

In 1887 the Congregational Church established an institution in Provo known as the Proctor Academy, which continued until about 1912 or 1914 or about the time Provo High School was established. One of the teachers in the latter part of its history was Professor S. H. Goodwin, an accomplished naturalist. He and some of his students apparently took considerable interest in the local bird fauna. One of his pupils was Robert G. Bee, who later adopted ornithology as a hobby and gathered an extensive collection of eggs and several volumes of notes and photographs, all of which are now at Brigham Young University. Goodwin published a few notes in the Condor which include observations on the nesting of the White Pelican on Rock Island in Utah Lake (1904b), the California Gull (1904a), and the presence of the Bohemian Waxwing in Utah (1905).

Robert G. Bee began his collecting of eggs in 1892 when he was only 10 years old. Although throughout his later life he directed most of his efforts toward the collection of nesting data and eggs, he also kept extensive notes on other items of ornithology. A contemporary of Bee was John Hutchings, who was born in Lehi, Utah, and has lived there ever since. An accomplished taxidermist, he was brought many interesting and unusual bird specimens to mount. His early collections included many sets of eggs with full data. Part of this material is at Brigham Young University and the remainder is in a small museum in Lehi, Utah, built for him by the citizens of that area.

Bee and Hutchings (1942) summarized the records of breeding birds in Utah based on their previous years of collecting and observation. Most of these collections were made in Utah Valley and closely adjoining areas.

In more recent years Lloyd Gunther, who was superintendent of the Bear River Migratory Bird Refuge, has made a collection of bird eggs in Utah. His collection has recently been acquired by Brigham Young University. A small collection of eggs made by Merlin L. Killpack is also housed at Brigham Young University.

CONSERVATION ORGANIZATIONS

During Utah's biological "past history" several private organizations and interested groups have fostered the study of natural history and have been active in conservation.

During the 1880s a natural history movement under the auspices of the Agassiz Association gained momentum in Utah, and although it never became institutionalized like the University of Utah and the Deseret Museum, it continued as an important force for several years among enthusiastic members of the populace. This movement was designed to encourage the observation and study of natural phenomena including birds.

The founder, Harlan F. Ballard, in the November 1880 issue of St. Nicholas Magazine issued a general invitation for the formation of chapters. In response, Utah Chapter A was organized 1 August 1882, Chapter B in the spring of 1883, and Chapter C later that same season, all in Salt Lake City. They continued with varying degrees of enthusiasm until 1 November 1885, when they were combined into one chapter and reorganized.

This organization initiated a small monthly publication under the title of Agassiz Notes, which ran through seven numbers between November 1885 and May 1886 before publication was suspended. During the life of the organization many field trips were conducted, many specimens collected (minerals, insects, bird nests and eggs, plants, etc.), cabinets installed, print-

ing press acquired, and notes published, all largely under the leadership of Marcus E. Jones, botanist, explorer, and general naturalist. Many of the members of this society were egg collectors on a semi-commercial basis and could scarcely be considered conservationists, although their efforts contributed something to the scientific knowledge of the birds of the area.

During the second decade of the twentieth century, a group of nature enthusiasts including such individuals as Claude T. Barnes, J. H. Paul, Walter Cluff, N. W. Reynolds, J. W. Sugden, E. G. Titus, C. T. Vorhies, A. O. Treganza, A. O. Garrett, J. Cecil Alter, G. O. Armstrong, Florence Knox, M. R. Cheeseman, F. A. Wrathall, Fred W. Chambers, Josephine Seamen, and Royal C. Barnes became active in bird study and formally incorporated the Utah Audubon Society on 3 January 1913 at Salt Lake City.

During that year they were instrumental in pushing two important laws through the legislature: one providing for the observance of bird day in all public schools on the last Friday of April, and the other providing for protection of all birds in the state except game birds in open season and a few pest birds that damage crops, poultry, or fish.

Certain members remained active for many years, but the group's activity gradually subsided. Soon after this, a chapter of the Cooper Club was organized in Salt Lake City. This group included such persons as the Treganzas, the Sugdens, Ashby Boyle, J. L. Mullen, G. Ray Walker, and others, most of whom were held together by a common interest in oology. In 1935 and 1936, after the previous movements had more or less subsided, a new group including A. M. Woodbury, William H. Behle, Charles W. Lockerbie, Rex B. Snow, J. Donald Daynes, Nettie Bradford, Beth Hansen, and others revived and reorganized the Utah Audubon Society. This society is still functioning. It has held monthly meetings, conducted monthly field trips, par-

Fig. 2. Great Blue Heron. Salt Creek Waterfowl Management Area, Box Elder County, Utah, 7 June 1973. Photo by R. J. Erwin.

ticipated in the Christmas bird census, kept field records, published mimeographed articles, sponsored the Junior Audubon Clubs, supported special programs for bird day in schools, promulgated winter bird feeding campaigns, and in general supported conservation movements.

Recently chapters of the Audubon Society have been organized at Provo (Mount Timpanogos Chapter), Logan (Bridgerland Chapter), and Vernal (Uinta Chapter).

STATE AND FEDERAL WATERFOWL PRESERVES

During the early expansion of Utah no restrictions were placed upon hunting. The time arrived, however, when not only game birds but big game animals as well were so reduced in numbers that many of the species were threatened with local extermination. Belatedly, the drastic game depletion was recognized and more definite steps were taken toward conservation and the restoration of reduced game populations.

One of the early steps was the establishment of a fish and game department by the legislature in 1893 which reported back to the legislature in 1895. It was this agency which first reported duck sickness around Great Salt Lake in 1910. In 1913 a comprehensive set of fish and game laws was placed in the statutes, providing for fairly adequate protection for many kinds of birds of the state. The law at one time (State Fish and Game Commissioner 1929) provided that:

> Except game birds as hereinafter enumerated, it shall be unlawful for any person or persons to take, kill, ensnare, net trap, or shoot at any native or imported bird in the state of Utah.
>
> Provided, that when farmers or poultrymen or others find it absolutely necessary to protect their interests, the following named birds may be destroyed, to wit: English sparrow, magpie, sharp-shinned hawk, Cooper hawk, goshawk and prairie falcon or bullet hawk.
>
> Provided, further; that the blue and black-crowned night heron and pelican may be destroyed under regulations issued by the state Fish and Game Commissioner.

Under the law "game birds" included both waterfowl and upland game birds. In accordance with federal regulations at that time, hunting of the following waterfowl could be permitted by the Commission: ducks, geese, swans, snipes, sandpipers, plovers, willets, curlew, godwits, avocets, and coots. The Commission has powers under certain conditions and with certain precautions to provide open hunting seasons of the following upland game birds: Pinnated Grouse, Blue Grouse, Ruffed Grouse, Willow Grouse, Sage Hen, Pheasant, Quail, Hungarian Partridge, and Mourning Dove.

Problems of game management, particularly of big game, led in 1917 to the establishment of the first game preserves, a number of which are now distributed through the state of Utah. The formation of such preserves was based on the idea that they could serve as breeding centers from which game would overflow into surrounding areas where it could be hunted.

Over the years the Utah State Department of Fish and Game, now known as the Division of Wildlife Resources, in cooperation with federal wildlife agencies, has been instrumental in expanding the number of gamebird management areas within the state. Such management areas include Locomotive Springs, Salt Creek Public Shooting Grounds, Ogden Bay, Farmington Bay, Timpie Springs, Harold Crane, and Howard Slough, all of which are around the borders of Great Salt Lake. Powell Slough and Rock Island management areas are located at Utah Lake. Other state owned areas are Clear Lake and Topaz Marsh, Millard County; Stewart Lake, Uintah County; Brown's Park, Daggett County; Desert Lake, Emery County; Bicknell Bottoms, Wayne County; and Olsen Slough, Sanpete County.

Federally owned and operated refuges include the large Bear River Migratory Bird Refuge in Box Elder County, Fish Springs Refuge in Juab County, and Ouray Refuge in Uintah County.

BIRD POPULATIONS IN UTAH

The abundance of water and shore birds around the Great Salt Lake was vividly described by Fremont (1845) and by Stansbury (1853). Quotations from their writing have been mentioned elsewhere. These early explorers as well as the early pioneers were understandably interested in the more conspicuous and larger birds as well as the game birds and predatory species. As has been previously mentioned, the early Mormon settlers soon after their arrival organized campaigns against the "vermin." In addition, market hunting of ducks, geese, and other edible species was a regular occurrence. The fact that these larger species were able to survive at all attests to the fact of their original abundance.

The abundance of upland game birds in favorable habitats throughout the state and in adjoining areas was evident in my (Hayward's) experience in the early 1900s in the Bear Lake area of northern Utah and southeastern Idaho. Sage Grouse, Sharp-tailed Grouse, Ruffed Grouse, and Blue Grouse were all present in large numbers in their particular habitats. Sage Grouse tended to gather around springs in late summer, and I have seen them rise in great clouds when disturbed. Some ruthless hunters would shoot these easy targets by the dozens, remove the breasts, and leave the rest of the carcasses in piles to decay.

In the vicinity of Utah Lake there was an abundance of waterfowl and wading birds similar to those of the Great Salt Lake area in the early days.

Fortunately Robert G. Bee obtained some information from early fishermen, trappers, and hunters around Utah Lake and recorded some of their statements in his notes.[9] Mr. Gus Slade of Lehi fished and hunted around Utah Lake before 1900. There was extensive fishing for bass from about 1894–1900, but the introduction of carp killed out the so-called "moss," and the bass largely disappeared for a time. Mr. Slade stated that in 1895 the "moss" was so thick you could hardly row a boat through it. There were "millions of ducks, so thick that when you shot a rifle you couldn't see through them as they arose." He mentions hunting ducks on Skippers Bay and killing 125 to 150 per day. He stopped the shooting in 1898 owing to the decrease in ducks and blamed the decrease to the destruction of the "moss" and other duck food by the carp. While Mr. Slade's descriptions seem to be somewhat exaggerated, he was no doubt impressed by the high populations of birds.

About the year 1896–97 a bounty was offered on all types of herons, pelicans, cormorants and all other fish-eating birds. At that time, and for some years before, states Mr. Slade, there were large heronries in the cedars (junipers) in the vicinity of Soldier Pass and Goshen Pass (west of Utah Lake). He estimated that the colony was three or four miles long and a mile wide and contained 100,000 birds. The Great Blue Heron also nested in the marshes of Goshen Bay. Mr. Slade visited this area with several other men, killed 1,290 birds (presumably nestlings) with sticks, cut their heads off, and placed them in sacks. They received $129 bounty for this kill.

Ad Robbins was another early hunter and trapper interviewed by Mr. Bee. Robbins also participated in market hunting of ducks, on one occasion killing 75 to 100 in a single day. The principal ducks killed were teal, scaup, and canvasbacks. On the market these brought from $1.25 to $1.75 per dozen. He also took part in the killing of what he called "quaks" and "cranes." These were Black-crowned Night Herons and Great Blue Herons. He reported being at the rookery before daylight and collecting heads and eggs. Many birds were shot.

Robbins mentions visiting Rock Island (year not given) and killing 1,000 pelicans "until the smell made us all sick."

Pete Johnson of Provo who was interviewed by Mr. Bee in March 1937 was then 79 years of age. He was another of the early trappers, fishermen, and hunters. He stated that he made $6 to $7 a day hunting fish-eating birds for bounty. He estimated that 10,000 herons and four or five hundred pelicans were slaughtered but there is no indication in the notes concerning the length of time involved. He said that in 1928 he killed over 1,200 mudhens (coots). They ate the hearts and gizzards, saved the feathers, and then threw the remaining parts of the birds away.

The destruction of fish-eating birds in the vicinity of Utah Lake continued into the thirties. When I (Hayward) first came to Brigham Young University to teach in 1930, the State Fish and Game Department furnished ammunition to hunters in Utah Valley to kill pelicans and other fish-eating birds. Thus many of these birds, along with numerous hawks, were killed.

During the past 46 years important changes affecting bird life in the central valleys of the state have been evident. Habitats of the water and shore birds have fluctuated and changed considerably. Utah Lake has fluctuated from a point of nearly drying up during a series of low precipita-

---

[9]Robert G. Bee's unpublished notes and journals are in the Life Sciences Museum, Brigham Young University, Provo, Utah.

tion years in the early 1930s to a high peak where it flooded adjacent farmlands in 1948–49. Pumping of water from the lake in varying amounts for irrigation purposes has resulted in some seasonal fluctuations. The area of shallow water known as Provo Bay or Mud Lake, partially surrounded by swampy land and emergent vegetation, has been an important area for the nesting of wading birds and waterfowl. In early spring of 1936 certain irrigation interests dug drainage canals through the area in an attempt to carry the water into Utah Lake to reduce surface evaporation. There was no attempt to install headgates to control the drainage, and for a time this important resource was nearly drained. Protests by local conservation interests (Evening Herald 15 April 1936:18) retarded the process of this program. The drainage canal has since been abandoned and has partially filled up. For many years raw sewage from the cities and towns of the valley flowed into Provo Bay and other parts of the lake. However, within the past decade most of these communities have established sewage plants, although they have not been entirely effective. Another source of pollution, still not entirely controlled, has been the by-products of the Geneva Steel plant, installed during World War II, and other smaller industries of the area.

Various other activities of man on and around Utah Lake have had their influence on bird life. The construction of a small boat harbor at the mouth of Provo River and the establishment of several other boat landings at other points on the lake, together with the increasing popularity of boating, have undoubtedly increased the disturbance factor, especially during the nesting season.

Habitats for the nesting of certain species have varied markedly over the past years. Following the construction of the previously mentioned canal in Provo Bay, willow trees and poplars sprang up along its banks and on drained land. Later these trees were flooded and consequently died. For several years these dead trees served as important nesting sites for colonies of Great Blue Herons and Cormorants. During the drought years of the early 1930s tamarisks and willows became established on the exposed land as the lake receded. When the lake rose again, these dense stands became flooded and for a short time were ideal habitats for the nesting of the Yellow-headed Blackbird, Red-winged Blackbird, American Coot, Western Grebe, Marsh Wren, and other species.

The effects of housing expansion, construction of roads, development of industries, and the reduction of farm lands along the Wasatch Front over the past twenty years have had some effect on the land bird populations, but an exact measurement of the effect is difficult. Only general observations are possible. The riparian habitat of Provo River and other streams issuing from the mountains along the more densely populated Wasatch Front — an area important to many forest dwelling species of birds — is rapidly disappearing and being replaced by homes. Certain species that formerly inhabited these areas in the late 1920s and early 1930s seem to have nearly or completely disappeared. These include the Redstart, Veery, and Fox Sparrow. On the other hand, the establishment of housing units, parks, and university campuses where ornamental shrubs and trees bearing edible fruits have been introduced seems to have attracted more of the smaller birds that have adapted well to human occupation.

Water conservation activities in Utah over the past several years have resulted in the construction of a number of reservoirs that have had some effect on the distribution and populations of birds in the state. Most of these reservoirs are of value principally as resting areas for waterfowl, but do not afford suitable breeding grounds. An exception to this is Pelican Lake, a small shallow body of water in the Uinta Basin near Vernal. Because of the abundant growth of emergent vegetation, the ample food, and some open shores, this lake has become an important nesting ground for American Coots, Black-crowned Night Herons, Black and Forster's Terns, Eared and Western Grebes, American Avocets, Black-necked Stilts, and several kinds of ducks. It is also serving as a resting and feeding area for many kinds of shore birds, both in spring and summer migration. The creation of several waterfowl refuges by previously mentioned state and federal agencies has also helped to balance against the loss of habitats resulting from human occupation, industries, and the pollution resulting therefrom.

PHYSIOGRAPHY AND CLIMATE OF UTAH

GREAT BASIN. — That portion of the Great Basin lying in Utah was formerly a part of ancient Lake Bonneville, which extended from southern Idaho southward into Iron County and from Salt Lake City westward nearly to Nevada. With the disappearance of that lake, the drainage was broken into several separate basins which are now independent of each other. Some of these have brackish or salty lakes or playas in the bottom. The principal ones are the Great Salt Lake and Sevier Lake basins, but there are also several smaller ones.

Bordering the Great Basin on the east side are a series of high mountain ranges, peaks, and plateaus running in a north-south direction. The summits of these mountains range from 9,000 to 12,000 feet in elevation. Drainage from the westward slopes formerly ran into the lakes and other lower areas of the Great Basin, but now much of this water is held back by reservoirs from whence it can be released into the cities and farmlands of the basin for irrigation or culinary purposes.

Between this series of mountains and the Nevada line, rising out of the lowlands of the basin (4,200 to 5,500 feet), lie a large number of small mountain ranges rising 3,000 to 5,000 feet above the basin floor.

Most of these have north-south axes. Between these mountain ranges lie lowland areas on the floor of the basin, most of which present desert characteristics. The extreme in desert soil is illustrated in the Great Salt Lake Desert where large areas of "salt flats" occur. These flats are covered with crystalline salt on the surface and are completely barren of vegetation. Nearly all gradations from these extreme desert conditions to rich agricultural soil may be found somewhere in the basin.

COLORADO BASIN. — The Green River arises in northwestern Wyoming and then enters Utah about thirty miles west of the northeast corner of the state. From there it makes a detour around the east end of the Uinta Mountains, into northwestern Colorado, and back into Utah. After that it flows southward through half of the state before joining the Colorado River. The latter river arises in Colorado in the mountains of the continental divide, crosses western Colorado, entering Utah near the middle of the east boundary, and then flows southwestward through remarkable canyons before it passes into Arizona near the middle of the southern boundary of the state.

A series of tributary rivers — Uinta, Price, San Raphael, Fremont (Dirty Devil), Escalante, Paria, Kanab, Virgin, and many lesser streams — drain the eastern slopes from the Great Basin divide in Utah. The chief tributaries of the Green and Colorado rivers from the Colorado Rockies include Yampa, White, Dolores, and San Juan rivers. The slopes of the Uinta Mountains also contribute numerous tributaries to the Colorado River drainage.

The Uinta Mountains, with an east-west axis, lie just south of Wyoming and include the highest areas in the state: Kings Peak at 13,498 feet and six other peaks over 13,000 feet. South of the Uinta Mountains lies the Uinta Basin, underlaid by strata which rise slowly to the south and form high plateaus that break off in escarpments known as the Roan and Book cliffs.

Two isolated sets of mountains, La Sal

and Abajo, arise from the Colorado Basin to heights of more than 11,000 and 12,000 feet in the region southeast of the Colorado River. The Henry Mountains form a conspicuous landmark west of the Colorado River.

Green River enters Utah from Wyoming at an altitude of 5,855 feet. The Colorado River enters from Colorado at 4,330 feet. The two join at an elevation of 3,875 feet and pass out of Utah into Arizona at 3,160 feet. The lowest altitude of the state, however, is found in Washington County in the southwest corner where both the Virgin River and the Beaver Dam Wash pass into Arizona at an approximate altitude of 2,250 feet. The Virgin River Basin is consequently the lowest basin of the state and is the only portion that is similar to the Lower Sonoran or Southern Desert shrub communities of Arizona and southern Nevada.

COLUMBIA PLATEAU. — A small area in the northwestern corner of the state belongs to the Snake River drainage. Some small streams originating on the north slope of the Raft River Mountains flow northward into the Snake River.

CLIMATE. — Particularly in the summer, moisture-laden air may sweep into Utah from the Gulf of Mexico, but the major source of water is the Pacific Ocean. Winds from that source must cross ranges of high mountains that parallel the coast and abstract much of the moisture. Utah, lying in the rain shadow of these mountains, is a part of the driest physiographic province of North America.

The desert valleys receive four to ten inches of precipitation annually. Mountains get more according to their altitudes above adjacent valleys, roughly increasing about one inch for each 160 to 200 feet rise. Higher mountain passes, however, may receive 30 to 50 inches annually.

Precipitation is unequally distributed throughout the year. In southern Utah, there are on the average two periods of deficiency, one in late spring and early summer, the other in the fall, and two periods of maxima, one in late winter, the other in late summer. Farther north, this double cycle tends to be replaced by a single seasonal cycle in which the maximum occurs in early spring and the minimum in midsummer. The proportion of precipitation which falls as rain and snow varies from the Virgin River Basin, where snow seldom occurs, to the high Uinta Mountains where it is nearly all snow. Part of the summer rains occasionally come in the form of thunder showers. In some years these thunder showers assume torrential proportions.

The actual conditions of climate vary a great deal in different years from average conditions. Prolonged drought, heavy rains, or blizzards may cause a wide departure from normal in any given year. Such departures often subject living organisms to extremes of climate that tax their endurance.

Temperatures in Utah are extremely variable and wide ranging. There is often a 20- to 30-degree F difference between day and night and 100-degree F difference between winter minimum and summer maximum, occasionally much more. During warm weather the relative humidity is extremely low, especially during the day. This is correlated with a high evaporation rate, particularly in southern Utah at low altitudes. The combination of low precipitation, high evaporation, and low relative humidity results in extensive desert areas with scanty vegetation, especially in the rain-shadow of mountains.

The average relative humidity of Utah, like that of Nevada and Arizona, is near 50 percent in contrast with the sea coasts with averages of 75 to 80 percent, the plains with 70 to 75 percent, and the western mountain states with averages of 50 to 65 percent. The rate of evaporation in Utah, because of the low humidity and bright sunshine, is extremely high, amounting to 45 to 55 inches per year from a free-water surface in the valleys west of the Wasatch Mountains.

BIRD HABITATS IN UTAH

There are, perhaps, few areas of comparable size on the North American continent that offer a wider range of habitats suitable to birds than those found within the state of Utah. The aquatic habitats range from large freshwater and salt lakes in the lowlands to small natural glacial lakes of the mountains, from slow-running streams of the valleys to swift rivers and brooks in the mountains. Added to these natural water bodies are several man-made lakes and reservoirs at varying elevations. Land communities vary from a small area of hot desert in the Dixie country of southwestern Utah to true alpine in the Uinta Mountains of northern Utah.

Since birds are among the most mobile of vertebrates, it is difficult to define many of them in terms of their confinement to any special community. To attempt to assign birds to particular life zones or biomes often fails or applies to them only at certain seasons of the year. Attempts to assign birds to particular community types are usually based on their activities during the breeding and nesting seasons when the populations are most stable as to numbers and territorial needs or to resident species that do not migrate or wander far.

Nevertheless, in viewing the Utah avian population it is possible, as it is elsewhere, to describe several types of bird habitats and to predict certain species that one would expect to find there during each of the seasons.

Aquatic and Semiaquatic Habitats

Utah Lake, located west of the Wasatch Mountains in Utah County, is the largest natural freshwater body in the state. It is a shallow lake some 20 miles long and 8 miles wide. Its shoreline varies from swampy areas with much emergent vegetation to rocky or sandy beaches. Until the beginning of the last decade, much raw sewage from the towns on the east side of the lake was poured into the lake, and the water became badly polluted. Most of the settlements now have sewage disposal plants, but even so there is still considerable waste material from sewage and industrial products entering the lake.

While Utah Lake probably does not have the potential for water fowl that it had prior to the coming of the white man, it and the adjacent sloughs and ponds of the valley lowlands still produce a great variety of birds.

The open waters of the lake serve principally as a daytime refuge, especially in early spring and autumn, for large numbers of ducks and geese that fly to surrounding fields or marshlands to feed at night. These birds inhabit the lake as long as it is free of ice. In addition, the White Pelican, Double-crested Cormorant, and Western Grebe feed on fish in the open waters. Some of the larger refuges such as Farmington Bay and Bear River areas adjacent to the Great Salt Lake and Fish Springs Refuge of western Utah afford similar habitats of open water but are better controlled and less polluted.

The large man-made reservoirs including Lake Powell, Flaming Gorge, Deer Creek, Strawberry, and several others within the boundaries of the state are at present mostly areas of refuge and rest for waterfowl. In time they may develop surroundings suitable for breeding and feeding. The shallow reservoirs such as Pelican Lake in the Uinta Basin and Mona Reservoir in eastern Juab County seem to be more suitable for open water birds as well as for marsh and shore birds.

The Great Salt Lake supports no fish and is, therefore, not an important area for fish-eating birds, although there are colonies of White Pelicans, California Gulls, and other species of birds nesting on some of its islands. Dense populations of brine shrimp and brine fly occur in the salty water and are utilized for food by a few species of birds.

Marshlands that have developed around the lakes, particularly Utah Lake and the

Great Salt Lake, consist of areas subject to periodic flooding and draining and are somewhat unstable. However, they furnish cover, food, and nesting habitats for many kinds of birds. The tall tules (*Scirpus*), cat-tails (*Typha*), and reeds (*Phragmites*), as well as other emergent vegetation, afford valuable nesting habitats for several species. Colonies of Great Blue Heron, Snowy Egret, Black-crowned Night Heron, and White-faced Ibis occur from time to time but suffer considerable shifting about, depending upon the amount of disturbance and drainage. Numerous coots and grebes build floating nests in these marshes especially where their waters are continuous with those of the lake. Marsh Hawks and occasionally Black and Forster's Terns build platform nests or nest on the tops of musk-rat houses or masses of dead water plants.

Colonies of Yellow-headed and Red-winged Blackbirds nest in the marshes. Also characteristic are Long-billed Marsh Wrens and Yellow-throats.

On slightly higher ground the marshes with their emergent plants give way to wet meadow situations that are often flooded in spring and early summer but become dry later in the summer. Numerous species of grasses, sedges, and rushes grow here, and much of the land is used for pasture or the vegetation is cut for wild hay. The Red-winged Blackbird, Western Meadowlark, Bobolink, Wilson's Phalarope, Willet, Long-billed Curlew, and Common Snipe are char-acteristic nesting species in this habitat.

Shallow open waters on the margins of lakes and ponds as well as the shores them-selves afford an important feeding and nesting area for a number of species. Char-acteristic nesting birds of open beaches are the Killdeer, Snowy Plover, American Avocet, Black-necked Stilt, and Spotted Sandpiper. Numerous kinds of migrating shorebirds, with Western and Least Sand-pipers, Northern Phalaropes, and Sander-lings being the most common, feed in the shallows and wet mud flats near shore.

The state of Utah, particularly the Colo-rado River drainage portion, is crossed by numerous streams fed by the watersheds within the state and in bordering states. The largest of these are the Green and Colo-rado rivers. In the lowlands these streams flow slowly or form rapids, depending upon the topography. Within the Great Basin there are numerous streams flowing from the Wasatch and other mountain ranges. Among the larger of these streams are Bear, Weber, Sevier, and Provo rivers. In the canyons and at higher elevations where these streams have their origin the water usually runs swiftly over a rocky streambed.

The slow-flowing streams of the lowlands serve as refuges and resting places for a variety of waterfowl. Canada Geese some-times nest along the stream banks and may be seen in summer swimming with their young in the open water. Ducks, particular-ly of the diving type such as Common and Red-breasted Mergansers, Buffleheads, and Common Goldeneyes, frequent these streams in winter. Small, quiet estuaries, flooded by high water in spring, frequently develop pond situations with emergent vegetation and are inhabited by Cinnamon Teal, Pintails, Mallards, and other species.

Swift streams of steeper canyons support the Dipper and occasionally the Belted Kingfisher, although the latter is more fre-quent near smaller valley streams. High mountain lakes, especially abundant in the Uinta Mountains of northern Utah, do not support many waterfowl, although small flocks or individuals of most species of ducks common to Utah may be seen on them occasionally. Little if any nesting occurs around these high lakes since they are still frozen over at the regular nesting time for ducks.

Land Habitats

The lowland country of Utah, which occurs in valleys ranging in elevation from 2,800 to 6,000 feet, is taken up with agricul-tural lands, cities, and towns wherever there is sufficient water for irrigation and suitable soil. This, however, takes up a relatively small portion of the total area of the state. The remainder of the lowland country is semidesert and desert vegetated by a variety of low-growing shrubs and is used principally as winter range for livestock.

The lowland streams are typically bordered by a flood plain or riparian woodland composed of cottonwood and box elder trees and a variety of tall shrubs and willows. In agricultural areas this community has expanded along irrigation canals and a similar community type occurs in orchards, ornamental trees and shrubs of city streets and parks. As a result, there is probably a more extensive and productive habitat of this sort suitable for a large variety of smaller birds than there was prior to the settlement by white man. Summer bird inhabitants of these wooded communities include a large variety of passerine birds such as the Yellow Warbler, Yellow-breasted Chat, Gray Catbird, American Robin, Black-headed Grosbeak, Starling, Western Wood Pewee, and House Finch. Other kinds include the Mourning Dove, Broad-tailed Hummingbird, Screech Owl, Sharp-shinned Hawk, and Cooper's Hawk. In winter the buds, fruits, and berries of both native and ornamental shrubs and trees offer an increasing supply of food for such wintering species as Bohemian and Cedar Waxwings, Evening Grosbeaks, California Quail, American Robins, and Townsend's Solitaires.

The community type described above, while relatively small in comparison to the total area of the state, is of great ornithological value and interest since it supports the greatest variety and population of small birds, most species of which seem to be able to withstand the pressures of the continuing expansion of human populations. The principal factors detrimental to their success would seem to be the increasing use of insecticides and the growth of the predator population, especially the house cat.

The desertlands of Utah are of two general kinds. A small portion of the Mojave Desert extends into the lower elevations of extreme southwestern Utah. Its vegetation is characterized by such shrubs as creosote bush, mesquite, giant yucca, and numerous hot desert cacti. A few species of birds including LeConte's Thrasher, Crissal Thrasher, Abert's Towhee, and the Black Phoebe seem to be rather strictly confined to this community. The Mockingbird is common but by no means confined to it.

A second general desert type occupies most of the valleys and plains of the state. It has been variously described as the Upper Sonoran Life Zone or the Northern or Cold Desert. It is characterized in the main by a vegetation of low-growing shrubs, many of them of a dull gray appearance, the species of which depend often on the amount of salinity of the soil and the degree of human disturbance. Bird life is rather sparse, but a number of interesting species occur. The Horned Lark is the most widespread and conspicuous species. Other species include the Sage Thrasher, Brewer's Sparrow, Vesper Sparrow, Sage Sparrow, Black-throated Sparrow, and in limited areas the Sage Grouse.

Another type of community that partakes primarily of desert characteristics is the pinyon-juniper forest, sometimes called the pygmy forest. This community is widespread in Utah but is especially well developed on the low mesas and hills of the eastern portion of the state. The juniper is universally present in the community, and the pinyon pines, of which there are two species, are often present. Bird life in this community is sparse and widely scattered both as to numbers and kinds, but a few species are rather characteristic. These include the Pinon Jay, Plain Titmouse, Black-throated Gray Warbler, Gray Flycatcher, Ash-throated Flycatcher, and Blue-gray Gnatcatcher.

Another land community found within the state is the so-called mountain brush. This is mostly a deciduous chaparral type with the scrub oak (*Quercus gambelii*) being the predominant plant. Other common shrubs include the big-toothed maple (*Acer grandidenatum*) and hackberry (*Celtis douglasii*). Cliff rose (*Cowania stansburiana*), antelope-bush (*Purshia tridentata*), and mahogany (*Cercocarpus*) often grow on the more rocky ridges. This community is well represented above the pinyon-juniper in the more isolated mountain ranges of southeastern Utah and along the Wasatch front or the west slope of the Wasatch Mountains where pinyon-juniper is lacking as a distinct belt. The avifauna of this community consists of many of the species that live also in the riparian communities of the valleys. Perhaps the most characteristic species are the Rufous-sided Towhee, Virginia's Warbler, Orange-crowned Warbler, and Scrub Jay.

At elevations on the mountains above the mountain bush are several types of evergreen and deciduous forests. The yellow pine forest (*Pinus ponderosa*) is one of these. This community is rather sparsely represented in Utah, with the largest stands occurring along the south and east base of the La Sal Mountains and other mountains of southeastern Utah and in some portions of the Uinta Mountains. Perhaps the most characteristic bird of this community is the Pygmy Nuthatch. The White-breasted and Red-breasted Nuthatch, Western Bluebird, Clark's Nutcracker, and Solitary Vireo are also characteristic of the yellow pine forest.

The two more widespread types of coniferous forests found in the mountains of Utah are the Lower Montane Forest, in which the white fir (*Abies concolor*) and the Douglas fir (*Pseudosuga menziesii*) are the predominant trees, and the Upper Montane Forest, wherein the Englemann spruce (*Picea engelmanni*) and the subalpine or black fir (*Abies lasiocarpa*) are characteristic. A subclimax conifer forest of lodgepole pine (*Pinus contorta*) occurs, particularly in the Uinta Mountains following burns. While these coniferous forests are quite different botanically, the bird life seems to be rather similar in all of them. The Red-breasted Nuthatch, Golden-crowned Kinglet, Ruby-crowned Kinglet, Yellow-rumped Warbler, Western Tanager, Olive-sided Flycatcher, Hammond's Flycatcher, Steller's Jay, and the Northern Three-toed Woodpecker are a few of the common representatives.

A deciduous forest of aspen (*Populus tremuloides*) frequently occurs in the mountains of the state at the level of the Lower Montane Forest where there have been fires. Ultimately these forests are usually replaced by conifers, but the process is often slow and mature stands of old aspens may occur. Such forests, with large standing live or dead trees are particularly suitable for a variety of hole-nesting birds including the Tree Swallow, Violet-green Swallow, Purple Martin, House Wren, Black-capped Chickadee, Yellow-bellied Sapsucker, Downy Woodpecker, Hairy Woodpecker, and Common Flicker. Other common birds of the aspen forests are Western Tanager, Chipping Sparrow, Cassin's Finch, Black-headed Grosbeak, Western Wood Pewee, Yellow-rumped Warbler, Mountain Bluebird, and Hermit Thrush.

Alpine communities are represented in some of the higher mountain ranges of Utah, particularly in the Uinta Mountains, Wasatch Mountains, and La Sal Mountains. They occur usually at elevations above 11,000 feet and are most extensive in the Uinta Mountains. These treeless, cold areas are rather inhospitable to most birds. The Rosy Finch and Water Pipit and sometimes the Rock Wren nest there but migrate to lower elevations in winter. Several kinds of birds feed in the alpine meadows in late summer. These include the American Kestrel, Green-Tailed Towhee, and several species of sparrows.

More specific habitat relationships will be considered under the accounts of the Utah species.

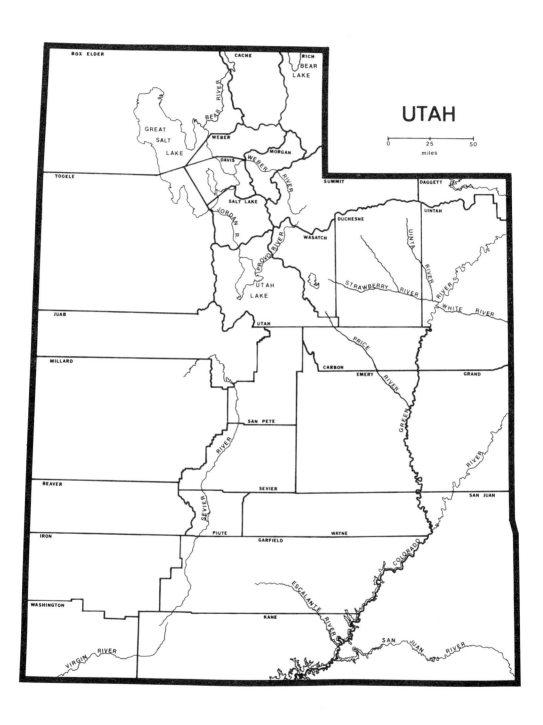

ACCOUNTS OF THE SPECIES

FAMILY GAVIIDAE
Gavia immer (Brunnich)
Common Loon

STATUS: The Common Loon is a rather habitual and consistent migrant in both spring and fall, and a few may remain throughout the summer, especially in the northern part of the state. There seem to be no records of nesting.

RECORDS: Specimens taken at Great Salt Lake in 1849 or 1850 were reported by Baird (1852:324–325) who stated that this record "enables us to give to it a locality more western than any yet recorded." Remy (1860 [2]:450) included the loon in a list of birds of Utah observed in 1855. Henshaw (1875:488) reported that "this diver was said by the fishermen of Utah Lake to be rather common, remaining in their waters till quite late in the fall." More recent collection records include the following: mouth of Jordan River, Salt Lake County, 30 October 1885; near Brigham City, Box Elder County, 9 June 1928; Utah Lake, Utah County, 30 October 1932; Veyo, Washington County, 27 October 1933; Gunnison Island, Box Elder County, 31 July 1938; Jordan Fur Farm, Davis County, November or December 1938; north of Scipio, Juab County, 14 August 1939 (Long 1940: 122). There are numerous sight records in recent years including observations by Donald Nielson of a single individual in a brinepond near Wendover, Tooele County, 10 June 1942 (Behle 1955:111) and Dugway, Tooele County, 18 May 1960 (Behle et al. 1964:450) and by Hayward and Frost of two specimens at Pelican Lake, Uintah County, 15 May 1970 (field notes).

FIG. 3.   White Pelican. Tremonton, Box Elder County, Utah. Photo by R. J. Erwin.

Fig. 4. Snowy Egret. Salt Creek Waterfowl Management Area, Box Elder County, Utah, 23 June 1973. Photo by R. J. Erwin.

Gavia arctica pacifica (Lawrence)
Arctic Loon

STATUS: A rare transient probably accidental in the state.

RECORDS: Hardy (1941a:125) reported that a bird of the subspecies *pacifica* was found dead near Beaver, Beaver County, 18 October 1940.

Gavia stellata (Pontoppidan)
Red-throated Loon

STATUS: A rare and seemingly accidental visitor to Utah.

RECORDS: A specimen in the University of Utah collection was found at the Bear River Migratory Bird Refuge during the summer of 1973. According to Behle (1973b:243), the bird was first seen at the refuge on 28 July 1973. It was later captured and died from the effects of a catfish spine lodged in the esophagus. A picture of this specimen is in American Birds (Able 1974:22).

FAMILY PODICIPEDIDAE

Podiceps auritus (Linnaeus)
Horned Grebe

STATUS: The Horned Grebe is a sparse but rather consistent migrant in Utah both in spring and fall. Formerly nesting in

Fig. 5.　Goshawk. Snow Basin, Weber County, Utah, 10 July 1970. Photo by R. J. Erwin.

northern Utah (AOU Check-list 1957:5).

RECORDS: Allen (1872b:173) collected a specimen near Ogden, Weber County, in September 1871. Henshaw (1875:489) reported that it was present in small numbers at Rush Lake, Iron County, in September 1972. A specimen in the U.S. Biological Survey collection was taken at Bear River,

Box Elder County, 4 September 1916, by Fisher. Webster (1947:40) published a sight record for Pine View Reservoir, Weber County, 19 April 1945, and Behle et al. (1964:450) reported two females taken at Farmington Bay, Davis County, 8 April 1962.

Podiceps nigricollis californicus Heerman
Eared Grebe

STATUS: This is the most common grebe found on the lakes and reservoirs of the state, appearing often in large numbers especially in spring. It breeds commonly in suitable habitats throughout the area. Most of the nesting records are for early June, July, and August.

RECORDS: Robert Ridgway (1877:369) noted this grebe especially in the vicinity of the Jordan River marshes and Great Salt Lake in Salt Lake County as early as 1869 but took no specimens. Young collected specimens near the lake in April 1897. These specimens are in the U.S. National Museum of Natural History, Washington, D.C.

Numerous specimens are in the University of Utah and Brigham Young University collections. Dates of collections and observations range from April through December. Cottam (1929:80) reported that on the night of 13 December 1928 many hundreds of grebes were forced to the ground by heavy storms at Caliente, Lincoln County, Nevada; at Enterprise, Washington County; and at Uvada and Modena, Iron County, Utah. They were undoubtedly in mass migration, but it is not certain from whence they came. Wauer (1969:331) reported a migration through the Virgin River Valley from 20 April to 14 May and from 30 September through 27 October.

Aechmophorus occidentalis (Lawrence)
Western Grebe

STATUS: The Western Grebe is a common migrant and breeding species in Utah. It is most abundant from mid-March to mid-November, but a few individuals occur in winter. Cottam et al. (1942:51) saw them at the Bear River Migratory Bird Refuge, Box Elder County, and near Ogden, Weber County, 14, 27–28 December 1941 and 10 January 1942. For breeding purposes these grebes prefer the marshy borders of the

larger lakes and reservoirs, although they often feed in rivers and larger canals especially if these are bordered by marshlands.

RECORDS: Early records of this species in Utah include the observations of Ridgway (1877:369) who saw it in ponds and marshes near Great Salt Lake in May and June 1869. Henshaw (1875:488) recorded collecting a specimen at Utah Lake, Utah County, 24 July 1872. There is an abundance of sight records and numerous collected specimens especially from northern and central Utah where more extensive habitats occur that are suitable for breeding. There are also many records of nesting in May and early June. Behle (1960a:21) reported seeing two migrants on the Colorado River at river mile 163 near Red Canyon, San Juan County, 5 July 1958.

Podilymbus podiceps podiceps (Linnaeus)
Pied-billed Grebe

STATUS: A resident throughout the year in the state wherever there are suitable habitats. Less common in winter than in other seasons, this grebe is more likely to inhabit small slow-flowing streams and secluded ponds than are the Eared and Western Grebes. The Pied-billed Grebe is usually seen as individuals or pairs especially during breeding and is less common than either the Western or Eared Grebe.

RECORDS: Early-day ornithologists reported that this species was common around Great Salt Lake and Ogden, Weber County (Allen 1872b:173; Ridgway 1877:369). Henshaw (1875:490) found it to be rather numerous at Rush Lake, Iron County, in September 1872. Most of the more recent records are from the northern counties of the state. However, Hardy and Higgins (1940:95) reported a migrant taken from the Virgin River at St. George, Washington County, 24 November 1934. Although it appears periodically in streams and ponds of southern Utah, presumably as a transient, nesting has been reported only in northern Utah.

Fig. 6. Sharp-shinned Hawk. Ogden Canyon, Weber County, Utah, 10 July 1956. Photo by R. J. Erwin.

FAMILY PELECANIDAE

Pelecanus erythrorhynchos Gmelin
White Pelican
Fig. 3, p. 30

STATUS: A nesting species on islands in Great Salt Lake and a migrant through the state. The White Pelican occurs in the area mostly from March to September, although there are reports of a few individuals wintering (Young 1951:169, Wilson 1952:159). The White Pelican occupies somewhat barren islands for resting and nesting and feeds on fish from freshwater bodies nearby. The history of these birds in Utah has shown considerable fluctuation in the number of breeding birds from year to year

over the past 40 or 50 years. From the earliest records Gunnison and Hat Island in Great Salt Lake have been the principal nesting areas for these pelicans. Stansbury (1852:179) gave the first account of the pelican nesting on Gunnison Island under date of 8 May 1850. Behle (1935:33) counted 3,300 nests and 6,600 adults on Gunnison Island, 29 June 1932. That same year he found 1,500 nests on Hat Island. Behle (1936b: 220) reported that Hat Island had been deserted as a nesting area in 1935 and 1936; however, Cottam and Williams (1939:150–155) visited the island on 11 and 12 June 1938 and reported seeing about 425 young pelicans. It was reported to Behle (1944b: 199) that pelicans nested on Hat Island in

Fig. 7. Sharp-shinned Hawk. Ogden, Weber County, Utah, 10 April 1973. Photo by R. J. Erwin.

1943. When Behle (1949b:268) revisited the island on 1 June 1947, there were no nesting pelicans found.

The nesting colony on Gunnison Island had been reduced to 1,250 nests when Behle visited it on 11 June 1948 (Behle 1949b:268–270). Lies and Behle (1966:286) reported that in 1964 the nesting colony on Gunnison Island, Great Salt Lake, was still intact but apparently reduced in size. They counted 897 young on 9 July 1964. Pelicans are known to have nested on Rock Island, Utah Lake, Utah County, on only one occasion (probably June 1904, Goodwin 1904b: 126–129).

RECORDS: Fremont (1845:149) was the first to mention the presence of the White Pelican near Great Salt Lake at the mouth of Bear River, Box Elder County, 3 September 1843, where one was shot as it flew by. Stansbury (1852:179, 191, 195) visited Gunnison Island 8 and 30 May and 1 June 1850 and described the large nesting colonies there. Remy (1860[1]:154, [2]:450) in 1855 mentioned pelicans as being present in the Salt Lake Valley. Numerous specimens have been collected from Box Elder, Cache, Tooele, Salt Lake, Kane, and Washington counties, and sight records are available from most of the counties of the state. Prior to the restrictions on egg collecting, hundreds of sets were collected for exchange purposes. On 16 May 1894 W. H. Parker took 500 sets of eggs from the colonies on Hat and Gunnison islands. Numerous sets were also taken by Treganza, Boyle, and

Fig. 8.   Swainson's Hawk. Ogden, Weber County, Utah, 30 August 1970. Photo by R. J. Erwin.

others in May 1906 and 1907. In the spring of 1918 Hat Island was visited by C. G. Plummer who reported that representatives of Utah Fish and Game Commissioner had shot many adults and clubbed to death nearly all the young birds presumably on the basis that they were detrimental to fishing interests. The fish consumed by this species are normally the rough or coarse fish, little used for human consumption (Cottam and Uhler 1937:5). S. H. Goodwin (1904b:126–129) found a nesting colony of about 200 young on Rock Island, Utah Lake, in June 1904. White Pelicans have been reported in migration from Kanab, Kane County, 10 and 28 April 1935 (Behle et al. 1958:38); Bryce Canyon, Garfield County, 14 June 1937 (Presnell 1937:259); St. George, Washington County, 20 October 1938 (Hardy and Higgins 1940:95–96). Re-

Fig. 9. Red-tailed Hawk. Ogden, Weber County, Utah, 15 April 1973. Photo by R. J. Erwin.

cently Knopf and Street (1974:428–433) analyzed eggs from the Gunnison Island colony and found that DDD, DDE, and Dieldrin levels were comparable to those reported for this species elsewhere.

Pelecanus occidentalis Linnaeus
Brown Pelican

STATUS: The Brown Pelican is possibly a rare, accidental transient in the state.

RECORDS: This species is included in the Utah list on the basis of a few sight records. No collected specimens from this locality are known to us. Woodbury (1937:225) reported a pelican of brown plumage with a flock of 20 to 30 White Pelicans observed near the Jordan River northwest of Salt Lake City, 28 April 1934. Another record is that of Claude T. Barnes (1946:258–259), who described in some detail a bird seen by him

Fig. 10. Red-tailed Hawk. Ogden, Weber County, Utah, 15 April 1973. Photo by R. J. Erwin.

at Farmington Bay Project, Davis County, 27 May 1944. Lockerbie (1947:162) reported that L. D. Pfouts saw two Brown Pelicans in a flock of White Pelicans on 13 April 1947 at Utah Lake, Utah County. Hayward (1966:305) reported a specimen seen by Merlin L. Killpack and him at Pelican Lake, Uintah County, 18–19 May 1963. Huser and Kashin (Kingery 1973:92) reported one seen at Lake Powell, San Juan County, in October 1972.

FAMILY PHALACROCORACIDAE

Phalacrocorax auritus (Lesson)
Double-crested Cormorant
Fig. 1, p. 11

STATUS: This is a summer resident in Utah usually from April through September. It is known to nest on several islands and in trees in a number of localities.

RECORDS: Stansbury (1852:161, 188, 207) gave the first descriptions of cormorant colonies on Egg Island, Great Salt Lake, which he visited on 9 April, 20 May, and 16 June 1850. The birds were nesting there at the time of his visits. This species was found around Great Salt Lake by Ridgway (1877:369). Numerous specimens have been collected from the Utah area, particularly from Box Elder County, and are now located in the U.S. National Museum of Natural History, Colorado Museum of Natural History, Louis B. Bishop, University of Utah, Utah State University, and Brigham Young University collections. Nesting records are numerous. Beginning in 1906 many sets of eggs were taken at Egg Island, Great Salt Lake, during early April. There is a record of a set of eggs taken by Aldous, 10 May 1901, at White Rock on the northwest side of Antelope Island. Dolphin Island in

Fig. 11. Ferruginous Hawk. Promontory Point, Box Elder County, Utah, June 1955. Photo by R. J. Erwin.

Great Salt Lake was once used as a nesting site (Lewis 1929:7), but it has since been abandoned (Behle 1936a:79). A nesting colony at Bass Pond Reservoir, Millard County, was reported by Pearson (1927: 382). Nesting has occurred in dead trees along Little Bear River, Cache County. This colony was visited by Stanford (1937: 195), 7 July 1936 and 28 April 1937 and by Hayward (field notes), 13 May 1938. Since the establishment of artificial islands in some of the units at Bear River Migratory Bird Refuge, Box Elder County, cormorants have utilized them for nesting sites. Their use began in 1936 and has continued to the present time. Migrants have been observed at St. George, Washington County, 6 May 1940, and collected at Ivins Reservoir, Washington County, 20 April 1940 (Hardy and Higgins 1940:96); observed at Kanab, Kane County, 21 April 1931 (Behle et al. 1958:38); and observed on the Colorado River at mile 109 in Glen Canyon, 16 July 1958 (Behle 1960a:21).

Periodically, cormorants have nested in Utah Valley. In the late 1940s and early 1950s a colony in the Provo Bay area nested in dead trees that had been flooded by high water. A similar nesting colony also in dead trees was established south of Provo City Airport, Utah County, in the late 1950s and early 1960s. During the latter part of the 1960s, as the trees rotted and fell and boating activities on the lake increased, cormorants became very scarce in the vicinity of Utah Lake. Frost (field notes) reported colonies at Geneva Steel dike and south of the Provo airport, Utah County, estimated at 40 nests, 20 May 1970. Mitchell (1975: 927–930) has summarized the history of this species in Utah and indicated a great decline in nesting pairs in the past 50 years.

SUBSPECIES: Peters in Check-list of Birds of the World (1931[1]:86) indicated that both the western race *P. a. albociliatus* and the eastern race *P. a. auritus* are to be found in Utah. The more recent AOU Check-list of North American Birds (1957:35–36) shows only *P. a. auritus* as being in Utah and

limits *P. a. albociliatus* to western Nevada (Pyramid Lake) and Arizona (lower Colorado River, Roosevelt Lake). Behle (1936a: 76–79) concluded that the Utah specimens he examined came closer to *auritus*, in which the plumes found in older breeding birds of both sexes are predominantly black rather than white as they are in *albociliatus*. Our own observations tend to confirm Behle's conclusion.

FAMILY ARDEIDAE

Ardea herodias treganzai Court
Great Blue Heron
Fig. 2, p. 19

STATUS: The Great Blue Heron is a common summer-breeding resident in the lower valleys and along the streams throughout the state. In localities where there is open water, a few remain throughout the winter. Henshaw (1875:464) found it on the borders of Utah Lake in December and assumed that some birds remained through the winter. Frost and Murphy (1965:181) observed it along the Colorado River below Moab, Grand County, every month of the year. It has been observed in January, February, and March in the St. George area (Hardy and Higgins 1940:96). Nests may be built in trees, on the ground in marshes, or occasionally on cliffs.

RECORDS: The earliest record for Utah seems to be that of Stansbury (1852:161, 188, 207), who found these herons on Egg Island, Great Salt Lake, 9 April, 21 May, and 16 June 1850. Allen (1872b:172), Henshaw (1875:464), and Ridgway (1875:31) were other early writers who reported them for the state.

Nesting records are known for many localities around Great Salt Lake and from Egg, Gunnison, and Hat islands on the lake from whence many sets of eggs have been collected. There have been and still are many nesting records from the vicinity of Utah Lake where they have nested in marshes and in trees at various locations in the valley. There have also been many nesting records from the Bear River Migratory Bird Refuge area in Box Elder County. Small nesting colonies occur along the major rivers of the state, especially the Green and Colorado rivers (Behle 1960a:21; Frost and Murphy 1965:181; Hayward 1967:17–18). In 1970 a few herons built their nests on narrow ledges of the sheer cliffs of Lake Powell a few miles south of Bullfrog Marina, Kane County (Hayward field notes).

SUBSPECIES: Great Blue Herons of the Utah area are considered to be *A. h. treganzai* described by Court (1908:291–296), the type locality being Egg Island, Great Salt Lake. The type specimen, now in the collection of the U.S. National Museum of Natural History, was taken by A. O. Treganza, 10 April 1907. Certain authorities (Parks 1955:287–288; Mayr and Short 1970:31) consider *A. herodias* to be conspecific with *A. cinerea.*

Butorides striatus (Linnaeus)
Northern Green Heron

STATUS: The Green Heron is an uncommon summer resident and occasional winter resident in the state and is known to breed in the marshes near the mouth of Bear River. Specimens with gonads in breeding condition have also been taken in the Virgin River area in southwestern Utah.

RECORDS: A breeding male was taken by Huber and Hull near the mouth of Bear River, Box Elder County, 21 June 1927. Two birds were seen at this time. Hardy (1941a:125) recorded a specimen in the collection at Dixie College obtained 17 September 1936 at St. George, Washington County. Behle (1943a:34) collected a male and a female along Santa Clara Creek near St. George, 15–16 May 1940. Behle et al. (1964:450) obtained a female at Spring Run, Salt Lake County, south of Salt Lake City, 27 December 1960, and another near the Salt Lake airport, Salt Lake County, 9 October 1961. Wauer (1969:331) reported it nesting in a cottonwood along Santa Clara Creek, Washington County, 18 and 24 May 1966. There have been a number of sight

records reported in recent years: Behle et al. (1958:39), Kanab, Kane County, 9 June 1935; Hardy and Higgins (1940:96), St. George, Washington County, 9 April 1940; Lockerbie (1956:208), Salt Lake City, 26 December 1955; Ferris (1963:63), Jordan Narrows, Utah County, 13 October 1963; Scott (1964:60), Jordan River, Salt Lake County, 13 October 1963, and (1967:591), Fish Springs, Juab County, 6 August 1967. Scott (1974:489) reported one at Zion National Park, Washington County, 17 December 1973.

SUBSPECIES: A male in breeding condition taken at the mouth of Bear River by Huber and Hull 21 June 1927 was examined by Oberholser and Cottam, who judged it to be of the subspecies *B. v. virescens,* the smaller race common to eastern North America. Other specimens have been determined to be *B. v. anthonyi,* which ranges through the western Pacific states and less commonly into the intermountain area (Hardy 1941a:125; Behle 1943a:34; Behle et al. 1964:450; Wauer 1969:331). *B. virescens* is now considered conspecific with *B. striatus* (American Ornithologists' Union 1976:786).

Florida caerulea caerulea (Linnaeus)
Little Blue Heron

STATUS: A rare summer visitor to the state.

RECORDS: Scott (1958:48) reported a specimen collected at Bear River Migratory Bird Refuge, Box Elder County, 4 September 1957, supposedly the first record for Utah. Subsequently Wilson and Reid (1958:214) reported on the same specimen, indicating it was apparently sick from botulism and died the day it was captured. Scott (1963:422) and Behle (1966:396) noted a specimen that has been found dead near Draper, Salt Lake County, 25 May 1963. This specimen was placed in the University of Utah collection. An immature white-phased bird was seen by Kashin at Farmington Bay, Davis County, in the fall of 1974 (Kingery 1975:93).

Fig. 12. Peregrine Falcon. Ogden, Weber County, Utah, June 1952. Photo by R. D. Porter.

Bubulcus ibis ibis Linnaeus

Cattle Egret

STATUS: This old-world egret, which has emigrated in recent years to parts of Central and South America, has spread northward into the United States and has been reported in Utah on several occasions during the past six or seven years.

RECORDS: Kashin (1964a:55) reported what seemed to be Cattle Egrets at Farmington Bay, 9 August 1964. Two birds were seen by Frost and Hayward near the Bear River Migratory Bird Refuge, Box Elder County, 29 April 1969. These birds had been previously noted by personnel at the refuge and by a party from the University of Utah. Frost and Hayward (field notes) saw a specimen south of Provo, Utah County, 16 April 1971. The bird was observed closely with a spotting scope and was in full breeding plumage. Kingery (1971:775) reported a specimen west of Logan, Cache County, 6 May 1971. A winter record has been reported by Beall (1974: 487) at Bear River Migratory Bird Refuge, Box Elder County, 17 December 1973. This species has now appeared in southern Utah at Zion National Park, Washington County, 18 May 1975 (Kingery 1975:886).

Casmerodius albus egretta (Gmelin)
Great Egret

STATUS: The Great Egret is a rare migrant or wanderer in Utah. No firm record of nesting within the state has been established.

RECORDS: A mature male was captured alive at St. George, Washington County, in May 1934. It was later prepared as a mounted specimen and is now in the collection of Brigham Young University. Ridgway (1877:369) found this species near Salt Lake City in 1869 and suspected that it might be breeding. A specimen was seen by Henshaw (1875:465) near Beaver, Beaver County, 22-25 September 1872. Later sight records include: Hull (letter), near mouth of Bear River, Box Elder County, summer 1926; Wilson, mouth of Bear River, 25 April 1933; Marshall (letter), Bear River Migratory Bird Refuge, mid-October 1936; Twomey (1942:368), near Jensen, Uintah County, 3 and 5 May 1937; Beck (letter), Provo Bay area, Utah County, spring 1940; Cottam (field notes), near Jensen, Uintah County, 12 September 1941; Scott (1959:51),

Fig. 13.   American Kestrel. Ogden, Weber County, Utah, 30 September 1973. Photo by R. J. Erwin.

Bear River Migratory Bird Refuge, Box Elder County, 28 November 1958; Scott (1959:311), Farmington Bay, Great Salt Lake, Davis County, 9 March 1959; (Utah Audubon News 1963:38), Farmington Bay, 20 May 1963; Bent (1926:144), listed the Bear River marshes and Salt Lake Valley in the breeding range of the Great Egret, but there appear to be no nesting data to substantiate this statement.

Egretta thula brewsteri (Thayer and Bangs)
Snowy Egret
Fig. 4, p. 31

STATUS: A common summer resident breeding in marshes around Great Salt Lake, Bear Lake, Cache Valley, Utah Lake, and more recently at Pelican Lake, Uintah County. Wanderers and nonbreeders may be seen around lakes and reservoirs or along streams almost anywhere in the state during the summer. In Utah the Snowy Egret seems to prefer nesting in remote marsh areas where it may occur in company with Great Blue Herons and Black-crowned Night Herons.

RECORDS: Surprisingly there are no early records of this egret in Utah unless the accounts of Ridgway (1875:31; 1877:369) and Henshaw (1875:465) were of this species under the name *Herodias alba egretta*. In their 45-year history of the Snowy Egret in Utah, the Treganzas (1914:245–250) mentioned that Mr. Knudsen had observed what he called the "white squak" near the mouth of Bear River as far back as about 1869. Mr. Knudsen obtained a specimen for Treganza in 1904. There are indications that the egret has increased in numbers after the settlement of the Utah valleys by white man. Collections of eggs in marshes near the mouth of Bear River, Box Elder County, were made by Aldous as early as 1906. Since that time there have been numerous collections of both birds and eggs and hundreds of sight records in various localities within the state.

Nycticorax nycticorax hoactli (Gmelin)
Black-crowned Night Heron

STATUS: A common summer resident, especially in the central valleys of the state. A few individuals may remain into late fall and even through the winter. Henshaw (1875:466) saw it around Utah Lake in December. Kashin (1968:361) reported seeing one in the Salt Lake area, 24 December 1967. There are numerous nesting colonies in less accessible marshes often in company with the Great Blue Heron and the Snowy Egret. Colonies may also nest in trees or tall bushes.

RECORDS: Early writers (Allen 1872b:172; Henshaw 1875:466; Bailey field notes) found this heron common around Great Salt Lake, Utah Lake, and Bear Lake. Numerous nesting records are available from these areas. Twomey (1942:369) found a small nesting colony in marshes south of Jensen, Uintah County, in the spring of 1937. Another nesting colony has been noted at Pelican Lake, Uintah County, by Frost and Hayward (field notes 1964 and 1970; Hayward 1967:18). Hardy and Higgins (1940:96) suggested that it might be "a summer resident in limited numbers" in the St. George area. Most of the collection and sight records are for March through October, but there are several examples of winter occurrence as noted above.

Ixobrychus exilis hesperis Dickey and van Rossem
Least Bittern

STATUS: An uncommon species known to breed at least formerly in the marshes around Great Salt Lake. Since the Least Bittern is shy and retiring in habits, it may be more common than the few records would indicate.

RECORDS: Hardy (1939:86) recorded a specimen collected near the Virgin River, Washington County, 20 May 1938. G. W. Browning and J. W. Sugden collected a set of eggs from Hot Springs Lake north of

Salt Lake City, 8 April 1884. The species was known to breed in this area before the marsh was drained. Several sight records are available: Bailey reported it from the Bear River Gun Club, 10 June 1936; Hull and Wilson added it to the list of Bear River Migratory Bird Refuge birds in 1937; and Cottam (1945b:172) found it at Bear River Migratory Bird Refuge, 2 June 1943, all localities in Box Elder County. Wauer and Russell (1967:420) observed it along the Virgin River, south of Washington, Washington County, 27 June 1965 and 28 August 1965.

Botaurus lentiginosus (Rackett)
American Bittern

STATUS: A summer resident of marshes all through the state, especially around the borders of the Great Salt Lake and Utah Lake. A few remain in the state throughout the winter (Killpack 1959:238). Since the bittern is solitary and tends to live in remote areas of the marshlands, it is rarely seen, but it may be more common than the records indicate.

RECORDS: The first recorded specimen taken in the state was obtained by the Stansbury expedition in 1850 (Baird 1852:320). Other early workers (Allen 1872b:172; Henshaw 1875:466–467; Nelson 1875:348; Ridgway 1877:369, 618) referred to it as being common in the early days of settlement. Numerous collections and observations have been made in more recent years, with specimens being found in several collections throughout the country. Most of the numerous nesting records are for May and a few for early June.

FAMILY CICONIIDAE

Mycteria americana Linnaeus
Wood Stork

STATUS: A sparse though somewhat regular summer wanderer in the state, at least formerly. Henshaw (1875:462) stated: "At Rush Lake I saw several different flocks, none composed of more than ten indivi-

duals." Most of the collection and observation records, other than Henshaw's (1875: 462), seem to have been made in the 1930s. We have not noted any published records in recent years.

RECORDS: The following records of collected specimens are known to the writers: Rush Lake, Iron County, two specimens taken by Henshaw, 1 October 1872 (Henshaw 1875:463); Hooper, Weber County, 8 August 1930 (Stanford 1938:136) and now in the Utah State University collection; Springer (1931:120) recorded a specimen from Holladay, Salt Lake County, 8 August 1930; marshes at mouth of Bear River, Box Elder County, 19 July 1934, an adult male now in University of Utah collection; near Lehi, Utah County, summer 1935, mounted by John Hutchings and now in Brigham Young University collection; Clear Lake, Millard County, 16 September 1938, U.S. Biological Survey; Virgin City, Washington County, 28 August 1939 in University of Utah collection (Long 1940:122). Several observations have been recorded for Box Elder, Davis, Salt Lake, Millard, and Piute counties, all in the 1930s. Palmer (1962: 512) indicated on his map a record for extreme southwestern Utah. This may be the record reported by Long (1940:122). Kraft reported one at Fish Springs, Juab County, 24 June 1973 (Kingery 1974:83).

FAMILY THRESKIORNITHIDAE

Plegadis chihi (Vieillot)
White-faced Ibis

STATUS: A common summer resident, breeding in large colonies, often associated with several species of herons. Occasionally occurring also in winter (Kashin 1963b: 263). The known nesting colonies are in marshes around Great Salt Lake and Utah Lake. In early spring they often feed in large flocks in open fields that have been flooded, as noted by Tanner (1941:86), southwest of Hurricane, Washington County, 6 May 1941.

RECORDS: Early ornithologists who visited the state all recorded the White-faced Ibis. Allen (1872b:172) reported it as common around Great Salt Lake in 1871 but indicated that it might not have occurred prior to that time. Henshaw (1875:463) found it common in spring and fall around Utah Lake. Ridgway in 1869 (1877:369, 615) saw a few near Great Salt Lake and considered it to be an abundant breeder (1875:31). Numerous specimens have been collected and are deposited at the University of Utah, Brigham Young University, and in other collections within the state and throughout the country. Large nesting colonies have been located in Box Elder, Davis, Salt Lake, and Utah counties, and many sets of eggs have been collected from some of these colonies.

Ajaia ajaja (Linnaeus)
Roseate Spoonbill

STATUS: A very rare visitor to the state.

RECORDS: There is only one authentic record known to us. Barnes (1919:565) stated that on 2 July 1919 a specimen was brought to him for identification. The specimen had been killed by Joseph Condley near Wendover, Tooele County, and was one of five that appeared on his ranch. Barnes had the bird mounted and displayed it on several occasions. Later it disappeared from his home and was considered lost (Behle 1944a:69). Behle (1955:17) reported that the specimen has been relocated and is now in the University of Utah collection. The AOU Check-list (1957:57) indicates that it occasionally wanders to northern Utah. This statement probably is based on Barnes's record.

FAMILY PHOENICOPTERIDAE

Phoenicopterus ruber Linnaeus
American Flamingo

STATUS: A very rare and apparently accidental visitor to the state.

RECORDS: The inclusion of this species in the state list is based on sight records. A specimen was seen by Don E. Neilson at Clear Lake Waterfowl Management Area, Millard County. It was observed on 25 July 1962 and again on 12 October (Worthen 1968:129). Color photographs were taken of the bird through a telephoto lens, amd there seems to be no doubt of the identification. W. E. Ritter and Reuben Dietz saw one at Buffalo Bay, Antelope Island, Great Salt Lake, 3 August 1966 (Behle and Perry 1975:9). Kingery (1971:883) reported two sight records, one at Bear River, Box Elder County, and the other at Farmington Bay, Davis County, both in June and August 1971. Contact with the Salt Lake City Zoo indicated that no bird had escaped from that institution. These records were substantiated by photographs.

FAMILY ANATIDAE

Olor columbianus (Ord)
Whistling Swan

STATUS: A common migrant and sometimes a winter resident. During migration the birds may congregate in large flocks.

RECORDS: Stansbury (1852:108, 159) recorded immense flocks of this swan near the mouth of the Bear River, 22 October 1849, and at the mouth of the Jordan River, 4 April 1850. His party collected two specimens in this area on 10 March 1850 (Baird 1852:321). Beckwith also collected a specimen at Salt Lake City (Baird 1858:758). Several other specimens have been collected in Box Elder, Weber, and Salt Lake counties and are in various museums around the country. One specimen in the Colorado Museum of Natural History was taken near Moab, Grand County, 10 November 1925. One was reported shot during the spring of 1945 at Kanab, Kane County (Behle et al. 1958:39). It has been found in December along the Virgin River near St. George, Washington County (Hardy and Higgins 1940:96), and along the Colorado River near Moab, Grand County, in February 1952 (Behle 1960a:22). Sherwood (1960:

370–377) discussed the status of this swan in Salt Lake Valley.

Olor buccinator Richardson
Trumpeter Swan

STATUS: Formerly common and probably a nesting species in the northern part of the state in early days. Presently occurs only as a rare straggler.

RECORDS: Six immature birds were captured and sent to the New York Zoological Park, 5 January 1901. These birds were obtained near Salt Lake City (Coale 1915:87). A mounted specimen in the University of Utah collection was taken at Spring Lake, Millard County, in April 1892 and was presented to the university by J. H. Clive. One was shot on Great Salt Lake, 23 November 1959 (Scott 1960:328). Several sight records have been recorded, but since this swan is difficult to distinguish from the Whistling Swan in the field, these observations are to be looked upon with some caution. This is especially true at the present time since the Trumpeter is inclined to stay close to its nesting ground at Red Rock Lake, Montana; Yellowstone Park, Wyoming; British Columbia; and southern Alaska. Bartonek (1966:521), who is acquainted with the calls of both the trumpeter and whistler, recorded hearing a trumpeter in an area about five miles south of Bear River Migratory Bird Refuge, Box Elder County, 27 December 1965. One was observed at Fish Springs National Wildlife Refuge, Juab County, during the summer of 1968 (Behle and Perry 1975:9).

Branta canadensis (Linnaeus)
Canada Goose

STATUS: The Canada Goose is a common summer breeder throughout much of the state. Many individuals migrate through the areas, and, depending somewhat on the severity of the weather, others remain in the state throughout the winter. The most common breeding areas are around Great Salt Lake, especially at Farmington Bay Refuge, Davis County, and Bear River Migratory Bird Refuge, Box Elder County; but other lakes and reservoirs throughout the state are also used. Nesting also occurs along the larger waterways, especially the Green and Colorado rivers.

RECORDS: Baird (1858:765), Remy (1860 [2]:449), and Ridgway (1877:620) stated that this goose was found in the Salt Lake Valley. Ridgway (1877:620) collected an egg on Carrington Island, Great Salt Lake, 17 June 1869. Many recent records for this species are found in the literature.

SUBSPECIES: The common breeding race of the Canada Goose in Utah is B. c. moffitti, but several other races have appeared in the population apparently as migrants or winter residents. Because the several subspecies of B. canadensis are based largely on measurements (Delacour 1954:164–178) and because there is much size intergradation among the races, it is difficult to place individual birds in their proper categories. As far as we are aware, no substantial series of Utah specimens have been assembled for taxonomic study. The best we can do here is list the records of the nonbreeding races available to us. Three specimens from Bear River Marshes, Box Elder County, 25 November 1933 and 23 October 1941 (University of Utah), were identified as B. c. leucopareia. One mounted specimen in the Bear River Gun Club collection taken about 1907 was identified as B. c. hutchinsii, and several other small specimens taken in Cache, Piute, and Millard counties were considered to be of this race (Cottam, Williams, and Gunther pers. comm.). Worthen (1968(136–138) lists several specimens in the University of Utah collection that represent nonbreeding races: A specimen approaching B. c. parvipes was taken at Fool Creek Reservoir near Oak City, Millard County, 4 January 1964. Another specimen from Deseret, Millard County, 13 December 1953, appears to be B. c. taverneri. B. c. minima was collected at Clear Lake, Millard County, 8 November 1962.

Branta bernicla nigricans (Lawrence)
Black Brant

STATUS: The Black Brant is considered to be accidental or casual in Utah. It is generally a coastal and saltwater species.

RECORDS: Brant were seen at Rush Lake, Iron County, 1 October 1872 (Henshaw 1875:472). A pair were taken on the Bear River Marshes, Box Elder County, in the fall or winter of 1913 and were mounted and placed on display at the Bear River Gun Club. Behle and Perry (1975:10) reported a specimen from Ogden Bay Waterfowl Management Area, Weber County, 29 October 1955.

Anser albifrons (Scopoli)
White-fronted Goose

STATUS: This goose is known principally as an uncommon spring and fall migrant through Utah. However, there have been a few December and January records in recent years.

RECORDS: A specimen of White-fronted Goose was taken by the Stansbury party (Baird 1852:321) at the mouth of Jordan River, Great Salt Lake, in March of 1850. Since that time a few additional collections have been made: Alexander Wetmore took an immature male at the Bear River Marshes, Box Elder County, 10 October 1916, and examined another taken by a hunter at the same place on 12 October 1915; Syninger reported a specimen which he captured alive near the mouth of the Jordan River, Davis County, in the fall of 1926 and kept alive for several years on his game farm; Hull collected a juvenile female 18 miles west of Brigham City, Box Elder County, 28 September 1928, and four birds on 29 September 1928 north of Bear River Bay; Behle and Selander (1952:26) reported a specimen taken at Bear River Gun Club, Box Elder County, 28 September 1928; Hayward (1944:204) published a record of a specimen in the Brigham Young University collection taken at Lehi, Utah

County, 22 April 1933; a specimen taken illegally by a hunter near Corinne, Box Elder County, 10 November 1937, was confiscated and mounted for display at the Bear River Migratory Bird Refuge; Behle and Selander (1952:26) reported an additional specimen taken at Lake Front Gun Club, Salt Lake County, 10 October 1948; Hayward (1966:305) reported a specimen in the Brigham Young University collection taken at Utah Lake, Utah County, 8 November 1964.

Several additional sight records have been published: Van den Akker (1949b: 178), south of Salt Lake City, Salt Lake County, 3 January 1949; Lockerbie (1952: 160), Salt Lake County, 23 December 1951.

SUBSPECIES: It appears that two subspecies of the White-fronted Goose may occur in Utah. Most of the collected specimens studied are of the smaller *A. a. frontalis* in which the length of the culmen is about 51 or 52 mm. A specimen obtained near St. George, Washington County, 24 September 1939, and now in the collection of Dixie College, has been identified as the larger race *A. a. gambelli*, sometimes known as the Tule Goose (Hardy and Higgins 1940:96). The culmen on this specimen measures 58 mm. Observant hunters in the state have also recognized two different-sized geese in their hunting experience.

Chen caerulescens caerulescens (Linnaeus)
Snow Goose

STATUS: A common spring and fall migrant often appearing in large flocks especially in freshwater bodies around the borders of Great Salt Lake. In spring the Snow Geese appear in late February or early March and remain until about mid-April. In fall they occur usually from late September until the freeze-up.

RECORDS: All of the early ornithologists who visited Utah noted the Snow Goose (Stansbury 1852:161; Remy 1860[2]:449; Allen 1872b:172; Henshaw 1875:470; Ridgway 1877:619), but apparently there were

Fig. 14. Golden Eagle. Dugway, Tooele County, Utah, spring 1954. Photo by R. D. Porter.

no collections made by them. In more recent years several specimens have been taken and are now in the U.S. National Museum of Natural History, Utah State University, University of Utah, and Brig-

ham Young University. The widespread occurrence of this goose in the state is indicated by many sight observations in such localities as Bear River Migratory Bird Refuge, Box Elder County; mouth of Jordan

River, Davis County; Utah Lake, Utah County; Clear Lake Refuge, Millard County; Minersville Reservoir, Beaver County; and Virgin River, Washington County.

SUBSPECIES: Examinations of Snow Geese taken in Utah indicate that they are all of the race *C. c. caerulescens*. Sight records of the dark morph that has been known as the "Blue Goose" have been reported from time to time. They are as follows: Marshall (1937:128) observed one at Bear River Migratory Bird Refuge, Box Elder County, 13 October 1936; Scott (1954:322) has recorded two specimens seen at Farmington Bay Refuge, Davis County, 15 March 1954; a field party (Scott 1960:59 and 1967:63) noted one each at the Bear River Migratory Bird Refuge on 5 November 1959 and in the fall of 1966.

Chen rossii (Cassin)
Ross' Goose

STATUS: Ross' Goose is a casual though regular migrant through Utah.

RECORDS: Several ornithologists have taken specimens at the Bear River Migratory Bird Refuge, Box Elder County. Wetmore took one on 22 October 1914; Marshall stated several were taken by hunters at the public shooting grounds in the fall of 1924; Hull reported five killed in one day in the fall of 1929. Marshall recorded one taken on 30 November 1936; Behle and Selander (1952:26) reported a specimen from Bear River Migratory Bird Refuge, 27 October 1949; Scott (1954:354–355) also gave a sight record for Salt Springs, western Utah, 31 May 1954. Behle (1956:72) gave another record for Desert Lake, 15 miles southeast of Price, Carbon County, about 1 December 1955. Behle et al. (1964:450) reported a mounted specimen at the headquarters of the Utah Division of Wildlife Resources in Salt Lake City taken at Flowell, Millard County, 3 April 1961. Scott (1966:77) reported one that had been collected at Bear River Migratory Bird Refuge in the fall of 1965.

Dendrocygna bicolor helva Wetmore and Peters
Fulvous Whistling-Duck

STATUS: A casual or accidental visitor to the state.

RECORDS: A specimen taken by V. T. Davis at Bear River Marshes, Box Elder County, in November 1908, was mounted and placed on display at Bear River Gun Club. Behle et al. (1964:451) reported a female taken by Donald E. Neilson at Clear Lake, Millard County, 20 May 1959. Scott (1969:612) reported two seen near Cedar City, Iron County, 10 May 1969, by Murie.

Anas platyrhynchos platyrhynchos Linnaeus
Mallard

STATUS: A common permanent resident of the state where it breeds around shallow waters. Less common in winter than summer but present in winter wherever there is open water. The Mallard is perhaps the most widespread duck in the state, since it inhabits any type of shallow water including small ponds or even ditches and canals. It is most abundant at elevations ranging between 4,000 and 7,000 feet.

RECORDS: Hundreds of collection and sight records are available from virtually all the counties of the state where the habitat is suitable.

Anas rubripes Brewster
Black Duck

STATUS: The Black Duck is regarded as a casual migrant and occasional winter resident. Although this duck has been introduced into Utah on several occasions, it is doubtful that it was ever a regular native resident. Yarrow (reported by Henshaw 1875:473) saw what he believed to be this species "having seen a number" at Rush Lake, Iron County, in November 1872. Later Yarrow (1877:4) wrote that he collected Black Ducks at Rush Lake and stated ". . . I have killed too many Black Ducks not to know them when I see them." Subsequent observations, however, have not supported Yarrow's observation. Specimens liberated at the Bear River Migratory Bird Refuge and eggs of black ducks exchanged for mallard eggs in nests found in the wild have not established this species as a common bird in Utah. Black ducks are natives of marshes and streams of the eastern United States and do not seem to be well adapted to western conditions. This species commonly hybridizes with the Mallard.

RECORDS: One was collected at Bear River Gun Club, Box Elder County, 10 November 1938. Another at the same locality was taken on 8 December 1942 and is on display at Bear River Migratory Bird Refuge (Williams et al. 1943:159). Behle and Selander (1952:26) reported a specimen now in the University of Utah collection taken at Farmington Bay, Davis County, 22 November 1951. Another specimen was collected near Farmington Bay Refuge, Davis County, 16 October 1965 (Behle 1966:396). Most specimens studied appear to have been crosses with mallards. A few sight records of the Black Duck are noted: pond near Jordan River, Salt Lake County, 20 December 1937 (T. Evans and A. Nielson); Bear River marshes, Box Elder County, November 1939 and 24 April 1941 (V. T. Wilson); Follett (1960:253), Hyde Park, Cache County, 26 December 1959; Scott (1967:63), Bear River Migratory Bird Refuge, fall 1966.

Anas strepera Linnaeus
Gadwall

STATUS: A common breeding species throughout the state but more abundant northward. It is most commonly found from mid-February to mid-November, but a few may remain throughout the winter where there is open water.

RECORDS: Stansbury's party took a speci-

men in Salt Lake Valley as early as 1850. Specimens were collected by McCarthy for Simpson at Utah Lake in January and April 1859 and reported by Baird (1876:381). Ridgway (1877:369) reported this species as being in the sloughs and marshes near the Jordan River and in open ponds near the Great Salt Lake. Since the time of these earliest records, numerous specimens have been collected and innumerable sight records noted in appropriate habitats in all sections of the state.

Anas acuta Linnaeus
Pintail

STATUS: During spring and autumn migration the Pintail is probably the most common duck in Utah. Many remain throughout the winter when the weather is not too cold, and a goodly number nest here, particularly in the northern part of the state. Like the Mallard, the Pintail is primarily a shallow-water bird, often feeding in temporary ponds during migration, especially during spring.

RECORDS: Early observers (Baird 1852: 323; Remy 1860[2]:450; Allen 1872b:173; Baird 1876:381; and others) collected specimens and considered this duck to be common. Since that time many specimens have been observed throughout most of the counties. Sight records are abundant.

Anas crecca carolinensis Gmelin
American Green-winged Teal

STATUS: The Green-winged Teal is a common migrant duck in Utah where it appears in large flocks from about 1 March to 15 April and again from 1 September to 1 December. A few pairs occasionally nest within the state on the high lakes of the Uinta Mountains, sometimes as high as 10,000 feet (I. Rasmussen and C. L. Hayward field notes). Wherever water remains open, a few may winter in Utah (Grater 1943:75).

RECORDS: Collections of Green-winged Teal were reported by most of the early ornithologists who worked in the state in the 1800s (Baird 1852:322; Baird 1858:778; Remy 1860[2]:450; Ridgway 1877:623). Since then many collection and observation records have been published.

Anas discors discors Linnaeus
Blue-winged Teal

STATUS: This teal is a consistent though not abundant spring and fall migrant and nests sparingly especially in the northern part of the state. A few may also remain throughout the winter (Grater 1943:75). According to Henshaw (1875:477), it was as numerous as the Green-winged Teal in 1872.

RECORDS: A few specimens were seen or taken by early explorers such as Henshaw (1875:477), Nelson (1875:345), Baird (1876: 381), and Ridgway (1877:369), but there is no reference to the species existing in great abundance except in the case of Henshaw's report. Numerous more recent records are available.

Anas cyanoptera septentrionalium
Snyder and Lumsden
Cinnamon Teal

STATUS: The Cinnamon Teal is a very common summer resident and breeds in great numbers throughout the state wherever there are suitable marshlands. A few remain throughout the winter especially in southern Utah, but the bulk of the population is migratory.

RECORDS: Baird (1852:322–323) reported three specimens collected by the Stansbury expedition along the Jordan River as being the second, third, and fourth individuals obtained in North America. This species was first described from birds collected in the Straits of Magellan. The first specimen from North America was collected near Opelousas, Louisiana, by Dr. Pilate and sent to the Philadelphia Academy of Science. Because the Louisiana bird had not been described and also because there was no description of a North American specimen, Baird (1852:323),gave a detailed account of a male and female from the Salt Lake area. All of the early-day ornithologists attest to the abundance of this species.

Fig. 15. Marsh Hawk. Ogden Bay, Weber County, Utah, spring 1948. Photo by R. D. Porter.

The many collections that have been made up to the present time further attest to the species' abundance. Records of occurrence indicate that fall migrations are completed by the last of September. Most of the spring migration takes place in April except in southern Utah where they have been reported in February and March (Hardy and Higgins 1940:97).

Anas penelope Linnaeus
European Wigeon

STATUS: This is a species of casual or accidental occurrence in Utah.

RECORD: Wilson and Young (1956:390) recorded a specimen taken at Bear River Migratory Bird Refuge, Box Elder County, 19 October 1956. Behle and Perry (1975: 11) reported a sight record by Bill Pingree at Lakefront Gun Club, eight miles northwest of Salt Lake City, Salt Lake County, 15 December 1963.

Anas americana Gmelin
American Wigeon

STATUS: The American Wigeon is an uncommon although consistent spring and summer resident in Utah. A few of these ducks are usually seen in any mixed concentration of waterfowl from March through the summer. A few occurrences have also been recorded in winter (Kashin 1968:361). Nesting takes place in the northern counties of the state.

RECORDS: Beginning with the Stansbury expedition (Baird 1852:322), when specimens were taken on the Jordan River, 4 April 1850, all of the early visitors to the state reported the American Wigeon. Henshaw (1875:475) considered it to be abundant in Utah in the fall, remaining around certain warm springs and sloughs all winter in the Provo area. Specimens have been collected and numerous sightings recorded for most of the counties of the state. Nesting records with eggs being laid as early as 2 March (Boyle collection) are known to

us from Box Elder, Weber, Davis, Tooele, Salt Lake, Wasatch, and Uintah counties.

Anas clypeata Linnaeus
Northern Shoveler

STATUS: One of the more common of the Utah ducks, the Shoveler breeds in abundance in marsh edges around the Great Salt Lake as well as in other marshlands of the state. It is primarily a summer resident, although a few remain through the winter where there is open water (Foster 1971:463; Allen 1972:478).

RECORDS: The first known collection in the state was made by McCarthy at Utah Lake, Utah County, 20 March 1859 and reported by Baird (1876:381). Ridgway (1875: 31) regarded it as a breeder of questionable abundance in Salt Lake Valley in 1869. Numerous collections are on record up to the present time. Breeding records are numerous especially for the northern counties of the state. Most of these records are for April, May, and June.

Aix sponsa (Linnaeus)
Wood Duck

STATUS: An uncommon visitor or casual transient in Utah. Allen (1872b:172) reported this species at Ogden, Weber County. Some early records indicate that it may have been a summer resident in former times and probably bred near the mouth of Bear River (Woodbury et al. 1949:8).

RECORDS: Most of the more recent records available seem to be for the fall. They are as follows: Hyrum Canyon, Cache County, 11 November 1934 (Stanford 1938: 136), Lake View, Utah County, November 1936 (BYU collection); Circleville, Piute County, 16 October 1942 (Behle and Ross 1945:168); Blacksmith Fork, Cache County, 2 July 1944 (Webster 1947:40); Springville, Utah County, 2 November 1946 (BYU collection); Clear Lake, Millard County, 1957, 1959, and 1961 (Behle et al. 1964:451), Farmington Bay, Davis County, 10 October

1962 (Behle et al. 1964:451); St. George, Washington County, December 1964, and along Santa Clara Creek, Washington County, 29 December 1964 (Wauer 1969: 331); Salt Lake City, 20 September 1965 (Scott 1966:77); Cedar Valley, Iron County, 1 October 1966 (Scott 1967:63).

Aythya americana (Eyton)
Redhead

STATUS: A summer resident throughout the state, breeding in marshes with deep channels of water. Common in northern Utah, more sparingly in the south. Most abundant during migration in March-April and August-September.

RECORDS: Some of the earlier collections in Utah were those of the Beckwith party in 1854 near Salt Lake City (Baird 1858: 794) and others reported by Baird (1876: 381) as being taken at Utah Lake, Utah County, 21 March 1859. Many specimens have been collected and observed since that time in most of the counties of the state.

Aythya collaris (Donovan)
Ring-necked Duck

STATUS: A rare summer resident in northern Utah and a casual migrant throughout the state. There are a few records of nesting.

RECORDS: Henshaw (1875:479) obtained a young female at Rush Lake, Iron County, in September 1872. A specimen in the U.S. Biological Survey collection was taken at the mouth of Bear River, Box Elder County, 21 October 1916. Specimens in the University of Utah collection were taken at Willard Spur, Box Elder County, in November 1929, and at the mouth of Bear River, Box Elder County, 12 October 1932. There is also a specimen taken at Bear River, 1 November 1937, in the Utah State University collection (Stanford 1938:136) and one from Ivins Reservoir, Washington County, 20 April 1940, collected by Harold Higgins

(Hardy 1941:125). The Brigham Young University collection contains a specimen taken at the Bear River Migratory Bird Refuge, 15 March 1966, by Lloyd Gunther and another from Mona Reservoir, Juab County, 14 November 1969. The University of Utah collection contains specimens taken at Clear Lake, Millard County, 12 April 1965, 7 November 1965, and 4 March 1966 (Worthen 1968:152–153).

Aythya valisineria (Wilson)
Canvasback

STATUS: Uncommon breeder of the Great Salt Lake marshes and a common migrant during March-April and October-November. Uncommon in winter.

RECORDS: There appear to be no records of early collections of the Canvasback in Utah. However, Ridgway (1877:625) considered it to be an abundant bird in winter on the lakes and marshes of the Great Basin. Specimens from the Bear River Marshes, Box Elder County, taken 11 August 1914 and 23 September 1916, are in the U.S. National Museum of Natural History collection. Other specimens from the same locality are in the Brigham Young University, University of Utah, and Utah State University collections, taken 4 November 1928, 14 November 1929, and November 1937, respectively. Most of the nesting records are from localities around Great Salt Lake. Low and Nelson (1945:131) reported seeing two broods at Ogden Bay Refuge, Weber County, one on 7 July 1943 and the other in mid-July 1943. At Clear Lake, Millard County, 27 June 1944, they saw a brood of nine young about three weeks old.

Aythya marila nearctica Stejneger
Greater Scaup

STATUS: A rare migrant through the state. There is no certain evidence that it nests in Utah.

RECORDS: The Greater Scaup was con-

Fig. 16.   American Kestrel.   Ogden, Weber County, Utah, 15 June 1959.   Photo by R. J. Erwin.

sidered by Allen (1872b:172) to be a common duck around Great Salt Lake in the fall and by Henshaw (1875:479) at Utah Lake and up the Provo River as the lake froze in November 1872. Several specimens were shot at that time. The status of this species has definitely changed, since at the present time it is rarely taken or seen, being far less common than the Lesser Scaup. Several specimens now in the U.S. National Museum of Natural History were taken by Wetmore in the Bear River Marshes, Box

Elder County, October 1916. A specimen taken from the same locality, 19 October 1932, and one from Farmington Bay Refuge, Davis County, 27 March 1949, are in the University of Utah collection (Behle and Selander 1952:26). A bird killed by botulism was picked up by Cottam at Ogden Bay, Weber County, 9 September 1942. Stanford (1931:4) recorded birds of this species at Redmond Lake, 15 April 1929, and at Salina Canyon, 27 March 1929, both localities in Sevier County. It is not clear whether these birds were collected or only observed. Barnes (1943:102) observed birds at Farmington Bay, Davis County, 21 March 1942. Kingery (1975:721) reported 20 birds at Bear River late in February 1975.

Aythya affinis (Eyton)
Lesser Scaup

STATUS: A common migrant through the state in March-April and October-November; uncommon summer resident and breeder of northern Utah.

RECORDS: The earliest collection records seem to be 10 specimens taken by Wetmore at the Bear River Marshes in October 1916. That this species was present earlier is implied by Henshaw (1875:470): "I did not secure any evidence of the presence at this time of the closely allied species *Fulix affinis,* though if not there then it had been a little earlier, as the gunners distinguish between them, and assure me of its abundance." Several other specimens in the collections of the University of Utah, Brigham Young University, and other institutions have been assembled. Mayr and Short (1970:34) called attention to the close taxonomic relationship of the Greater and Lesser Scaups.

Bucephala clangula americana (Bonaparte)
Common Goldeneye

STATUS: A common migrant through the state in February-April and October-

December. Also a rather common winter bird living on the larger streams that stay open. It may occasionally linger into the spring as illustrated by Carter's (Monson 1963:423) finding two at Beaver Dam Wash, Washington County, 14 May 1963.

RECORDS: Beckwith's party (Baird 1858: 796) took a specimen near Salt Lake City in 1854. Henshaw and Yarrow collected a specimen on Utah Lake, Utah County, 2 November 1872, and Henshaw (1875:480–481) reported it as a common duck in late fall and winter on Utah Lake and Provo River, Utah County. Specimens in the Brigham Young University collection include two from the Bear River Marshes, Box Elder County, 4 and 15 November 1928; one from near Provo, Utah County, 23 December 1932; and one from Utah Lake, Utah County, 4 April 1933. There are no certain records of nesting within the state. It has been seen at Kanab, Kane County, 21 April 1931 (Behle et al. 1958:42). Hardy and Higgins (1940:97) reported one collected at Leeds, Washington County, 14 April 1940. It has also been observed in Glen Canyon on the Colorado River by Behle (1960:23), 16 April 1947.

Bucephala islandica (Gmelin)
Barrow's Goldeneye

STATUS: Barrow's Goldeneye is considered to be a casual migrant through the state with a few birds remaining over winter.

RECORDS: Specimens were taken by Henshaw (1875:482) at Utah Lake, Utah County, 11 November and 1 December 1872. A mounted specimen taken in the Bear River Marshes, Box Elder County, about 1908, is in the Bear River Gun Club collection. Another specimen reported by Cottam et al. (1942:52) was taken at the same locality during the hunting season of 1939. Recent sight records are as follows: Kanab, Kane County, 20, 22, 27 April 1931 (Behle et al. 1958:42); a male near the Virgin River at St. George, Washington County, 20 April

1940 (Hardy and Higgins 1940:97); and seven on Sevier River near Hatch, Garfield County, 14 February 1942 (Behle et al. 1958:42); Logan, Cache County, January and March 1949, reported by Van den Akker (1949:179); and at Bear River Migratory Bird Refuge, Box Elder County, 28 December 1964, reported by Wilson (1965: 309). Scott (1963:346) recorded a collection at Bear River Migratory Bird Refuge, Box Elder County, 27 March 1963.

Bucephala albeola (Linnaeus)
Bufflehead

STATUS: The Bufflehead is a fairly common duck during spring migration from late February to early May and again in the fall from mid-October to early December. It is also a sparse winter and summer resident, although there appears to be no evidence that it nests within the state.

RECORDS: Early observers in Utah found the Bufflehead present in the state. The Stansbury party (Baird 1852:324) took a specimen on Provo River, Utah County, 22 February 1850. Birds were also reported by Remy (1860[2]:450), and two specimens were collected by Henshaw and Yarrow at Provo, 25 November 1872 (Henshaw 1875: 482). Numerous specimens taken more recently are in the U.S. Biological Survey, University of Utah, Utah State University, Brigham Young University collections, and others.

Clangula hyemalis (Linnaeus)
Oldsquaw

STATUS: A rare transient of northern Utah. Records available indicate that the Oldsquaw is a late fall and early winter migrant.

RECORDS: The following collection and observation records are available: Bear River Marshes, Box Elder County, a male, 20 December 1929 (University of Utah); near Benson, Cache County, a pair taken about 1915, mounted in Utah State University collection; mouth of Weber River, We-

ber County, male taken in November 1927 was mounted and put on display in Ogden, Weber County (Hull); Bear River Marshes, a female taken 19 November 1933, University of Utah collection, and two females taken 22 November 1936 (Marshall); Utah Lake, Utah County, taken about 1936 and mounted in Brigham Young University collection; Cottam et al. (1942:52) reported one seen at Bear River Migratory Bird Refuge, Box Elder County, 10 October 1941, and mentioned that 13 specimens had been taken during the hunting season of 1934; Williams et al. (1943:159–160) report one seen flying near Perry, Box Elder County, in December 1942; Ogden Bay, Weber County, two seen in fall 1948 and two taken by hunters at Bear River in the fall of 1948, reported by Van den Akker (1949:25); Wilson and Norr (1950:27; 1951:31) noted specimens that were collected at Bear River Migratory Bird Refuge by hunters, 11 November 1949 and 24 November 1950; adult female from Clear Lake, Millard County, 27 October 1956 (Worthen 1968:157).

Histrionicus histrionicus (Linnaeus)
Harlequin Duck

STATUS: Accidental in Utah.

RECORD: Two birds were taken on Box Elder Creek near Brigham City, Box Elder County, 13 April 1913, by James Hull. One of the birds was mounted and placed on display in a local hotel where it was examined and identified by Alexander Wetmore (field notes). This is the only record of the Harlequin Duck from Utah known to us. The present location of this specimen is unknown to us. Behle (mimeographed list 1971) and Behle and Perry (1975:12) regard the occurrence of this species in the state as hypothetical.

Melanitta deglandi deglandi (Bonaparte)
White-winged Scoter

STATUS: The white-winged Scoter is an uncommon fall migrant appearing on the

Fig. 17. Common Snipe. Monte Cristo, Rich County, Utah, 30 June 1963. Photo by R. J. Erwin.

larger bodies of water in northern Utah. Also an occasional spring visitor to the state.

RECORDS: Two specimens in the Colorado Natural History Museum were taken near Corinne, Box Elder County, 9 October 1914. While Alexander Wetmore was stationed at the Bear River marshes, Box Elder County, he had reports of specimens being shot by hunters in that area in November 1914 and 1915 and of a specimen being given to him by H. M. Porter that was taken on 8 October 1916. Specimens in the University of Utah collection include females taken at the public shooting grounds near Little Mountain, Weber County, 30 November 1930 and 26 October 1932. Cottam et al. (1942:52) reported a specimen collected at the Bear River Migratory Bird Refuge, Box Elder County, 1 October 1941, and two shot during the 1941 hunting season. The only spring records available to us are those of Webster (47:40) who saw them at Pineview Reservoir, Weber County. He recorded two birds on 29 March 1945, eight on 5 April, and two on 9 April. Wilson and Norr (1951:31) reported seeing 50 birds at Bear

River Migratory Bird Refuge, Box Elder County, 30 November 1950. Shaffer stated that a specimen was collected by a hunter and brought to the Tracy Aviary in late October 1952, where it died the following month (Utah Audubon News 1952:52). The locality is not indicated. Lloyd F. Gunther, former manager, Bear River Migratory Bird Refuge, Box Elder County, collected a specimen in the fall of 1966 at the refuge (Scott 1967:63). Worthen (1968:158) stated that a specimen was taken by a hunter at Clear Lake, Millard County, in 1955 or 1956, and was sent to the State Division of Wildlife Resources. However, this specimen has not been located since.

Melanitta perspicillata (Linnaeus)
Surf Scoter

STATUS: A rare transient in Great Salt Lake and probably Utah valleys.

RECORDS: Wetmore obtained an immature female killed at the Duckville Gun Club, Box Elder County, 24 October 1916. Bent (1925:151) referred to a migration of the Surf Scoter in the Bear River area at this same period. There was a mounted specimen at one time on display at the State Capitol that was supposedly taken in Salt Lake Valley. Mushback (1932:9) considered the Surf Scoter to be a rare migrant on the Bear River Migratory Bird Refuge, Box Elder County.

Oxyura jamaicensis rubida (Wilson)
Ruddy Duck

STATUS: A common summer resident, breeding near deep water over much of the state, especially in northern Utah. It is a common migrant from late February to early May and in the fall from September to November. A few are known to remain in the state throughout the winter.

RECORDS: Simpson's party (Baird 1876: 381) took a specimen in Utah in 1859. Ridgway (1877:369) found it in sloughs and marshes near the Jordan River in the Salt Lake Valley in 1869. Specimens were collected by Allen (1872b:172) in Weber County, 16 and 23 September 1871, and are now in the Museum of Comparative Zoology. Henshaw (1875:483) recorded a specimen taken at Provo, Utah County, 27 November 1872. Numerous specimens in the University of Utah, Brigham Young University, and other museums of the West have been collected in recent years.

Mergus cucullatus Linnaeus
Hooded Merganser

STATUS: A sparse migrant through the state. A few may remain in Utah throughout the winter, and there is a possibility that it may be a rare summer resident.

RECORDS: Henshaw (1875:484) recorded this species as being common in Utah. A mounted specimen on display at the Bear River Gun Club, Box Elder County, was supposed to have been taken on the Bear River Marshes, Box Elder County, about 1908. The Colorado Museum of Natural History has one collected in Utah about

1925 or 1926. Three specimens in the University of Utah collection were taken near Perry, Box Elder County, 19 November 1933, and C. S. Williams reported one taken in Bear River Migratory Bird Refuge, Box Elder County, in late November 1938, by a hunter. An adult male in the University of Utah collection was taken at Clear Lake, Millard County, 7 December 1955 (Worthen 1968:160). There have been numerous sight records from the Bear River Marshes. Clifton Greenhalgh (Utah Audubon News 1955:30) reported a flock estimated at 150 seen on Bear Lake, Rich County, Utah, 20 April 1955. Murie (Scott 1967:527) reported seeing two specimens in southwestern Utah, 25 April 1967.

Mergus merganser americanus Cassin
Common Merganser

STATUS: This species is a casual summer resident in Utah and an uncommon migrant throughout the state mainly from mid-February to early May and from early October to December.

RECORDS: Early collection records include a specimen taken at Utah Lake in the spring of 1849 by the Simpson party (Baird 1876:381). Allen reported it to be common in Salt Lake Valley in 1871 (1872b:172), and Henshaw (1875:483) reported it to occur in the state. There are several specimens in the University of Utah and Brigham Young University collections. The BYU collection includes one collected by Cottam at Bear River Migratory Bird Refuge, Box Elder County, 4 November 1928; one at St. George, Washington County, in March 1936; one from Lehi, Utah County, 8 March 1937; two on the Colorado River, 20 miles south of Moab, San Juan County, 20 December 1962. Webster (1947:40) collected one west of Logan, Cache County, 15 December 1945, and observed this species on the Weber River, west of Ogden, Weber County, 8 December 1945, 31 December 1945, 19 January 1946, and 2 February 1946.

Mergus serrator serrator Linnaeus
Red-breasted Merganser

STATUS: A rather common migrant through Utah from late February to late April and from early October to December. A few may remain all winter. The summer status seems uncertain. R. G. Bee stated in an unpublished report that it was a nesting species at Farmington Bay, Davis County, in July 1939. Irvin G. Emmett is supposed to have found it nesting near Great Salt Lake in 1919.

RECORDS: Allen collected a specimen near Ogden, Weber County, 4 September 1871. This specimen is in the Museum of Comparative Zoology. Henshaw (1875:484) found it to be rather common at Utah Lake, Utah County, in November 1872. Hayward (unpublished ms 1934) found it to be common in Bear Lake Valley, Utah-Idaho, in early spring and again in the fall and found a few in the summer with evidence of nesting. Several specimens from Utah are in the collections of the University of Utah and Brigham Young University. It has been reported from St. George, Washington County, 5 November 1935, and from Ivins Reservoir, Washington County, 20 April 1940 (Hardy and Higgins 1940:97). Other southern Utah observations are sight records: 21 April, 5 and 10 May 1931, and 15 April 1947, Johnson Reservoir, near Kanab, Kane County; 50 at Lower Reservoir, near Kanab, Kane County, 15 April 1947 (Behle et al. 1958:42).

FAMILY CATHARTIDAE

Cathartes aura teter Friedmann
Turkey Vulture

STATUS: Widely distributed throughout the state somewhat less commonly now than formerly. Sometimes seen roosting in small flocks in trees in more remote areas. Nesting usually in caves along the mountain ranges wherever such sites are available.

RECORDS: All of the early ornithologists that visited Utah collected or recorded the Turkey Vulture. These included Allen (1872b:170), Ridgway (1875:34), Henshaw (1875:428), Fisher (1893:34), and Bailey (field notes). In recent years collections or observations have been made of this species in every county of the state. Most observations are of a single bird or a pair of birds. However, on the Green River, Uintah County, Twomey (1942:375) during the summer of 1937 reported "forty or fifty birds often were seen feeding on a carcass." Hardy and Higgins (1940:97) also reported "a large flock numbering fifty or more" in cottonwoods at the junction of the Santa Clara and Virgin Rivers, Washington County, 28 September 1939.

Vultur californianus Shaw
California Condor

STATUS: Formerly a rare visitor probably limited to the southern part of the state.

RECORDS: Henshaw (1875:428) reported:

> A very large vulture, seen near Beaver, Utah, November 25 [1872], was believed to be of this species. In company with a flock of the Red-headed Vultures [Turkey Vultures] it had been feeding upon the carcass of a horse, and, as they all made off at my approach, I was enabled to note the comparative sizes of the two; the bird supposed to be this species greatly exceeding the others in size.

A taxidermist who formerly lived in Iron County told Woodbury (1932) that condors were occasionally seen by sheepherders during the winter in western Iron County where they fed on sheep carcasses, especially during severe winters.

FAMILY ACCIPITRIDAE

Accipiter gentilis atricapillus (Wilson)
Goshawk
Fig. 5, p. 32

STATUS: A year-round resident of Utah, probably more common in winter because of migration from more northern areas. This species breeds in scattered localities

Fig. 18. Long-billed Curlew. Ogden Bay, Weber County, Utah, 21 June 1916. Photo by R. J. Erwin.

throughout the montane forests as well as in floodplain woodlands (White et al. 1965).

RECORDS: Numerous specimens are in the Utah State University, University of Utah, and Brigham Young University collections. Most of the specimens have been taken in late autumn and winter and may be either local individuals or migrants. There is a tendency for the local breeding population to drift down into the valleys in winter. Breeding birds tend to use the same nesting site or alternate closely located sites year after year. To our knowledge, a nesting area at Aspen Grove, Mt. Timpanogos, Utah County, was used from at least 1925 to 1945. Nests are constructed either in dense coniferous growths or in more open aspen forests.

SUBSPECIES: Formerly the western population of Goshawks in North America went under the subspecies name of *A. g. striatulus* (Check-list of Birds of the World [1] 1931: 208). It now seems to be the general consensus that the western birds should be included in the subspecies *A. g. atricapillus* (Friedmann 1950:150; American Ornithologists Union 1957:102). Todd (1963:211) considered the new-world *atricapillus* to be specifically distinct from *gentilis*.

Accipiter striatus velox (Wilson)
Sharp-shinned Hawk
Figs. 6, 7; pp. 34, 35

STATUS: A widely distributed resident of the state preferring wooded areas along canyon and valley streams. Since this is a hawk of more or less dense woodlands, it seems to be more likely to survive than those species living in more open habitats.

RECORDS: Early ornithologists in Utah (Baird 1852:314; Remy 1860[2]:449; Henshaw 1875:417; Ridgway 1877:375) recorded and collected the Sharp-shinned Hawk, and all regarded it as common when white men first settled in the area. Many collections have been made and are now in the museums of the state institutions. Many sets of eggs have been collected, indicating that the nesting season ranges from late April through June, which is somewhat later than most raptors of the area. Platt (1976:102–103) reported that Utah Sharp-shinned Hawks appeared at the nest site up to four weeks before egg laying. Nesting occurs 15–20 days earlier in Washington County than in Cache County, 350 miles to the north.

Accipiter cooperii (Bonaparte)
Cooper's Hawk

STATUS: A fairly common summer resident in Utah being more common in migration and sparse in winter. Like the Sharp-shinned Hawk, Cooper's Hawk tends to prefer wooded areas as a habitat.

RECORDS: This species was first noted in Utah by Ridgway (1877:375), who regarded it as an uncommon breeding species in 1869. Henshaw (1874:10) indicated that it was not common but generally distributed and a resident in the state. Many specimens are in the collections of the various institutions of the state and elsewhere. There are numerous accounts of nesting, mostly for late May and June.

Buteo jamaicensis (Gmelin)
Red-tailed Hawk
Figs. 9, 10; pp. 37, 38

STATUS: A permanent resident throughout the state. It is adapted to a wide range of habitats and is found in deserts, mountains, and populated valleys. It may nest either on cliff ledges or in tall trees.

RECORDS: Baird (1852:314) listed a specimen near Great Salt Lake in 1850. Red-tailed Hawks were observed or collected by Remy (1860[2]:450) in 1855, and Ridgway (1877:375, 582–584) found them nesting in the Wasatch Mountains in 1869. Reference was made to them by Stevenson (1872:462), Allen (1872b:170), Nelson (1875:347), Henshaw (1875:424), and others. Specimens collected early in Utah are in the U.S. National Museum of Natural History and in the American Museum. Many newer collection records of birds and eggs have been made in recent years from every county of the state.

SUBSPECIES: The Utah population of the Red-tailed Hawk has usually been assigned to the subspecies *B. j. calurus*. The race *B. j. kriderii* has been reported by Parker and Johnson (1899?). Porter and Bushman (1956:152) recorded two collections of this subspecies: one immature male from Willard Bay, Box Elder County, 15 October 1951, and an immature at King's Pasture, Garfield County, 24 August 1953. These specimens were verified by Herbert Friedmann. Recently Behle, C. White, and G. Kashin published sight records of two more birds (Utah Audubon News 1962:32) west of Delta, Millard County, 25 May 1962, and at Memory Grove, Salt Lake City, 30 May 1962. Twomey (1942:378) collected specimens in Uintah County which he identified as belonging to the race *B. j. fuertesi*. However, some doubt exists as to the accuracy of this identification (Behle 1944a:71). A specimen of *B. j. harlani* in the University of Utah collection (no. 20931) was taken at the Lorin Peck farm, six miles west of Delta, Millard County, 4 November 1967 (Worthen 1968:172; 1973a:79). Wauer (Snider 1966:447) reported sighting a *harlani* at St. George, Washington County, from 22 January to 4 March 1966.

Buteo lineatus lineatus (Gmelin)
Red-shouldered Hawk

STATUS: Of accidental or casual occurrence in Utah.

RECORDS: Knowlton and Harmston (1943: 589) took a specimen at Elgin, Grand County, 28 September 1939. It seems, however, that the specimen was not saved (Behle letter). Kashin (1963a:16) reported seeing one in Parley's Canyon, Salt Lake County, 10 February 1963. Murie (Scott 1965:567) reported that one was seen regularly at Cedar City, Iron County, from 8 August to September 1965.

Buteo swainsoni Bonaparte
Swainson's Hawk
Fig. 8, p. 36

STATUS: A summer and possibly an occasional winter resident throughout the state. It occurs both in valleys and at lower elevations in the mountains. Its numbers have declined recently because of heavy persecution.

RECORDS: A specimen in the U.S. National Museum of Natural History was taken in the Wasatch Mountains in 1868. Ridgway (1877:584) found it nesting abundantly in oaks and aspens around Parley's Park, Summit County, and in the nearby valley. He reported that these hawks in the valley were feeding on Mormon Crickets and grasshoppers (1877:586–587). Numerous specimens of birds as well as their eggs are in the collections of the institutions of the state and elsewhere. A sight record by Gleb Kashin for Salt Lake City, Salt Lake County, 14 December 1960, indicated that it may occasionally remain in Utah throughout the winter (Scott 1961:348).

Buteo lagopus sanctijohannis (Gmelin)
Rough-legged Hawk

STATUS: A rather common migrant and winter resident in the state. Reports by some early naturalists (Henshaw 1875:426; Ridgway 1877:375) stating that it was present in summer may have resulted from misidentification since there are, to our knowledge, no nesting records or specimens taken in summer.

RECORDS: Henshaw (1875:426) found it to be common around Utah Lake in late November and early December 1872 when he and Yarrow collected 11 specimens. Bailey collected and found this hawk to be common in St. George, Washington County, in late December 1888 (specimens in U.S. National Museum of Natural History). Numerous specimens taken in more recent years are in the collections at Utah State University, Brigham Young University, and the University of Utah.

Buteo regalis (Gray)
Ferruginous Hawk
Fig. 11, p. 39

STATUS: A widely distributed species in the state but found mainly in open desert country. It is primarily a summer resident with only a few records for winter months.

RECORDS: McCarthy, of Simpson's expedition, collected a bird, its nest, and eggs on 3 May 1859 in Rush Valley, Tooele County, and another on the same day at Camp Floyd, Utah County (Baird 1876: 377). The species is still fairly common in these desert valleys. Weston (Murphy et al. 1969:25–34) during 1967–68 studied the nesting ecology of this species in west central Utah. There have been numerous collection records of birds and eggs in more recent years. Nests may be built in low trees, especially junipers, on ledges and rock pinnacles, on mounds, or on level ground (Weston and Ellis 1968:111).

Buteogallus anthracinus anthracinus (Deppe)
Black Hawk

STATUS: A rare nesting bird in southern Utah, known to occur in the state since 1962.

RECORDS: Carter and Wauer (1965:82–83) first found this hawk nesting near Springdale, Washington County, in early May 1962. The hawks were seen in the vicinity of two nests located in cottonwood trees.

However, on 13 May 1963 a bird was seen on one of these nests, although the final outcome of the nesting was not determined at that time. Photos of the birds were taken for positive identification. Wauer and Russell (1967:420) reported seeing the mating of a pair of Black Hawks on 8 May 1964 at Beaver Dam, Arizona, and later in the summer (August 25) found a single juvenile, indicating that nesting had been successful. They also recorded a single adult bird seen near Hurricane, Washington County, 27 June 1965. Wauer (1969:331) collected a specimen at Wash-

Fig. 19. Spotted Sandpiper. Pigeon Lake, Bayfield County, Wisconsin, no date. Photo by R. D. Porter.

ington, Washington County, 21 April 1966. This is the first collected specimen for the state and is found in the museum collection at Zion National Park, Washington County. Northward movement of this species is evidenced by a sight record at Capitol Reef National Monument, Wayne County, in the fall of 1971 (Kingery 1972:96).

Aquila chrysaetos (Linnaeus)
Golden Eagle
Fig. 14, p. 49

STATUS: A resident bird throughout its breeding range mainly in rugged country. It usually nests on cliffs but sometimes in trees or even on flat ground. This is a steadily declining species because of persecution and probably the effects of insecticide and poisonous baits. (Ellis et al. 1969: 165–167).

RECORDS: All of the early naturalists reported the eagle in the state (Remy 1860[2]: 222; Ridgway 1875:34, 1877:375; Allen 1872b:170; Henshaw 1875:426; Bailey field notes). Numerous specimens are in collections of the various institutions of the state and elsewhere. There are many records of nests and eggs from almost every county. Recently Camenzind (Murphy et al. 1969: 4–15) discussed the nesting ecology and behavior of the Golden Eagle in west central Utah.

Haliaeetus leucocephalus (Linnaeus)
Bald Eagle

STATUS: A fairly common winter resident in Utah. Early observations indicate that the Bald Eagle also nested in some numbers in former times. Breeding records at the present time are not well confirmed.

RECORDS: Allen (1872b:170) reported that the Bald Eagle was more or less frequent around Ogden, Weber County, in early fall of 1871. Henshaw (1875:427) and Yarrow found it regularly visiting Utah Lake, Utah County, for fish and assumed that it nested in nearby mountains. Bailey (field notes)

found it near Provo, Utah County, and in Sevier, Kane, and Garfield counties in the winter of 1888. He also saw it in late June at Fairfield, Utah County, in 1890. Most of the nesting records are from the notes of Treganza who observed nesting sites at Upper Provo River, Wasatch County, 1 May 1914; head of Emigration Canyon, Salt Lake County, 15 May 1918; Low Pass, Tooele County, 15 March 1922; and Mt. Baldy, Summit County, 1 April 1922. The first nest contained almost fully fledged young. Apparently no egg sets were taken by Treganza. Wolfe (1928:97) made reference to a nest east of Alpine, Utah County. A nesting site has been reported near Bicknell, Wayne County (Hayward 1967:23). Large concentrations of Bald Eagles are common in several localities in the state during the winter. Scott (1957:284) reported a peak of 120 birds at Bear River Migratory Bird Refuge, Box Elder County, 3 March 1957, and Murie (1963:46) counted 18 in the area around Parowan, Iron County, during the winter of 1962–63. The population dynamics of this species and the Golden Eagle in the Great Basin have been studied by Edwards (1969:1–142).

SUBSPECIES: The Bald Eagles of Utah have been considered to be of the larger northern race, H. l. alascanus (AOU Check-list 1957:114), although the Check-list (113–114) indicates that the southern race H. l. leucocephalus may have formerly bred in Utah. It is presumed that the birds wintering in the state are migrants from the north, but there is no confirmed evidence of this. Two female specimens in the Brigham Young University collection, taken in Utah County in December and January, have wing measurements of 606 mm and 620 mm — well within the size range of the northern race.

Circus cyaneus hudsonius (Linnaeus)
Marsh Hawk
Fig. 15, p. 52

STATUS: A common summer resident

usually found around marshy areas in the lower valleys but sometimes feeding over mountain meadows and in desert country. Behle (1960a:25) observed one flying over the crest of the Abajo mountains near Cooley Pass, San Juan County, 24 August 1956, at an elevation of about 10,350 feet. Primarily a migrant species, although a few remain in lower valleys throughout the winter.

RECORDS: All the early ornithologists who visited Utah soon after its settlement by the Mormons recorded the Marsh Hawk as being common to abundant, particularly in the Salt Lake and Utah Lake valleys. However, it is found in many localities throughout the state: near Yost, Box Elder County, 7 September 1932 (Behle 1958:16); St. George, Washington County, 25 March 1934 (Hardy and Higgins 1940:98); along the Green River, Uintah County, summer 1937 (Twomey 1942:381); Fish Springs, Juab County, 23 June 1946 (Behle 1955:18); south of Kanab, Kane County, 20 May 1947 (Behle et al. 1958:45). There are numerous nesting records.

FAMILY PANDIONIDAE

Pandion haliaetus carolinensis (Gmelin)
Osprey

STATUS: Formerly a sparse but regular summer resident in Utah; now greatly reduced in numbers and considered to be rare and endangered.

RECORDS: Early notations by Allen (1872b:170) and Henshaw (1874:10) indicate that the Osprey was present around the marshes of Great Salt Lake in the early days of settlement. Henshaw said it was rare at Utah Lake, while Allen stated that it was common in summer near Great Salt Lake. A few specimens have been taken within the state as follows: mouth of Weber River, Weber County, 13 October 1914 (Wetmore); Maple Creek Trout Hatchery, Mantua, Box Elder County, 25 April 1925; Springville Fish Hatchery, Utah County,

spring 1926 (reported by Cottam); mouth of Provo River, Utah County, 23 April 1927 (killed by a hunter); Murray Fish Hatchery, Salt Lake County, 15 October 1927; Ogden, Weber County, 1 May 1930 (taken by a hunter); two miles south of Gunlock, Washington County, 23 April 1945 (specimen in Dixie College collection). Numerous sight records are available from various parts of Utah. One was seen by Hayward at Lincoln Beach, Utah County, several times in spring of 1969. All nesting records have been from mountain areas where there are lakes or reservoirs. The birds have nested at Fish Lake, Sevier County, as reported by Wolfe (field notes), Cottam (field notes), and Bee and Hutchings (1942:67). Nesting records from Summit, Wasatch, and Duchesne counties were reported by Hayward (1931:151), Twomey (1942:382), and Bee and Hutchings (1942:67). All of the nesting sites were in tall trees. Kingery (1973:644) saw one at Zion National Park, Washington County, in late March 1973.

FAMILY FALCONIDAE

Falco mexicanus Schlegel
Prairie Falcon

STATUS: Formerly considered to be common in Utah but lately becoming increasingly more rare. It is a permanent resident found at all elevations but more commonly in the lower canyons and valleys.

RECORDS: Some of the early naturalists (Henshaw 1875:410–411; Ridgway 1877: 368, 375, 577; Fisher 1893:39) recognized the Prairie Falcon as a rather common species in the state. Hayward (field notes) recorded it frequently in the Utah Valley area and westward. Nesting pairs occurred on cliffs in most of the canyons along the Wasatch Front in the 1930s and 1940s. Brigham Young University collection contains the following specimens from Utah: Utah Lake, Utah County, 18 November 1932; St. George, Washington County, 30 September 1934 and 3 November 1935; Lost

Fig. 20. Black-necked Stilt. Ogden Bay, Weber County, Utah, spring 1953. Photo by R. D. Porter and R. J. Erwin.

Lake, Uinta Mountains, Summit County, 29 August 1940. There are numerous records of nesting throughout the state. Recently Porter and White (1973:1–74) have discussed competition between the Prairie Falcon and Peregrine Falcon in Utah.

Falco peregrinus Tunstall
Peregrine Falcon
Fig. 12, p. 42

STATUS: The Peregrine Falcon, or Duck Hawk as it has sometimes been called, is a sparse permanent resident in the state, especially in areas near marshlands. It has been greatly reduced in numbers here as elsewhere in recent years and is in grave danger of extermination.

RECORDS: Some of the early investigators in the state considered this falcon to be rather common (Allen 1872b:170; Henshaw 1874:9). Neither Ridgway nor Merriam encountered it. Specimens from Bear River Marshes, Box Elder County, are in the collections of the U.S. National Museum of Natural History and Academy of Natural Sciences of Philadelphia. The University of Utah collection contains specimens from near Bountiful, Davis County, and from near Salt Lake City and elsewhere. Bent (1938:67) reported that a specimen banded

at King's Point, Yukon, Canada, 30 July 1924, was shot at Duchesne, Duchesne County, 20 February 1925. A specimen taken west of Utah Lake 2 August 1935 was mounted by John Hutchings of Lehi. A specimen in the Louis B. Bishop collection was taken at Cedar City, Iron County, 12 May 1936. Specimens in the Royal Ontario Museum (Canada) and the Carnegie Museum were taken in the Uinta Basin. Wolfe (1928:101) collected a specimen at St. George, Washington County, and there is a specimen in the Zion Park Museum from Zion Canyon, Washington County, 16 July 1939. Nesting sites have been reported from Box Elder County (Treganza letter); Weber County (Dee Porter); Tooele County (Wolfe letter 30 June 1930); Utah County (Johnson 1899b:45; Bee and Hutchings 1942:67–68); Clear Lake Refuge, Millard County (Gunther and Nelson field notes); and Uintah County (Twomey 1942:383–384). Porter and White (1973:1–74) have listed numerous specimens and nesting records for the state and have discussed the ecology of the species in detail.

SUBSPECIES: The systematics of the Peregrine Falcon has been treated by White (1968:1–195). It appears that both *F. p. anatum* and *F. p. tundrius* have been taken in Utah during the winter months.

Falco columbarius Linnaeus
Merlin (Pigeon Hawk)

STATUS: A sparse resident of Utah breeding in scattered areas in the mountains. There is some migration of at least three races through the state, and a few winter in the area. It seems that no specimens of breeding birds have been taken, and the race nesting in the state is unknown.

RECORDS: There are a few records of Pigeon Hawks having been collected in Utah in the early days of settlement. Stevenson (1872:462) reported a specimen taken on Green River in early October 1871 by the Hayden Expedition. Allen (1872b:170) regarded it as being moderately frequent around Ogden, Weber County, in 1871, and took one specimen at West Weber, Weber County, 16 September, and another at Ogden, 4 October. A specimen was taken near Minersville, Beaver County, 12 December 1934, and reported by Stanford. Another was taken by Ralph Hafen, 11 December 1939, near St. George, Washington County (Hardy and Higgins 1940:98). Behle et al. (1964:451) published an account of a specimen shot in the Salt Lake City Cemetery, Salt Lake County, 9 March 1937, and another collected at the Tracy Aviary, Salt Lake City, 1 February 1954. Both are now in the collection of the University of Utah. Porter and Knight (1952:84–85) recorded specimens taken at Plymouth, Box Elder County, February 1948, and Ogden, Weber County (both in Weber State College collection). There are two specimens in the Brigham Young University collection taken in Utah. One was collected at St. George, Washington County, 21 December 1926, and the other at Provo, Utah County, 26 January 1964. Both are females.

Sets of eggs are known to have been collected in Utah. Wolfe (1946:97) referred to a set of eggs in the J. P. Morris collection taken in the Wasatch Mountains, 29 May 1868. These eggs were collected by Rickensecker and are now in the collection of the Western Foundation of Vertebrate Zoology.

Another set taken by Rickensecker in 1869 in the Wasatch Mountains is in the U.S. National Museum collection.

SUBSPECIES: It seems that three or four subspecies may appear in the Utah population. A specimen in the U.S. National Museum of Natural History listed by Coues (1874:348) as having been taken in Box Elder Creek, Utah, was placed in the subspecies *F. c. richardsonii*. A specimen in the Brigham Young University collection taken at St. George, Washington County, was identified by H. C. Oberholser as *columbarius*. However, the latter specimen seems to be definitely of the race *F. c. richardsonii*, according to Freidman's key (1950:619). The specimen mentioned above collected in the Salt Lake Cemetery is of the race *columbarius*. The race *F. c. suckleyi* is a winter visitor in Utah. The previously mentioned specimen taken at the Tracy Aviary, Salt Lake City, and those reported by Porter and Knight (1952:84–85) for Plymouth, Box Elder County, and Ogden, Weber County, are of this race. A female specimen in the Brigham Young University collection taken at Provo, 26 January 1964, is also *suckleyi*. *F. c. bendirei* has been assumed to be the race breeding in Utah (Behle 1943a:24), but there seems to be no positive proof of this. Hardy and Higgins (1940:98) recorded a specimen of *bendirei* collected at St. George, 11 December 1939.

Falco sparverius sparverius Linnaeus
American Kestrel (Sparrow Hawk)
Figs. 13, 16, 24; pp. 43, 55, 78

STATUS: A permanent resident in Utah but less common in the northern part of the state during winter. This falcon seems to maintain its population somewhat better than most of the other birds of prey. Owing perhaps to its small size, it is less conspicuous and is persecuted less frequently by man than are most of its larger relatives.

RECORDS: All of the early writers on Utah ornithology commented on the great abundance of this small species in the state (Allen 1872b:170; Henshaw 1875:414; Ridgway 1877:578–580; and others). It has been observed and collected from many localities throughout the state. Recently Smith et al. (1972a:73–83) studied the ecology of this species in central Utah.

FAMILY TETRAONIDAE

Dendragapus obscurus (Say)
Blue Grouse

STATUS: Formerly a common grouse in the higher mountain ranges of the state. Now, as a result of hunting pressure and livestock grazing, it is reduced in numbers. It ranges in altitude from the foothills to timberline but is perhaps most characteristic of coniferous forests where there is an abundance of wild berries on which it feeds.

RECORDS: Early observers collected specimens and noted the abundance of Blue Grouse in Utah mountains (Allen 1872b: 170; Henshaw 1875:435–436; Ridgway 1877: 598). Many records of specimens from the major mountainous areas of the state are in collections throughout the country. Breeding records available are mainly those of broods of young. Sets of eggs on record indicate that nesting begins in mid-May.

SUBSPECIES: The subspecies recognized from most areas of the state is *D. o. obscurus*, which is also found in central Wyoming, Colorado, parts of northern New Mexico, and Arizona. Behle and Selander (1951b:125–128) have described a paler colored race which they call *D. o. oreinus* that is found in the Deep Creek Mountains of central western Utah and westward into parts of Nevada. The type specimen was collected by Robert K. Selander and is in the University of Utah Museum of Zoology, no. 10779. It was collected three miles north of the Queen of Sheba mine, west side of Deep Creek Mountains, 7,500 feet elevation, Juab County, 23 April 1950.

Bonasa umbellus incana Aldrich and Friedmann
Ruffed Grouse

STATUS: The Ruffed Grouse was formerly rather common at lower elevations in northern Utah at least as far south as Sanpete County. It is an inhabitant of brushy canyons and aspen forests where there are frequent open areas and nearby streams. In some localities it has been called the Willow Grouse.

RECORDS: Fremont (1845:143) was the first to record this species, noting that it was abundant in areas that later became the Utah-Idaho border. It was also recorded by Allen (1872b:171), by Simpson's party (Baird 1876:380), and by Ridgway (1877: 599). Numerous specimens have been collected in more recent years. Sets of eggs are few, but many broods of young have been noted. Mullen (pers. comm.) found a nest containing five eggs in Big Cottonwood Canyon, Salt Lake County, 22 June 1931. The nest was located under the curved base of an aspen. Hayward and Bee (Bee and Hutchings 1942:68) found a nest in identical habitat on Mt. Timpanogos, Utah County, 17 May 1942, which eventually contained seven eggs by 23 May.

SUBSPECIES: The Utah population has been placed in the race *B. u. incana* (AOU Check-list 1957:129). The type specimen is an adult male, no. 155869, in the U.S. National Museum of Natural History, collected at Barclay, 15 miles east of Salt Lake City, Salt Lake County, 1 May 1897, by E. A. Preble.

Tympanuchus phasianellus columbianus (Ord)
Sharp-tailed Grouse

STATUS: Originally widespread and rather common throughout much of northern and central Utah wherever there was a suitable habitat of grassland and sagebrush. Since much of its native habitat was taken up for agriculture, it is now restricted

Fig. 21. Black-necked Stilt. Ogden Bay, Weber County, Utah, spring 1953. Photo by R. D. Porter and R. J. Erwin.

to a few areas in the northern part of the state.

RECORDS: These grouse were reported by early naturalists for the Salt Lake and Ogden areas as well as for Utah Valley (Allen 1872b:170; Henshaw 1874:10; Nelson 1875:347; Ridgway 1877:599; Bailey field notes; Osgood field notes). There are few specimens in the museums of the state. The Museum of Comparative Zoology has one taken in Weber County, 26 September 1871; specimens were collected near Blue Spring Hill in Box Elder County, 17 August to 5 September 1928; specimens in the collection of the Colorado Natural History Museum were taken near Tremonton, Box Elder County, 28 May and 7 June 1929; a specimen collected three miles west of Huntsville, Weber County, 24 March 1940, is in the University of Utah collection. Nesting records are very scarce. A set of nine

eggs collected by Aldous (now in the Daynes collection) was taken in Davis County, 20 May 1917. Hayward (field notes), while living and hunting in Bear Lake Valley during the 1920s, found the Sharp-tailed Grouse, or Prairie Chicken as it was locally called, common on the foothills and sometimes along the valley streams on the west side of the valley. The birds inhabited the parkland country and usually sought groves of aspens or tall shrubs around springs, especially in winter. They often fed in autumn in dry farm grain fields and were nearly as common as the sage grouse. In those days it was not uncommon for a hunter to take Sage Grouse, Blue Grouse, and Sharp-tailed Grouse in the same general locality. Low and Gaufin (1946:180) reported a flock of 23 east of Providence, Cache County, 22 March 1946.

Centrocercus urophasianus urophasianus (Bonaparte)
Sage Grouse

STATUS: Originally widespread and very common throughout the state wherever sagebrush or mixed grasslands and sagebrush were prevalent. Since much of the original habitat has been taken up by agriculture, the grouse have been restricted to rangelands but have been able to survive under reduced hunting pressure and conservation measures.

RECORDS: All the early naturalists who visited the area mentioned the abundance of Sage Grouse even in places near settlements (Baird 1852:319; Remy 1860[2]:450; Merriam 1873:699; Ridgway 1877:368, 375, 600). There are many collected specimens in local museums and others throughout the country. At the present time their principal habitat is sagebrush communities where there are small streams or springs. In 1970 hunters obtained 15,877 birds, and in 1971 this species provided 20,013 individuals for hunters (State of Utah Division of Wildlife Resources 1972:19).

FAMILY PHASIANIDAE

Colinus virginianus (Linnaeus)
Bobwhite

STATUS: The Bobwhite, at times referred to as the Eastern Partridge, is not a native to Utah but has been introduced into the state several times and in a variety of localities. According to Allen (1872a:395), this quail was introduced into Utah around Ogden prior to 1871 and for a time gave promise of multiplying rapidly and becoming thoroughly naturalized. Henshaw (1875:439) found them near Provo and stated that "everything would seem to indicate their rapid increase. In July, the call notes of males were frequently heard, and a number of coveys were seen here in the fall near the thickets and hedges." Wyman (1889:123) and Bent (1932:31) both

referred to this early introduction into Utah. Birds resulting from these early plantings soon died out under pressure from hunters and had mostly disappeared by about 1900. In more recent years the Bobwhite has been introduced into Utah several times. They were planted near Moab, Grand County, in 1915; near Vernal, Uintah County, in 1930; at Jensen, Uintah County, in 1935; and near Richfield, Sevier County, in 1938 (information from Utah Division of Wildlife Resources). Plants were also made near Deweyville and Brigham City, both in Box Elder County, in 1947, and also near Grantsville, Tooele County, in 1946. Most, if not all, of these birds have disappeared, and further introductions seem unjustifiable.

Lophortyx californicus (Shaw)
California Quail

STATUS: The California Quail, also called the Valley Quail or California Partridge, is not native to Utah but was introduced a short time before 10 November 1869 by General Gibbon who was stationed at Camp (now Fort) Douglas. He brought to Utah 14 pair of quail and liberated them in the Salt Lake Valley for the express purpose of propagating them (Deseret Evening News 1869:3). During the 1870s and 1880s several more introductions were made, mostly in the northern and central valleys of the state. (Popov 1949:138–143). The birds survive best in city parks and in agricultural areas and adjacent foothills where there are ample shrubs or thickets for cover. Under limited hunting these quail survive rather well in the central and northern counties of the state.

RECORDS: Early collectors in Utah, including Ridgway, Merriam, Nelson, and Henshaw, did not report this quail since it had not become widespread in their time. Specimens were recorded in the Deseret Museum Catalogue in 1892, and a pair of birds taken at Ogden, Weber County, in 1883, are in the Colorado Natural History Museum. In more recent years numerous specimens have been assembled in the several collections within the state and elsewhere.

SUBSPECIES: Since numerous introductions of this quail have been made with stock from several areas, the subspecies in the Utah population are ill defined. It seems that the first introductions were of the subspecies *brunnescens*, a native of the more humid western coast. This olive brown and darker race seemingly did not survive in the dry interior, but the Colorado Museum specimens taken at Ogden in 1883 appear to be of this subspecies. The present Utah population seems to resemble more closely the race *L. c. californicus.*

Lophortyx gambelii Gambel
Gambel's Quail

STATUS: Gambel's Quail is a native inhabitant of the warmer deserts in the Colorado and Virgin River drainage areas of southern Utah. It is known to occur as far north as Wayne County (Grater field notes), and Porter (1954:362) has reported it from Green River, Emery County. It has adapted rather well to human settlements and often feeds in grain fields.

RECORDS: Yarrow and Henshaw (Henshaw 1875:440–441) collected this quail along the Virgin River in October 1872 and reported that it lived near settlements. They stated that flocks of 100 were not infrequent. Vernon Bailey (field notes) found it to be common in the same area in January 1889. Numerous collections and observations are on record for more recent years.

SUBSPECIES: In some of the earlier literature (Woodbury et al. 1949:11) the population of the Virgin River and north to Wayne County was assigned to the race *L. g. gambelii,* and the birds of southeastern Utah, especially in the Moab area, were assigned to the western Colorado subspecies *L. g. sanus.* Behle (1960b:16–17) considered the birds in the extreme southwestern part of Utah to be *L. g. gambelii,* although atypical.

Specimens from the Kanab, Kane County, and Moab, Grand County, areas appear to be *L. g. sanus,* according to Behle's account; however, Phillips (1958:365) placed the race *sanus* in synonymy under *L. g. gambelii.*

Phasianus colchicus Linnaeus
Ring-necked Pheasant

STATUS: The first pheasants were introduced into Utah near Salt Lake City by M. H. Walker about 1890 (Popov 1949:144–153). Twomey (1942:388) wrote that they were also released in the Uinta Basin in 1900. The birds seemed to thrive well, and several eggs were taken in Salt Lake County as early as 1899 and 1904. In 1922 the State Division of Wildlife Resources established a pheasant farm in Springville, Utah County, and has since released many hundreds of birds into all the agricultural areas of the state. While pheasants occur more abundantly around farm and pasture lands, they have also spread into foothill areas, particularly along the Wasatch Front. During 1970 and 1971 hunters obtained over 250,000 birds each year (State of Utah Division of Wildlife Resources 1972:19).

RECORDS: Collections have been made in nearly all counties in the state. However, both collection and sight records would indicate that pheasants are more numerous in the Great Basin (especially in settlements along the Wasatch Front) and in the Uinta Basin, owing to the greater extent of irrigated farmlands in those areas.

SUBSPECIES: The AOU Check-list (1957:146) does not assign subspecific names to the North American stock, inasmuch as the birds have been introduced from England as well as from their native Asia where there are some 30 races. Several of these races have been introduced and have intermingled to the extent that the present-day population in America cannot be subspecifically identified.

Alectoris chukar (Gray)
Chukar

STATUS: A native of southern Europe and Asia, the Chukar or Chukar Partridge has now been successfully introduced into many localities in the western United States including Utah. The first birds were apparently released in Box Elder County in March 1936 (Popov 1949:126–131). Since that time, many releases have been made and the species has become established in semidesert country throughout the state. They seem to survive well under seasonal hunting. In 1970 hunters harvested 56,053 Chukars and in 1971, 61,151 were taken (State of Utah Division of Wildlife Resources 1972:19). The largest harvest came from Box Elder, Utah, Cache, Tooele, and Morgan counties. The Chuckar adapts well to native desert country and is not so dependent on agricultural lands for survival.

RECORDS: Collections of specimens have been made from many parts of the state. The Brigham Young University collection contains one specimen from Dog Valley, Juab County, 23 November 1956; three from Roosevelt, Duchesne County, 15 April 1958; and one from Sterling, Sanpete County, 15 November 1958.

SUBSPECIES: According to the AOU Check-list (1957:147), there are over 20 geographic races of the Chukar in its native range. Several of these have been introduced into the United States, and the subspecific status of the present population is uncertain.

Perdix perdix perdix (Linnaeus)
Gray Partridge

STATUS: The Gray Partridge, also called Hungarian Partridge, is native to northern and central Europe and Asia. Porter (1955: 93–109) has reviewed the status of this species in Utah. One hundred twenty birds were introduced from Canadian stock in the spring of 1912 and distributed to seven counties in Utah. In 1923 an additional 400 birds were released. By 1940 all introductions were considered unsuccessful.

Fig. 22. Wilson's Phalarope. Ogden Bay, Weber County, Utah, 20 June 1961. Photo by R. J. Erwin.

However, populations are established in Rich, Box Elder, Tooele, and Juab counties. These individuals are believed to have spread from the neighboring states of Idaho and Nevada where introductions have been successful. The State of Utah Division of Wildlife Resources (1972:19) reported 9,407 Hungarian Partridges harvested in 1971.

FAMILY MELEAGRIDIDAE

Meleagris gallopavo merriami Nelson
Turkey

STATUS: Whether or not the Turkey occurred natively in Utah is questionable. If it did, it most likely lived in the mountains of the southeastern part of the state. There is evidence that it was native in some of the counties of Colorado, Arizona, and New Mexico adjoining Utah (Hayward 1967:26). Turkey bones and feathers have been found in cliff dwellings (Hargrave 1939:208; Shroeder 1955:159; Sharrock and Keene 1962:62; Sharrock 1966:77–78, 80, 82), but these could have been domesticated birds or else birds brought into the area from elsewhere. Many introductions of wild stock have been made in various parts of the state. A number of introductions from eastern stock were made between 1925 and 1948 as follows: Antelope Island, Great Salt Lake, 1925; east of Milford, Beaver County, 1936, 1938, 1939–1941; Iron County, 1941; Washington County, 1942; south fork of Provo River, Utah County, 1943, 1948. Apparently none of these introductions was successful for any great length of time (Popov 1949:154–160). Behle (1960a:26–27) gave an account of its introduction into the La Sal, Abajo and Henry mountains by the State Division of Wildlife Resources beginning in 1953. Worthen (1968:193) has furnished information regarding the release of turkeys west of Milford in 1936 and mentioned several scattered records from the Tushar Mountains, Beaver and Piute counties. Populations have also been established on Boulder

Mountain, Garfield County, and near East Zion, Kane County, and Beaver Mountain, Beaver County. These plantings have been successful to the point where limited hunting is now allowed. Eighty-six birds were harvested in 1971 (State of Utah Division of Wildlife Resources 1972:19).

FAMILY GRUIDAE

Grus canadensis (Linnaeus)
Sandhill Crane

STATUS: Formerly a common summer resident in northern Utah (Baird 1852:319; Remy 1860[2]:450; Ridgway 1877:364, 376) but now a regular though uncommon migrant. John Hutchings (Bee and Hutchings 1942:69) saw an adult with young near Lehi, Utah County, in the summer of 1939. A party consisting of R. G. Bee, James Bee, and C. L. Hayward found a nest at Fish Springs, Juab County, 3 May 1946. As many as five birds were seen together at that time in the Fish Springs area (Bee and Hutchings 1942:68–69). Within the last five years nesting has occurred on the Strawberry River, Wasatch County. In June 1969 a nest was destroyed by cattle in this area, but the two eggs were saved. The Utah State Division of Wildlife Resources donated one egg to the University of Utah and the other to Brigham Young University. In recent years the Sandhill Crane has become well established as a migrant and breeding species along the Bear River and in nearby marshlands of Bear Lake Valley. Although this valley lies partly in Utah, it is doubtful if any nesting takes place in the state, owing to lack of extensive marshlands in that part of the valley lying in Utah. However, nesting birds should be looked for along the Bear River in Rich County in the vicinity of Woodruff and Randolph. Bear Lake Valley has always been a favored migration route for the Sandhill Crane, and some birds have no doubt nested there rather consistently for many years. Hayward, who was born and raised in that area, recalls as a small boy seeing and hearing cranes frequently in spring and fall and remembers that they were sometimes shot for food. When he made a rather extensive study of the birds of the valley (approximately 1927–1930), a few Sandhills were seen in the valley throughout the summer, but no nests were actually found. However, at that time they were not nearly as common as they have been in the last 10 years.

RECORDS: Most of the records in print are apparently sight records, many of which have been published. Two specimens taken by the Stansbury party in Salt Lake County in 1849–50 are in the U.S. National Museum of Natural History. These are probably the same birds that Baird (1858:654) mentions. Yarrow saw birds of this species at Fish Springs in August 1872 (Henshaw 1875:467). A set of two eggs undated, in the U.S. National Museum of Natural History, is labeled "Simpson Lake Charles McCarthy Exp. in Utah." A mounted specimen, taken by John Hutchings at Lehi, Utah County, in March 1936, is in the Brigham Young University collection. Sugden (1938:18–22) summarized the known records of this species in Utah and southern Idaho. While there have been several nesting records mentioned over the years, there are apparently few actual sets of eggs available. A set of two eggs taken near Utah Lake was brought to Johnson, 3 May 1900 (Johnson's Journal). Two sets of two eggs each are in the Brigham Young University collection, taken 4 May 1940 and 2 May 1946 at Fish Springs, Juab County. The Sandhill Crane has been observed in southern Utah at the junction of the Santa Clara and Virgin Rivers, Washington County, 9 April 1940 (Hardy and Higgins 1940:98), and in the northwestern part of the state, two miles south of Lynn Reservoir, Box Elder County, 20 June 1956 (Behle 1958:18).

SUBSPECIES: It appears from the information available that the race *G. c. tabida* is the common migrant and breeding bird in

Utah. However, an unknown number of *G. c. canadensis*, a smaller subspecies sometimes called the Little Brown Crane, appear as transients. The mounted specimen cited above in the Brigham Young University collection from Lehi, Utah County, taken in March 1936, is of this smaller race. The measurements of this specimen are culmen 93 mm, tarsus 189 mm, and wing 452 mm.

FAMILY RALLIDAE

Rallus limicola limicola Vieillot
Virgina Rail

STATUS: A breeder, migrant, and regular winter resident in marshlands throughout the state wherever such habitats occur.

RECORDS: All of the early collectors obtained specimens or reported this rail in Utah. Ridgway (1877:369) in 1869 found it near Salt Lake City; Henshaw (1875:468) recorded it from nearly all areas of the state visited by him in 1872; Rowley (collection of American Museum of Natural History) took a specimen at Bluff, San Juan County, 14 May 1892. Many specimens have been collected in recent years. Specimens at Brigham Young University from Utah are as follows: near Utah Lake, Utah County, 24 December 1927, 17 May 1934, and 12 October 1955; one specimen found dead on Brigham Young University campus, Utah County, 15 December 1958; Myton, Duchesne County, 27 December 1958. There are also numerous nesting records, including several for southern Utah (Hardy and Higgins 1940:98; Wauer 1969:331). Sets of eggs have been taken as early as 20 April and as late at 10 June, but most of the records are for May.

Porzana carolina (Linnaeus)
Sora

STATUS: The Sora or Sora Rail is a rather common breeding species and migrant in marshy habitats, especially in the more northern counties of Utah. Because of its secretive habits, it would appear to be less common than it actually is. Although it is primarily a bird of lower valleys, it may occur at higher elevations where there are suitable habitats. It is known to occur sparsely in winter.

RECORDS: Early records include those of Ridgway (1877:369, 376, 612–613), who found it to be common in the marshes around Salt Lake City, Salt Lake County, in 1869, and who also collected one at Parley's Park, Summit County, 26 July 1869. Allen (1872b:172) reported it as common near Ogden, Weber County, in September 1871, and Henshaw (1875:469) found it in 1872 near ponds and lakes in Utah. Many

more recent collections have been made. Specimens in the Brigham Young University collection include one from Logan, Cache County, 27 June 1931; two from near Utah Lake, Utah County, 21 April 1928 and 28 September 1943; and one from Roosevelt, Duchesne County, 1 June 1950. One in the University of Utah collection was obtained at Dugway Proving Ground, Tooele County, 26 August 1957. This specimen was far from any water (Behle et al. 1964: 451). Although most of the known breeding records are from the northern counties of the state (especially Weber, Salt Lake, Utah, and Wasatch), Hardy and Higgins (1940:98) reported an immature bird taken in Washington County, 19 May 1938.

Fig. 23.   Black Tern.   Rochester, Monroe County, New York, 11 July 1967.   Photo by R. J. Erwin.

Porphyrula martinica (Linnaeus)
Purple Gallinule

STATUS: The Purple Gallinule occurs only accidentally in Utah.

RECORDS: A mounted female specimen in the collection of the University of Utah was taken at Haynes Lake, about 12 miles south of Salt Lake City, Salt Lake County, 23 November 1924 (Sugden 1925:210). There is also one sight record from Salt Creek Canyon about 4 miles east of Nephi, Juab County, 10 July 1939 (Woodbury et al. 1949:12).

Gallinula chloropus cachinnans Bangs
Common Gallinule

STATUS: This species occurs only casually in Utah, but there is some evidence that it may occasionally nest in the state.

RECORDS: A single bird was observed and studied closely with field glasses at the Ogden Bay Bird Refuge, Weber County, 24 June 1947 (Cottam and Low 1948:459). Wauer (1963:263) first reported this species in southern Utah at St. George, Washington County, 29 December 1962. Nine were counted in the same locality on 19 December 1963 (Wauer 1964:292) and one at St. George on 12 March 1964 (Snider 1964: 377). Fledglings were observed on 9 July 1964 near Washington, Washington County (Snider 1964:527), and on 1, 17, and 21 August 1965. Juveniles were observed, an indication that it is a breeding bird in southern Utah (Wauer and Russell 1967:421). A specimen was collected at Washington, 5 May 1966, and is in the collection at Zion National Park, Washington County (Wauer 1969:331). One was observed at Bear River Migratory Bird Refuge, Box Elder County, spring 1966 (Scott 1966:536). Hayward (field notes) observed three Common Gallinules, presumably two males and one female, at one time at Powell's Slough, Utah Lake, Utah County, on several dates in April and May 1969, and one bird in the same area in May 1970. On 10 May 1969 two of the birds were seen fighting in a small area of open water in the otherwise dense growth of cattails and tules. The males would periodically display with the tail raised to show conspicuously the white under-tail coverts. Not wishing to disturb the birds, Hayward conducted no systematic search for a nest, but the fighting and display of the males and the persistence of the birds in the area strongly support the possibility of nesting. Winter records for northern Utah are reported by Beall (1974:487) at Bear River Migratory Bird Refuge, Box Elder County, 17 December 1973, and by Kingery (1975:721) at the same location in January and early February 1975.

Fulica americana americana Gmelin
American Coot

STATUS: An abundant breeding species and migrant throughout the state wherever there are ponds, lakes, or marshes. Coots prefer water bodies with open shorelines where they can come out to sun on the beaches but can quickly retreat to the water whenever disturbed.

RECORDS: The earliest explorers in the area attest to the abundance of the Coot in Utah. Beckwith's party (Baird 1854:15) took a specimen in 1854 at Salt Lake City, and Simpson (Baird 1876:381) collected one at Camp Floyd, Utah County, west of Utah Lake, 25 March 1859. Henshaw (1875:470) indicated that the lakes and ponds of the state in the fall were "fairly covered with the coots." Many collections and observations have been made since that time. Especially in the spring and fall when migration is at its peak, the Coot is by far the most common bird in lakes and ponds. There seems to be no indication that the numbers are diminishing. There are also numerous records of nesting, which takes place in late April and during May.

Fig. 24. American Kestrel. Ogden, Weber County, Utah, 27 February 1973. Photo by R. J. Erwin.

FAMILY CHARADRIIDAE

Charadrius semipalmatus Bonaparte
Semipalmated Plover

Status: The Semipalmated Plover is a casual migrant in both spring and fall reported from several areas in the state. It appears in small numbers often in association with Killdeer and Snowy Plovers.

RECORDS: A specimen from the Bear River Marshes, Box Elder County, taken 22 April 1916, is in the U.S. National Museum of Natural History. Behle et al. (1964: 451) recorded two specimens collected at Dugway Proving Grounds, Tooele County, 29 April 1961. The Brigham Young University collection has two specimens from Pelican Lake, Uintah County, 23 September 1961 and 29 Septermber 1962. One was observed by Webster (1947:40) at Harrisville, Weber County, 6 May 1945. Snider (1966:79) reported that Wauer observed one at St. George, Washington County, 24 August 1965. One was seen at Panguitch, Garfield County, 28 August 1974 (Kingery 1975:94). There have also been several sight records from Box Elder, Davis, Salt Lake, Utah, and Uintah counties.

Charadrius alexandrinus nivosus (Cassin)
Snowy Plover

STATUS: This is a rather common summer resident and breeding species on muddy flats or sandy beaches in the central valleys of the state. It seems to be rare in the Uinta Basin and other parts of the Colorado River drainage.

RECORDS: Ridgway (1877:604) stated,

"This handsome and graceful little Plover was exceedingly numerous in May on the bare mud-flats around Warm Springs Lake near Salt Lake City." Numerous collections have been made and sightings recorded of this species, especially in the vicinity of Great Salt Lake and Utah Lake. They nest regularly at Lincoln Beach at the south end of Utah Lake, Utah County (Hayward field notes). Most of the records of nests are for May, although sets of fresh eggs have been taken as late as 10 June (Sugden collection). An early spring sight record is for Kanab, Kane County, 28 March 1931 (Behle et al. 1958:48).

Charadrius vociferus vociferus Linnaeus
Killdeer

STATUS: An abundant summer resident and breeding species throughout the state in nearly all the valleys up to 8,000 feet elevation where there is water. Many birds also migrate through Utah in spring and fall, and a few remain in winter where there are warm springs or small streams that remain open (Webster 1947:40). Nesting occurs over a long period from early April to late July; there is some evidence that two broods may be produced.

RECORDS: Hundreds of collections and observations of birds and nests are on record for this abundant and conspicuous species.

Charadrius montanus Townsend
Mountain Plover

STATUS: The Mountain Plover, which is at home on the higher plains of eastern Montana, Wyoming, and Colorado, is only a casual migrant in Utah.

RECORDS: In 1872 a few specimens were seen south of Fort Bridger, Wyoming, a few miles north of the Utah border (Nelson 1875:342). Alexander Wetmore (field notes)

Fig. 25.   American Avocet. Willard Bay, Box Elder County, Utah, 6 May 1973. Photo by R. J. Erwin.

saw three birds near the mouth of Weber River, Weber County, 26 August 1915. Van den Akker (1946:246) collected a female 15 miles southwest of Brigham City, Box Elder County, 25 March 1946. This is the first collected record in the state. The specimen taken at Bear River Migratory Bird Refuge is in the refuge collection. Scott (1965:501) reported a specimen collected by Wauer near Rockville, Washington County, 29 March 1965. Wauer and Russell (1967:421) listed a specimen taken four miles below Rockville, Washington County, 11 April 1965, and indicated that it is deposited in the Zion Canyon National Park Museum. Snider (1966:537) reported that Wauer saw two birds of this species at St. George, Washington County, 24 April 1966.

Pluvialis dominica dominica (Müller)
American Golden Plover

STATUS: This is a sparse migrant through Utah in both spring and fall, although fall records are more numerous.

RECORDS: A mounted specimen bearing no data was on display at the Bear River Gun Club, Box Elder County; there is also a skin taken 19 September 1932 by Archie V. Hull. Another specimen in the University of Utah collection was taken at the New State Game Club on 28 October 1939. A specimen at Brigham Young University was collected at Pelican Lake, Uintah County, 23 September 1961 (Hayward 1966:305). Several sight records are available. Twomey (1942:390) saw two sizable flocks near Jensen, Uintah County, in May 1937, and a flock of eight at Strawberry Reservoir, Wasatch County, in August of the same year. Two Golden Plovers were seen with a flock of Black-bellied Plovers at Bear River Marshes, Box Elder County, by Cottam and Williams, 17 September 1941.

Pluvialis squatarola (Linneaus)
Black-bellied Plover

STATUS: An uncommon although regular migrant through the state from mid-April to early June and from August to mid-October.

RECORDS: Several specimens have been collected in the Bear River Migratory Bird Refuge area, Box Elder County. One taken by a hunter in the fall of 1908 is on display at the Bear River Gun Club, Box Elder County, and the collection of the U.S. National Museum of Natural History has six specimens taken by Alexander Wetmore in May 1915 and 1916. The Brigham Young University collection contains 10 specimens as follows: Utah Lake, Utah County, one specimen, 9 May 1936; Pelican Lake, Uintah County, nine specimens, 13 May 1961, 23 September 1961, 18 May 1963, and 1 June 1964. There are also many sight records mostly from Box Elder, Davis, Salt Lake, and Utah counties.

FAMILY SCOLOPACIDAE

Arenaria interpres morinella (Linnaeus)
Ruddy Turnstone

STATUS: The Ruddy Turnstone is a rare or casual migrant in Utah.

RECORDS: Cottam (1945a:79) recorded the following collection and sight records of this species: Archie Hull collected a male at Bear River Migratory Bird Refuge, Box Elder County, 4 August 1930; Hull and V. T. Wilson closely studied two birds in the same area in late May 1932, and three more in full breeding plumage were seen by Hull at close range on 17 May 1933; E. R. Quostrup saw a Turnstone on Willard Spur just outside of Bear River Migratory Bird Refuge, 28 May 1944. Behle and Perry (1975:17–18) reported sight records from northern Utah marshes, 3 June 1944, 29 April 1962, and 24 August 1973.

Capella gallinago delicata (Ord)
Common Snipe
Fig. 17, p. 58

STATUS: A common summer resident throughout the lowlands of Utah wherever there are swampy or boggy habitats or even temporary ponds. A few birds also remain throughout the winter where there are small running streams or seeps that do not freeze over.

RECORDS: All of the early naturalists to visit Utah recorded the Common Snipe or Jacksnipe as an abundant breeding species in the area (Allen 1872b:171; Nelson 1875: 348; Henshaw 1875:452–453; Ridgway 1877: 376, 606). Numerous birds and sets of eggs have been collected more recently. Most of the breeding records are for May and early June.

Numenius americanus Bechstein
Long-billed Curlew
Fig. 18, p. 61

STATUS: A fairly common summer resident and migrant in the state, especially through the central and more northern valleys. There are occasional reports of its occurrence in winter (Kashin 1963b:264). Less common in the Colorado River drainage. This species lives and breeds in higher and drier meadowlands than do many of the shorebirds. Its numbers seem to be gradually diminishing, a result of disturbances by man and livestock on its breeding grounds.

RECORDS: All of the early explorers and naturalists who visited the state were aware of these large and conspicus birds, and indications are that they were very common (Remy 1860[2]:450; Merriam 1873: 701; Nelson 1875:348; Ridgway 1877:369, 370, 376, 611). Stansbury (Baird 1852:320) was probably the first to collect a specimen (on Antelope Island), but there is evidence that the Mormon pioneers used them to some extent for food. Simpson (1876:46) on 3 May 1859 recorded that "McCarthy shot a curlew, from which he took, perfectly formed in the shell, an egg as large as a chicken's." Hundreds of collection records and observations have been pub-

lished. In past years, when egg collecting was permitted, numerous sets of eggs were taken since they were highly prized by collectors.

SUBSPECIES: Most of the specimens of curlews known from Utah have been referred to the subspecies *N. a. americanus.* Oberholser (1918b:195) placed a specimen from Fillmore, Millard County, under the name *N. a. occidentalis*, a short-billed subspecies not recognized in the AOU Checklist (1957:180–181). Some specimens from Utah seem to be of the currently recognized short-billed race *N. a. parvus*, but separation of this form from *N. a. americanus* seems to be uncertain where age and sex are unknown. It does appear to be certain, however, that the short-billed race is at the most a rare migrant through the state.

Numenius phaeopus hudsonicus Latham
Whimbrel

STATUS: This is a rare migrant known to pass through Utah in May.

RECORDS: Merlin L. Killpack and C. L. Hayward saw a flock of 28 birds at Montezuma Creek Reservoir, Uintah County, 18 May 1963. One female was taken from the flock and is now in the collection at Brigham Young University (Hayward 1966:305–306). Scott (1965:501) listed one seen by Dennis M. Forsythe near Logan, Cache County, 7 May 1965. McKnight (Scott 1967: 527–528) observed 10 Whimbrel at Fish Springs, Juab County, 21 May 1967.

Tringa[10] *macularia* Linnaeus
Spotted Sandpiper
Fig. 19, p. 64

STATUS: A common summer resident from late April to late September, breeding along the margins of streams, ponds, and lakes throughout the state. It has a wide altitudinal range from 10,000 feet down to

---

[10]We follow Mayr and Short (1970:45–46) and other authors listed by them in merging *Actitis* and *Totanus* into *Tringa.*

the lowest elevations. A few individuals remain in the state in winter.

RECORDS: Allen (1872b:171), Henshaw (1874:11), Ridgway (1877:369, 376, 610) and other early naturalists found the Spotted Sandpiper along all the streams and ponds they visited. In more recent years numerous collections and observations of both birds and eggs are on record. Nesting of this species seems to be somewhat later than most of the local shorebirds since the majority of the records are for June and early July.

Tringa solitaria Wilson
Solitary Sandpiper

STATUS: The Solitary Sandpiper is a casual summer resident especially in the Colorado River drainage area of the state where it may nest. Wauer (1969:331) considered it to be a regular migrant in the St. George Basin, Washington County, where it was seen from 8 April to 4 May and from 4 August to 12 September.

RECORDS: Early naturalists who visited the state recorded sightings of this Sandpiper in several areas (Allen 1872b:171; Nelson 1875:345; Henshaw 1875:459; Ridgway 1877:376, 610). In more recent years the following collections have been made: Bear River Marshes, Box Elder County, 29 August 1914 (Wetmore); Utah Lake, Utah County, 10 September 1927 (Cottam); Benson, Cache County, 28 April 1937 (Utah

Fig. 26.   Mourning Dove. Tremonton, Box Elder County, Utah, 30 June 1974.   Photo by R. J. Erwin.

State University collection) (Stanford 1938: 137); near Mexican Hat, San Juan County, 9 July 1937 (University of Utah); near Jensen, Uintah County, 22 July 1937 (Brigham Young University); 2 miles south of Jensen, summer 1937 (Twomey 1942:392); Zion Canyon, Washington County, 3 May 1942 (Grater); Springdale Ponds, Washington County, 29 April 1965 and 8 May 1965 (Wauer and Carter 1965:51). Evidence of nesting of this species in Utah seems to be based on our knowledge that the birds are consistent summer residents in small numbers. To our knowledge, no nests have actually been found. However, Behle and Selander (1952:26–27) reported a pair collected at Ibapah, Tooele County, 15 July 1950, one of which had testes 12 mm long. This pair was near an irrigation ditch and would not leave the area. Behle and Selander inferred that the birds were breeding. Porter and Bushman (1957:204) indicated that the testes measurement was in error and that the testes were 2 mm long, which would eliminate the likelihood that the birds were breeding. They also reported the collection of six more specimens in Skull Valley, Tooele County, 9, 12(2), 17, and 31 August and 13 September 1954.

SUBSPECIES: Woodbury et al. (1949:13) stated that the form *T. s. cinnamomea* is a casual summer resident breeding in Uintah and Kane counties. Behle and Selander (1952:26–27) reported that the Kane County

Fig. 27. Barn Owl. Ogden, Weber County, Utah, 8 August 1973. Photo by R. J. Erwin.

specimens (University of Utah nos. 2635 and 2636) were "Spotted Sandpipers (*Actitis macularia*)" in winter plumage and so were misidentified. These authors also commented on several other specimens taken in Utah. The specimen collected at Ibapah, mentioned above, and those reported by Twomey (1942:392) are referred to the race *T. s. solitaria* on the basis of Conover's (1944:537–544) discussion of the races of the Solitary Sandpiper; a specimen collected at Mexican Hat, 9 July 1937, and

Fig. 28.   Barn Owl. Ogden, Weber County, Utah, 8 August 1973. Photo by R. J. Erwin.

another in the University of Utah collection obtained at Farmington Bay, Davis County, 10 May 1950, are also of the race *T. s. solitaria.* Porter and Bushman (1957:203–206) carefully summarized the characteristics of the specimens from Mexican Hat, Ibapah,

Farmington Bay, and the six obtained in Skull Valley using Conover's (1944:537–549) diagnostic characters of races. Their analysis indicated that all the specimens were of the race *cinnamomea* except one collected at Skull Valley, 12 August 1954,

Fig. 29. Long-eared Owl. Promontory, Box Elder County, Utah, 30 June 1969. Photo by R. J. Erwin.

Fig. 30. Long-eared Owl (young). Hogup Mountains, Box Elder County, Utah, 25 June 1974. Photo by R. J. Erwin.

Fig. 31. Burrowing Owl. Ogden, Weber County, Utah, 8 August 1973. Photo by R. J. Erwin.

which was of the race *solitaria*. Wauer (1969:331) obtained a male at Washington, Washington County, 22 April 1966, which also represents the race *cinnamomea*.

Tringa melanoleuca (Gmelin)
Greater Yellowlegs

STATUS: The Greater Yellowlegs is a fairly common migrant through Utah mainly in April, May, and again in late July through September. There are some fall records for October and November, and Cottam et al. (1942:53) have published a record for 10 December 1941.

RECORDS: Allen (1872b:171) considered it to be abundant around Ogden during

Fig. 32. Short-eared Owl. Dugway, Tooele County, Utah, 23 March 1953. Photo by R. D. Porter.

September 1871. Earlier naturalists had missed it. Henshaw (1875:458) and Yarrow found it to be abundant at practically all ponds and lakes of the state they visited. They collected specimens near Utah Lake, Utah County, 26 July 1872, and at Deep Creek, Washington County, 12 August 1872.

Numerous collections and sight records are available in more recent years. One record of special interest is a specimen in the Brigham Young University collection taken at Kigalia Ranger Station, Elk Ridge, San Juan County, at 8,402 feet elevation, 24 June 1927, by Cottam. This specimen was

Fig. 33. Saw-whet Owl. Weber River bottoms, Weber County, Utah, 1948. Photo by R. D. Porter and R. J. Erwin.

a male in full breeding plumage with greatly enlarged gonads. It has been reported in migration in southern Utah by Hardy and Higgins (1940:99) and Behle et al. (1958:49).

Tringa flavipes (Gmelin)
Lesser Yellowlegs

STATUS: The Lesser Yellowlegs is a common migrant through Utah, especially from

Fig. 34. Saw-whet Owl (young). Weber River bottoms, Weber County, Utah, April 1948. Photo by R. D. Porter.

mid-March to early May and again in late summer and fall from mid-July to mid-September. A few stragglers may occur in northern Utah in October and as late as December (Kashin 1968:361).

RECORDS: Allen (1872b:171) and Henshaw (1874:11) considered this species to be uncommon in the state and apparently collected no specimens. Judging from the numerous collections and observations made by more recent ornithologists, it is probably more common in migration than the Greater Yellowlegs. In migration it passes through southern Utah where Tanner (1941:86) saw a flock of 20 in a small pond southwest of Hurricane, Washington County, 6 May 1941. Behle et al. (1958:49) collected one near Kanab, Kane County, 15 April 1947. Wauer and Russell (1967:421) reported a specimen collected at Springdale, Washington County, 29 April 1965, and

another near St. George, Washington County, 7 September 1965.

Catoptrophorus semipalmatus inornatus (Brewster)
Willet

STATUS: The Willet is a common shorebird in Utah from late March to early October, occurring rarely in winter. It inhabits the lowlands in grassy situations near the borders of streams and lakes especially in the more central and northern counties, but it appears in southern Utah during migration.

RECORDS: The earliest collection was made by the Stansbury party near Salt Lake City in the spring of 1850 (Baird 1852:320). Ridgway (1877:609) found it to be an abundant breeder in Salt Lake Valley from 2 May to 21 June 1869. Numerous collections of both birds and nests have been made more recently. In over 40 years of observation in Utah County I (Hayward) have not noted any marked decrease in the numbers of this species around Utah Lake.

Calidris canutus rufa (Wilson)
Red Knot

STATUS: An erratic migrant through the state. During some years flocks numbering 1,500 have been observed (Woodbury et al. 1949:14).

RECORDS: The University of Utah has a specimen collected at Bear River Marshes, Box Elder County, in May 1933. There are several observations of this species around Great Salt Lake. Two were seen at Farmington Bay, Davis County, 8 May 1954 (Scott 1954:322–323). Wauer and Russell (1967:421) obtained a specimen three miles southeast of St. George, Washington County, 12 September 1965. It was feeding with Killdeer and Least and Western Sandpipers in a flooded field. One was observed at Utah Lake, Utah County, 11 May 1968

Fig. 35. Horned Lark. Hogup Mountains, Box Elder County, Utah, 11 June 1972. Photo by R. J. Erwin.

Fig. 36. Willow Flycatcher. Blacksmith Fork, Cache County, Utah, 18 July 1954. Photo by R. D. Porter and R. J. Erwin.

(Scott 1968:561). Behle and Perry (1975: 19) reported a flock of 40 at Bear River Migratory Bird Refuge, Box Elder County, 10 May 1973, and Kingery (1975:887) listed one for Logan, Cache County, 5 May 1975.

Calidris melanotos (Vieillot)
Pectoral Sandpiper

STATUS: This species is an uncommon spring and fall migrant through Utah. Most of the records are from late March through May and from late June into October.

RECORDS: Two specimens in the U.S. National Museum of Natural History were taken at Bear River Marshes, Box Elder County, 18 and 22 September 1914. In the same area two were found dead of botulism on 28 August and 17 September 1929 by Hull. Wetmore (field notes) found the Pectoral Sandpiper to be common at Bear River Marshes in September and the first half of October 1916, and C. S. Williams noted the first arrivals in the same area on 21 March 1938. There is a sight record from near Salt Lake City, Salt Lake County, 12 August 1950 (Wilson and Norr 1951:32). Two males were collected by Wauer (1969: 331) at Washington, Washington County, 10 September 1965. Kingery (1975:887) reported a sight record in southern Utah on 9 May 1975.

Calidris bairdii (Coues)
Baird's Sandpiper

STATUS: A seasonal migrant through

Utah. From the available information, it would seem to be present April through June and in August and September.

RECORDS: This species was taken by Wetmore at Bear River Marshes, 5 September 1914 and 11, 19, 23 August 1915. The specimens are in the U.S. National Museum of Natural History. Other specimens collected in the same locality were taken 2 April 1933 (University of Utah), 6 August 1938 (Trowbridge), and 27 June 1941 (Cottam). Twomey (1942:393) observed "small scattered flocks of from three to ten birds during early May and September." They were seen by him on 4 May 1937 along the Green River, Uintah County, and in September 1937 at Strawberry Reservoir, Wasatch County, and at the Ashley Creek marshes, Uintah County, in company with Least and Semipalmated Sandpipers. Wilson and Norr (1951:32) reported seeing 3,000 at Bear River, Box Elder County, 16 September 1950. Two specimens were taken at Pelican Lake, Uintah County, 23 September 1961 (Brigham Young University). Wauer and Russell (1967:421) collected "an extremely fat (weight, 66.6 g) female of this species" near St. George, Washington County, 15 September 1965.

Calidris minutilla (Vieillot)
Least Sandpiper

STATUS: An abundant migrant in Utah, where it often appears on mud flats or around the borders of lakes and ponds in large flocks. It is more common in April-May and August-September but has been recorded for every month of the year. Small numbers winter in the state where warm springs keep the water open.

RECORDS: Ridgway (1877:369, 376, 608) found it near the shores of the Great Salt Lake and elsewhere in the summer of 1869. Allen (1872b:171) thought it to be uncommon around Great Salt Lake in the fall of 1871. Henshaw (1875:455) collected one at Utah Lake, Utah County, 26 July 1872. The Brigham Young University collection contains some 25 specimens from Utah and

southern Nevada. Specimens in the Brigham Young University collection were taken near Utah Lake on 3 and 24 December 1927 and 28 December 1960. Tanner (1927: 199) in his report on the birds of the Virgin River Valley in southwestern Utah stated, "Two specimens were taken in September, 1926, by Mr. Cottam." Cottam collected specimens in September, December, and January at St. George, Washington County (Hardy and Higgins 1940:99).

Calidris alpina pacifica (Coues)
Dunlin

STATUS: A casual but regular migrant through Utah, known mainly in Salt Lake and Utah Lake valleys and from the Uinta Basin. It is known to occur in the area from mid-April through May and again from mid-August to December.

RECORDS: The only one of the early naturalists to record the Dunlin in Utah was Allen (1872b:171), who found it common in Salt Lake Valley in September 1871. Specimens in the U.S. National Museum of Natural History were taken at Bear River Marshes, Box Elder County, 20 and 26 May 1916 and again 26 May 1932. Twomey (1942:393) mentioned a sight record by A. C. Lloyd in the Uinta Basin, 1 May 1935. Behle and Selander (1952:27) referred to specimens taken at the mouth of Bear River, Box Elder County, 26 May 1932, and Farmington Bay Refuge, Davis County, 10 May 1950. Wauer (1969:331–332) collected one of two specimens seen at the confluence of Santa Clara Creek and the Virgin River, Washington County, 28 December 1965. Hayward and Frost (field notes) found a small flock of about a dozen birds at Pelican Lake, Uintah County, 13 May 1966. A single female was seen and collected at Lincoln Beach, Utah County, 18 April 1970 (Brigham Young University).

Calidris pusilla (Linnaeus)
Semipalmated Sandpiper

STATUS: An uncommon migrant through

Fig. 37. Tree Swallow. Blacksmith Fork, Cache County, Utah, 17 July 1954. Photo by R. D. Porter and R. J. Erwin.

Utah, usually associated with Least and Western Sandpipers.

RECORDS: Early naturalists in Utah mentioned the occurrence of this sandpiper in Utah, but apparently few specimens were taken. Henshaw (1875:454–455) took one specimen at Sevier Lake, Millard County, in September 1872. Large flocks at the shore of Great Salt Lake noted by Nelson (1875:348) may have been mostly Western Sandpipers. One was collected near Nephi, Juab County, 13 June 1936 (Ross Hardy collection). Twomey (1942:394) reported three specimens of *C. pusilla* taken by him near Jensen, Uintah County, in 1937. On this basis he considered it to be the most numerous of the sandpipers migrating through the area. He later reported, however, that these specimens had been misidentified and were actually *C. mauri* (Twomey 1944b:90). Two specimens were collected by Wauer and Russell (1967:421) southeast of St. George, Washington County, 7 September 1965.

Calidris mauri (Cabanis)
Western Sandpiper

STATUS: An abundant migrant through the central valleys of Utah but also through the Uinta Basin of eastern Utah (Twomey 1944:90). Most of the migration occurs from mid-March to mid-May and from late July through October.

RECORDS: Shorebirds of the group often called "peeps" were noted by early naturalists, but few specimens were collected. The two closely related species *C. pusilla* and *C. mauri* were apparently often confused. Based on collections and observations in more recent years and up to the present, the Western Sandpiper is by far the more common of the two. Numerous collections and observations have been made (Hardy and Higgins 1940:99; Tanner 1941:86; Behle et al. 1958:50; Wauer and Russell 1967: 421).

Calidris alba (Pallas)
Sanderling

STATUS: The Sanderling is a regular though not common migrant through Utah in both spring and fall. It appears most commonly about the middle of May but may be found as early as mid-April. It is less common in the fall, although there are

records as early as 3 August and as late as 13 October.

RECORDS: This species seems not to have been noted by early naturalists in the state. The U.S. National Museum of Natural History has specimens from the Bear River Marshes, Box Elder County, 20 May 1916. Others have been taken in that some locality on 26 May and 17 September 1932. The University of Utah has specimens from Egg Island, Great Salt Lake, 18 May 1932 and 21 April 1940, and from Utah Lake, Utah County, 26 May 1932 (Behle 1942b:231). Twomey (1942:394) reported a female collected by A. C. Lloyd at Ashley Creek marshes, Uintah County, 21 May 1935, and another specimen obtained south of Jensen, Uintah County, summer 1937. Brigham Young University collection has specimens taken at Utah Lake, 8 October 1927, and eight specimens from Pelican Lake, Uintah County, 13 May 1961, 23 September 1961, 13 May 1966, 12 May 1970. Behle et al. (1964:452) reported a specimen from Dugway, Tooele County, 29 April 1961.

Micropalama himantopus (Bonaparte)
Stilt Sandpiper

STATUS: A rare or perhaps accidental migrant through Utah.

RECORDS: A mounted male specimen from the old Deseret Museum now at Brigham Young University is labeled "Utah, April 1893." The label is written on the bottom of the stand on which the specimen is mounted. The bird is in intermediate plumage between winter and breeding. The specimen reported by Woodbury et al. (1949:14) from Moab, Grand County, proved on closer examination to be a Long-billed Dowitcher (Behle and Selander 1952:28). Woodbury et al. (1949) also recorded a sight record of several birds at Bear River Marshes, 26 July 1932. To our knowledge, there have been no collections of this species in the state in recent years. Wauer (Snider 1965:502) sighted a Stilt Sandpiper near Washington, Washington County, 15

May 1965. Kashin (Scott 1969:87) reported one at Farmington Bay, Davis County, 5 September 1968.

Limnodromus griseus hendersoni Rowan
Short-billed Dowitcher

STATUS: An uncommon but probably regular migrant through the state. Positive records are few, but there is evidence that birds appear in both spring and fall.

RECORDS: Pitelka in his revision of the genus *Limnodromus* (1950:48) recorded an adult male taken at the mouth of Bear River, Box Elder County, 20 May 1915. Behle and Selander (1952:27) listed a female from the Bear River Migratory Bird Refuge, Box Elder County, 17 August 1946 (University of Utah). A series of specimens in the Brigham Young University collection all appear to be the common Long-billed Dowitcher. This includes two specimens formerly identified as *L. griseus* (Johnson 1935a:160).

Limnodromus scolopaceus (Say)
Long-billed Dowitcher

STATUS: The Long-billed Dowitcher is abundant during migration, especially through the central valleys of the state. It often appears in large flocks of hundreds. It is known for every month of the year except January and February, but is most abundant in May and August-September.

RECORDS: Allen (1872b:171) found this species to be abundant near Ogden, Weber County, in September 1871, and Henshaw (1875:453) regarded it as an abundant migrant in Utah. Yarrow and Henshaw (Henshaw 1875:453) collected a juvenile female at Rush Lake, Iron County, 1 October 1872. Numerous collections and observations have been made in recent years in various localities in the state, including St. George, Washington County, 4 May 1935 (Hardy and Higgins 1940:99, errata) and Kanab, Kane County, 1 May 1946 (Behle et al. 1958:49). The Brigham Young University

collection contains some 30 specimens, mostly from Utah Lake Valley, Utah County, and Pelican Lake, Uintah County. Dates range from 26 March to 23 September. Twomey (1942:393) collected 3 specimens east of Vernal, Uintah County, in May 1937, and Cottam et al. (1942:53) reported one seen at Bear River Marshes, Box Elder County, 12 December 1941.

Limosa fedoa (Linnaeus)
Marbled Godwit

STATUS: The Marbled Godwit is a common migrant through Utah, especially in the central valleys of Great Salt Lake and Utah Lake. Lesser numbers pass through the Uinta Basin. Most of the migration occurs in late April through May and from July to September, although stragglers may remain as late at 16 December (Cottam et al. 1942:53).

RECORDS: Many specimens were taken by the U.S. Fish and Wildlife Service in the Bear River Marshes, Box Elder County, from 1914 to 1916. Two specimens, Utah Lake, Utah County, 26 April 1929 and 12 May 1932, are in the Brigham Young University collecton. Twomey (1942:394) collected a specimen 12 miles east of Vernal, Uintah County, 6 May 1937. One specimen was taken at Lower Reservoir, 3 miles south of Kanab, Kane County, 15 April 1947 (Behle et al. 1958:50).

FAMILY RECURVIROSTRIDAE

Recurvirostra americana Gmelin
American Avocet
Fig. 25, p. 79

STATUS: This was formerly a common summer resident and breeding species on the mud flats and around the borders of lakes and ponds, especially near the Great Salt Lake and Utah Lake. It is still present in considerable numbers on the Bear River Migratory Bird Refuge, Box Elder County, and other sanctuaries where it has received

Fig. 38. Cliff Swallow. West Weber, Weber County, Utah, 15 July 1954. Photo by R. J. Erwin.

a measure of protection from disturbance during the nesting season. In recent years it has become more common around some of the reservoirs in the Uinta Basin where it regularly breeds. Occasionally a few may winter in the state (Kashin 1966:351, six seen on 2 January 1966 in the Salt Lake area.)

RECORDS: All of the early naturalists

(Baird 1852:320; Remy 1860[2]:450; Allen 1872b:171; Merriam 1873:701; Nelson 1875: 348; Henshaw 1875:448–450; Ridgway 1877:369, 605) found the American Avocet to be abundant around Great Salt Lake and Utah Lake, Utah County. Collections within the state as well as in most of the American museums and some foreign museums contain numerous specimens of both birds and eggs from Utah. In migration it has been observed and collected in southern Utah at Hurricane, Washington County, 6 May 1941 (Tanner 1941:86), and near Kanab, Kane County, 5 May 1931, 28 April 1935, 17–18 May 1946, 15 April 1947, 20 and 24 May 1947 (Behle et al. 1958:50).

Himantopus mexicanus mexicanus (Müller)
Black-necked Stilt
Figs. 20, 21; pp. 67, 70

STATUS: The Black-necked Stilt was formerly a common summer resident breeding along open shores of lakes and ponds, especially in the central valleys of Utah. Disturbances by man have caused it to be less common at present and somewhat less abundant than the American Avocet. It has become well established as a breeding species in the Uinta Basin and maintains itself rather well at the Bear River Migratory Bird Refuge, Box Elder County, and at other wildlife sanctuaries in the state. It has been recorded from early March to late November.

RECORDS: Allen (1872b:171), Merriam (1873:702, 711), Henshaw (1874:12), and Ridgway (1877:369–606) all reported the stilt as a common breeding species, especially in Salt Lake and Utah Lake valleys. Many collections and observations have been made in recent years. Migrants have been observed near Hurricane, Washington County (Tanner 1941:86), near Boulder, Garfield County, and south of Kanab, Kane County (Behle et al. 1958:50).

FAMILY PHALAROPODIDAE

Phalaropus fulicarius (Linnaeus)
Red Phalarope

STATUS: A rare, accidental migrant through Utah.

RECORDS: Two specimens now in the Dixie College collection were collected on the Virgin River near St. George, Washington County, 14 and 15 October 1934 (Hayward 1937:304). A partially paralyzed Red Phalarope was picked up by botulism workers at Bear River Migratory Bird Refuge, Box Elder County, in September 1951. The specimen is now in the U.S. National Museum of Natural History (Sciple 1953:205). Kingery reported (Snider 1965:65) seeing a Red Phalarope on Wahweap Creek, Kane County, 10 September 1964.

Phalaropus [11] *tricolor* (Vieillot)
Wilson's Phalarope
Fig. 22, p. 73

STATUS: A common summer resident in suitable habitats throughout the state where it breeds in grass or sedge habitats near water. It has been recorded from late March to mid-September. Often abundant in migration in July and August, when on stormy nights it may be seen in thousands milling around city lights.

RECORDS: Ridgway (1877:369, 604) found it on alkaline ponds around the southern shore of Great Salt Lake in May and June 1869. Allen (1872b:171) found it abundant near Ogden, Weber County, and Great Salt Lake in the early fall of 1871. It was also reported in the same area by Merriam (1873:701) and by Yarrow (Henshaw 1875: 451). The species seems to maintain itself rather well even under the pressure of expanding human population. Numerous collections and observations have been made in recent years.

---

[11]We follow Mayr and Short (1970:47) and other authors cited by them in considering the three species of phalaropes to be congeneric.

Phalaropus lobatus (Linnaeus)
Northern Phalarope

STATUS: A common and abundant migrant through Utah in spring and late summer. The peak of spring migration occurs about mid-May and the summer flight in August.

RECORDS: Many hundreds of observations and collections have been recorded, mostly from the central Utah valleys of Great Salt Lake and Utah Lake. However, it has also been recorded from southern Utah. Greenhalgh observed Northern Phalaropes at Kanab, Kane County, 9–10, 12 May 1931 (Behle et al. 1958:50); Hardy and Higgins (1940:99) reported it at St. George, Washington County, 3 September 1939; and it has also been reported from the northwest portion of Utah, near Yost, Box Elder County, 7 September 1932 (Behle 1958:18). In recent years there has also been a heavy flight through the Uinta Basin. Hayward and Frost (field notes) observed thousands of Northern Phalaropes on 15 May 1970 at Pelican Lake, Uintah County. Large restless flocks were swimming in the open water or wading in the small pools adjacent to the lake. They appeared to be feeding on the abundant midges on the water surface. Approximately three weeks later, 3 June 1970, not one Northern Phalarope was observed (Frost field notes).

FAMILY STERCORARIIDAE

Stercorarius parasiticus (Linnaeus)
Parasitic Jaeger

STATUS: A rare migrant or accidental, having been observed in spring, summer, and fall.

RECORDS: A male victim of botulism was taken at the Bear River Migratory Bird Refuge, Box Elder County, 2 September 1932, and another specimen (University of Utah) was collected in the same area by Hull on 8 October 1934. Several sight records by personnel of the Bear River Migra-

tory Bird Refuge are known for 21, 25 August 1934, September 1941, and September 1942 (Woodbury et al. 1949:15). Kingery (1972:884) reported two seen at Bear River Migratory Bird Refuge, Box Elder County, during the spring and summer of 1972.

Stercorarius longicaudus Vieillot
Long-tailed Jaeger

STATUS: A rare migrant or accidental known to occur in Utah in August and October.

RECORDS: A specimen now in the U.S. National Museum of Natural History was found dead at Bear River Migratory Bird Refuge, Box Elder County, 29 August 1944, by C. C. Sperry (Cottam 1945b:173). A. K. Fisher (1937:389–390) observed one at close range in the same locality on 3 October 1926.

FAMILY LARIDAE

Larus hyperboreus hyperboreus Gunnerus
Glaucous Gull

STATUS: This gull is usually considered to be an accidental visitor to the state, and most of the records are sight records.

RECORDS: Two birds were observed at the mouth of Provo River and Utah Lake, Utah County, from 22 February to 15 April 1934, and one (Brigham Young University) was finally collected (Johnson 1935a:160). One was collected at Bear River Migratory Bird Refuge, Box Elder County, 16 March 1955, by Vanez Wilson (Wilson and Young 1956:390). This specimen is now in the refuge collection. One was seen in west central Utah by Lockerbie during the winter of 1948–49 (Van den Akker 1949:179). Worthen (1968:475) mentioned a bird recently collected at Farmington Bay, Davis County. The Audubon Field Notes for 1963, 1964, 1965 (Scott 1963:347, 442; 1964: 376; 1965:405) reported a number of sight records for Farmington Bay and Bear River

Fig. 39. Loggerhead Shrike. Dugway Valley, Tooele County, Utah, May 1953. Photo by R. D. Porter and R. J. Erwin.

Marshes. All of the records available to us are for February, March, and April, except a report from Bear River for 17 December 1973 (Beall 1974:487).

Larus argentatus smithsonianus Coues
Herring Gull

STATUS: The Herring Gull is probably a regular transient in Utah where it has been reported in the spring, fall, and winter.

RECORDS: The first observation of this species in Utah was Nelson (1875:348), who reported, "I saw a large gull at the mouth of the Jordan which I am quite sure was this species." The first collection record is that in June 1915 by Wetmore, who found the remains of a specimen that had died the previous winter or spring (Williams et al. 1943:160). Marshall (1937:258) also reported a partially decayed carcass found at Bear River Migratory Bird Refuge, Box Elder County, 27 April 1937. Between 27 April and November another specimen was found, according to Marshall. This pos-

sibly could be the mounted skin on display at Bear River Migratory Bird Refuge Headquarters that was obtained 7 October 1937. Stanford (1938:139) recorded a bird obtained at Bear River Migratory Bird Refuge, 25 November 1937, now in the Utah State University collection. Behle (1942b:230) obtained a specimen from Bear River Migratory Bird Refuge that was collected in late September or early October 1939. Cottam et al. (1942:53) reported seeing a Herring Gull at Bear River Migratory Bird Refuge in September and again 16, 27, 28 December 1941. A specimen obtained by Beck (1942:54) at Utah Lake, Utah County, 27 February 1942, and later verified by Cottam, has unfortunately been lost. The remains of one bird were found by Behle (1942b:230–231) on Egg Island, Great Salt Lake, 8 May 1942. On the following day he observed one at Bear River Migratory Bird Refuge. During the winter of 1956–57 Lockerbie reported four birds wintering at Farmington Bay, Davis County (Scott 1957:284). Another winter report is that of

Kashin (1966:351) for the Salt Lake area in late December 1965 and early January 1966. Wauer (Scott 1965:405) reported sighting a Herring Gull at Springdale, Washington County, 14 February 1965.

Larus californicus Lawrence
California Gull

STATUS: This is an abundant summer resident of Great Salt Lake and Utah Lake valleys where it nests in large colonies on islands and dikes. Small numbers occur elsewhere in the state as nonbreeders or migrants. Banding records indicate that young birds hatched in Utah migrate to the West Coast where they remain for two or three years until they are ready to breed.

RECORDS: Early records of the California Gull in Utah are somewhat indefinite. Fremont (1845:158) related that his party on their visit to Great Salt Lake on 12 September 1843 had a supper of "sea gulls." Stansbury (1852:188) and Ridgway (1877:637) found them nesting commonly on the islands of Great Salt Lake in 1850 and 1869. Allen, Nelson, Merriam, and Henshaw did not mention them in their writings. It has been generally assumed that the "sea gulls" mentioned by the Mormons as saviors of the crops of 1848 and 1849 from the ravages of crickets (*Anabrus simplex*) were most likely California Gulls. In more recent years many hundreds of records and observations of birds and their nesting activities have been made.

Larus delawarensis Ord
Ringed-billed Gull

STATUS: A common winter resident in the central valleys of Utah. It is a regular though less common resident in summer. Some evidence indicates that it nests in small numbers.

RECORDS: A specimen of this species in the U.S. National Museum of Natural History was taken by Stansbury in Utah in 1850 (Allen 1872b:173). Henshaw (1875:485) re-

corded a female taken at Provo, Utah County, 30 November 1872. Nelson (1875:349) and Henshaw (1875:485) found it common around the larger bodies of water in the state but did not find the California Gull. There may have been some confusion in identification of the two species by these early naturalists. Twomey (1942:396) reported that Ring-billed Gulls nested in small numbers near Jensen, Uintah County, but this was based on hearsay and was not verified by Twomey. Hayward (field notes) has found this species to be a common summer resident at Pelican Lake, Uintah County. It is far more common there than the California Gull. However, we have found no evidence of nesting. It has been found in the following localities in southern Utah: along the Virgin River, near St. George, Washington County, 23 April 1940 (Hardy and Higgins 1940:99), and along the Colorado River, near the mouth of Last Chance Creek, river mile 49, Kane County, 16 April 1947 (Behle 1948b:306).

Larus pipixcan Wagler
Franklin's Gull

STATUS: A common summer resident in Utah where it breeds in marshy areas around the Bear River Migratory Bird Refuge, Box Elder County, and possibly other areas. It has been recorded in the state from 2 April to 22 October.

RECORDS: None of the early naturalists to visit the state identified Franklin's Gull; and it has been claimed by some that this species, which is the common gull eastward in the prairie country, has but recently moved westward. Goodwin (1904a:99) wrote that he was not able to find the bird in the state up to 1904. Wetmore (1916) found them rather common at Bear River Marshes in 1916 and apparently was first to discover a nesting colony there. Since that time, they appear to have increased greatly in the Bear River Migratory Bird Refuge area, Box Elder County. Twomey (1942:396) reported this species in the Uinta Basin on 10 May 1937. In recent years they have increased in that area (Hayward 1967:31). The Brigham Young University collection has four specimens taken at Pelican Lake, Uintah County, 22 July 1961, 2 June 1964, and 15 May 1966. Our observations indicated that Franklin's Gull is spotty in its distribution in the state. Areas of concentration seem to be the Bear River Migratory Bird Refuge and the Uinta Basin. It is rarely seen in Utah Valley around Utah Lake. This irregular distribution of the species may account for the fact that it was missed by early observers in the state. This species has been found in southern Utah at several different localities. One specimen from a flock of 20 was obtained on the Virgin River near St. George, Washington County, 23 April 1940 (Hardy and Higgins 1940:99). Behle (1948b:306) collected one on the Colorado River, near the mouth of Ticaboo Canyon, river mile 148, Garfield County, 13 April 1947. A flock of 12 was seen at Lower Reservoir, three miles south of Kanab, Kane County, 15 April 1947 (Behle et al. 1958:50).

Larus philadelphia (Ord)
Bonaparte's Gull

STATUS: An uncommon migrant and occasional winter resident in Utah. It is not known to breed within the state, but a few nonbreeding individuals may remain through the summer.

RECORDS: The only recording of Bonaparte's Gull by the early naturalist visitors was by Allen (1872b:173), who found a flock near Ogden, Weber County, about 2 October 1871. Five immature specimens collected at the Bear River Marshes, Box Elder County, 22 May 1915 and 8 June 1916, by Wetmore, are now in the U.S. National Museum of Natural History. Four specimens were collected by Cottam (Brigham Young University) at the Bear River Marshes on 13 November 1927 and 4 November 1928. Two were taken at Utah Lake, Utah County, 15 May 1933, and one

at the same locality on 21 October 1934 (Brigham Young University). One was collected near Kanab, Kane County, 15 April 1947 (University of Utah, Behle et al. 1958: 51). Behle et al. (1964:452) reported a collection near Camel Mountain, Tooele County, 25 April 1955. Hayward and Frost (field notes) observed several with a flock of Franklin's Gulls at Pelican Lake, Uintah County, 15 May and 3 June 1970. There have been numerous other sight records.

Rissa tridactyla tridactyla (Linnaeus)
Black-legged Kittiwake

STATUS: A species of seemingly accidental occurrence in Utah.

RECORDS: A male specimen was found dead at Fish Springs National Wildlife Refuge, Juab County, 12 March 1972, by Jim Harrison, a trapper. It was sent to the University of Utah and placed in their collection (Behle 1973b:243).

Xema sabini sabini (Sabine)
Sabine's Gull

STATUS: The few records would indicate that this gull is of accidental occurrence in Utah.

RECORDS: Allen (1872b:173) took a single specimen, the only one seen, at West Weber, near Ogden, Weber County, 28 September 1871. This specimen is now in the Museum of Comparative Zoology at Harvard. Behle (1949a:98) recorded a specimen found by C. W. Lockerbie at Decker's Lake near Salt Lake City, Salt Lake County, 26 September 1948. Five other birds were seen at the lake that day. There is also a sight record for Lockerbie (Scott 1954:33) of one near Salt Lake City, 8 October 1953. Kingery (1975:722) reported one observed at Vernal, Uintah County, for two weeks during March 1975.

Sterna forsteri Nuttall
Forster's Tern

STATUS: A common summer resident of Utah, breeding mainly from 25 May to 20 June in marshes around lakes and sloughs.

It is more abundant in the northern and central valleys of the state but is also known to breed at Pelican Lake, Uintah County.

RECORDS: Ridgway (1873a:173; 1875:31; 1877:369, 640) collected specimens and noted that it was an abundant breeder in Salt Lake Valley from 20 May to 21 June 1869. Henshaw (1874:13; 1875:486) collected specimens at Utah Lake in the summer (24 July) and fall of 1872. Many records of birds and nesting have been reported since then.

Sterna hirundo Linnaeus
Common Tern

STATUS: A migrant species through Utah, the Common Tern is usually considered to be rare, but it may be more common than has been supposed. Because of its close resemblance to Forster's Tern and its tendency to flock with that species, the Common Tern may be easily overlooked.

RECORDS: Stanford (1944:151) listed one collected at Gunnison Reservoir, Sanpete County, 7 June 1941. One in the U.S. National Museum of Natural History was found a victim of botulism at Bear River Migratory Bird Refuge, Box Elder County, 14 September 1941. At this same time Williams (1942:578) estimated that about one-fourth of the terns at the refuge were Common Terns. Several additional sight records are available, including a single bird at Kanab, Kane County, 5 May 1931 (Behle et al. 1958:51); six at Farmington Bay, Davis County, 20 May 1963, observed by Kashin and Webb (Utah Audubon News 1963:38); and one at Provo, Utah County, 30 April 1974 (Kingery 1974:833).

Fig. 40. Rock Wren. Big Bend National Park, Brewster County, Texas, May 1958. Photo by R. D. Porter and R. J. Erwin.

Sterna caspia Pallas
Caspian Tern

STATUS: An uncommon summer resident in Utah where it has bred at several localities from time to time depending upon the amount of disturbance by man and by other birds.

RECORDS: Ridgway (1875:31; 1877:369, 639) was the only one of the early naturalists to record this tern. He found it in the marshes near Salt Lake City, Salt Lake County, in June and July 1869. Wetmore took three specimens at Bear River, Box Elder County, in June and August 1916. Brigham Young University has two immature specimens taken at St. George, Washington County, 7 September 1926, and three others taken from Utah Lake, Utah County, in June 1927 and 1928. Various nesting sites of the Caspian Tern have been recorded, including Hat Island, Great Salt Lake, Rock Island, Utah Lake, Utah County (Hayward 1935a:140–141), and on certain dikes at the Bear River Migratory Bird Refuge, Box Elder County. Cottam (1946:94–95) found downy young at Bear River as late as 18 September 1945. Some of the colonies have been harassed by the predatory California Gull, especially when the two were nesting together. At the present time there is a nesting colony on an artificial island at the Bear River Migratory Bird Refuge. Kingery (1975:95) reported four seen at Zion National Park, Washington County, 11 September 1974.

Chlidonias niger surinamensis (Gmelin)
Black Tern
Fig. 23, p. 76

STATUS: A common summer resident of Utah where it breeds in small colonies in the marshes around Great Salt Lake and Utah Lake, Utah County. In recent years it has probably nested at Pelican Lake, Uintah County, where it is a common summer resident.

RECORDS: Henshaw (1875:487) found it at Utah Lake, Utah County, in July 1872, and Ridgway (1875:31) found evidence of its nesting in Salt Lake Valley. Numerous records of collections and observations of both birds and eggs have been recorded in more recent years. The Black Tern is now common in the Uinta Basin, especially at Pelican Lake. Birds are to be found there throughout the summer, with immature individuals being taken in late July (Hayward 1967:31–32). It has been reported north of Ibapah, Tooele County, 20 May 1942 (Behle and Ross 1945:169), and near Kanab, Kane County, 1 May 1946, 20 and 24 May 1947 (Behle et al. 1958:51).

FAMILY ALCIDAE

Synthliboramphus antiquus (Gmelin)
Ancient Murrelet

STATUS: The Ancient Murrelet is a rare and accidental visitor in Utah and in some of the other intermountain states.

RECORDS: One specimen was taken on Jordan River, Utah County, 21 December 1925, by John Hutchings and was prepared by him as a mounted specimen (Woodbury et al. 1949:16). A second specimen, a female, was obtained 12 November 1955 at Roosevelt, Duchesne County, by Merlin L. Killpack (Killpack and Hayward 1958:23). The bird was found on the ground in an exhausted state. This specimen is now in the collection at Brigham Young University. Verbeek (1966:510) reported a specimen found dead at Logan, Cache County, 24 November 1962. A carcass about two days old was found on Gunnison Island, Great Salt Lake, Box Elder County, 6 May 1974 (Kingery 1975:95).

FAMILY COLUMBIDAE

Columba fasciata fasciata Say
Band-tailed Pigeon

STATUS: An uncommon resident in the mountains of southern Utah at mid-elevations, especially in pinyon-juniper and yellow pine forests. Less common in the Uinta Basin of northeastern Utah and in recent years reported along the Wasatch front.

RECORDS: Sight records of this species, usually seen in small flocks, are numerous (Presnell 1935a:82; Benson 1935:445; Hardy and Higgins 1940:99; Cottam 1941b:122; Grater 1943:76; Wauer and Carter 1965:53). Grater (1937:14) reported this species as breeding at East Fork Mountain, Kane County, near Bryce Canyon (no date). Behle and Ghiselin (1958:4) reported a mounted specimen in the University of Utah collection taken at Hanna, Duchesne County, July 1930. The remains of a Band-tailed Pigeon were collected between 9 and 12 September 1946 in the vicinity of Elk Ridge, San Juan County (Behle 1960a:28). Behle and Selander (1952:27–28) took one at New Harmony, Washington County, 24 June 1950. Behle (1960a:28) collected a specimen in the La Sal Mountains, San Juan County, 17 July 1956. Worthen (1968: 214) reported three separate areas in the Tusher Mountains, six or seven miles northeast of Beaver, Beaver County, where three flocks were breeding in cottonwoods along streams. A flock of between 5 and 25 was seen by many observers in Salt Lake City, Salt Lake County, during the spring of 1975 (Kingery 1975:887). Pederson and Nish (1975:59–75) have summarized sight and collection records from all parts of the state up to and including 1972. For the 1970-72 period three additional reports are given for the Uinta Basin plus two reports for Wasatch County and seven for Utah County. One was collected at the head of Rock Canyon, Utah County, 20 September 1975, and is in the Life Sciences Museum at Brigham Young University (museum number 5425).

Columba liva Gmelin
Rock Dove

STATUS: Introduced and common around cities and farming communities throughout

the state. It may be domesticated by pigeon fanciers or occur in semiwild flocks in city streets or around farms. The common pigeon is composed of a mixture of several natural subspecies (AOU Check-list 1957: 260).

Zenaida asiatica mearnsi (Ridgway)
White-winged Dove

STATUS: This dove is an uncommon summer resident in Utah especially in the hot, dry desert country of the southwest.

RECORDS: Behle et al. (1964:452) have summarized the known records of this species. Most of these are sight records, but several specimens have been taken at Beaver Dam Wash, Washington County, 24 June 1961, 25 May 1962, and July 1962. Two specimens were taken in traps at Fish Springs National Wildlife Refuge, Juab County, 24 May 1961 and 8 September 1962. One was banded and the other, which expired in the trap, was prepared as a specimen. There are also sight records for East Canyon, Morgan County, 1 August 1939, and Liberty Park, Salt Lake City, 1 May 1962. It has also been reported for Bear River Migratory Bird Refuge, Box Elder County, 19 July 1965 (Scott 1965:567) and Beaver Dam Wash, Washington County, from 5 April to 4 August (Wauer 1969:332). A White-winged Dove was collected in a river bottom near the old Bennion Ranch northeast of McDowell (Keg) Mountain, Juab County, 8 September 1975. One wing was preserved and is in the Brigham Young University Life Sciences Museum (museum number 5429).

Zenaida macroura marginella (Woodhouse)
Mourning Dove
Fig. 26, p. 82

STATUS: The Mourning Dove is a common summer resident throughout the state. It is most abundant along the streams in the lower valleys where it builds flimsy nests of small sticks in trees or on the

Fig. 41. House Wren. North Fork Ogden River, Weber County, Utah, 11 June 1954. Photo by R. J. Erwin.

ground. A few individuals remain through the winter, particularly in the warmer valleys of the south.

RECORDS: Mourning Doves were reported by all the early naturalists (Allen 1872b: 170; Merriam 1873:710; Henshaw 1875:431–432; Ridgway 1877:596–597) who visited Utah. Many collections and observations have been made in recent years.

Scardafella inca (Lesson)
Inca Dove

STATUS: This dove is considered accidental in Utah.

RECORDS: Behle (1966:396) reported one collected at Beaver Dam Wash, Washington County, 5 miles north of the Utah-Arizona border, 9 July 1963. One was seen at Parowan, Iron County, 15 August 1963 (Behle and Perry 1975:22).

FAMILY CUCULIDAE

Coccyzus americanus occidentalis
Ridgway
Yellow-billed Cuckoo

STATUS: The Yellow-billed Cuckoo is an uncommon summer resident in favored habitats throughout the state from May to September. It lives in the woodlands along streams in the lower valleys.

RECORDS: Henshaw (1875:386) saw this species at Provo, Utah County, but took no specimens. Bailey (field notes 1893) reported that a pair lived on a farm near Ogden, Weber County, in July 1893. More recent collection records are as follows: Wellsville, Cache County, 17 June 1938, and Logan, Cache County, 10 June 1941 (Utah State University); near Hurricane, Washington County, 20 August 1932 (University of Utah, Woodbury 1939:157); St. George, Washington County, 11 July 1937 (Hardy and Higgins 1940:99). Brigham Young University has specimens from Bluff, San Juan County, 2 July 1927; Virgin River, Washington County, near Utah-Arizona border, 1934; Provo, Utah County, 20 June 1941. Merlin L. Killpack (pers. comm.) reported a male specimen taken near Santaquin, Utah County, 8 July 1973. Wauer and Carter (1965:59) considered it to be a rare summer visitor in the Virgin River Valley of southwestern Utah. Several sets of eggs have been taken in Weber, Salt Lake, Utah, and Washington counties.

Coccyzus erythropthalmus (Wilson)
Black-billed Cuckoo

STATUS: This cuckoo appears to be of rare occurrence in the state in summer.

RECORDS: Behle and Selander (1952:28) reported a specimen taken at Bountiful, Davis County, 9 July 1951. This was a female in breeding condition. Kashin (1963c:61) reported that one was seen and heard singing in Salt Lake City, Salt Lake County, 15 June 1963.

Geococcyx californianus (Lesson)
Roadrunner

STATUS: The Roadrunner is a fairly common resident of the lower deserts adjacent to the Virgin River Valley of Washington County. It is less common in southern Iron and Kane counties and accidental as far north as Provo, Utah County.

RECORDS: The occurrence of the Roadrunner in the Virgin River area of southwestern Utah was mentioned by Henshaw (1875:383) and some of the other early naturalists, but they apparently took no specimens. Specimens and observations of both birds and eggs taken in recent years are mostly from Washington County (Presnell 1935b:201; Hardy and Higgins 1940:99; Behle 1943a:39). A specimen taken near Parowan, Iron County, prior to 1936, is in the University of Utah collection (Worthen 1968:218). Behle et al. (1958:51) saw Roadrunners near Kanab, Kane County, 2 April 1947, 1 May 1946, 20 May 1947, and 29 November 1947. In July of 1932 a rather badly decomposed specimen was found on the foothills east of Provo by Reinwald Leichty (Hayward 1944:204). The head was saved in alcohol and was in the Brigham Young University collection for several years. Unfortunately it eventually was lost. Wauer and Carter (1965:54) considered the Roadrunner to be an uncommon permanent resident at lower elevations in the Zion Canyon area. Recently (21 August 1976) Laurence B. McArthur (personal communication) observed a Roadrunner for approximately 15 minutes at Beers Pass (elevation 6,300 feet), about three miles west of State Highway 21 in the extreme northwestern corner of Beaver County. This location is about a mile south of the Beaver-Millard County line and is over 100 miles north of the range of this species as given by Behle and Perry (1975:23).

FAMILY TYTONIDAE

Tyto alba (Scopoli)
Barn Owl
Figs. 27, 28; pp. 83, 84

STATUS: The Barn Owl is usually considered to be an uncommon resident in Utah, but it tends to be colonial. In certain localities where there are suitable nesting situations, it may be concentrated in considerable numbers (Smith et al. 1972b:229). It is known to live and nest through the length of the state in the central valleys and also in the Uinta Basin.

RECORDS: The early naturalists seem not to have noted the Barn Owl in Utah. Two specimens (University of Utah) were taken near Parowan, Iron County, prior to 1936. There are also several collections (University of Utah) from near Kanab, Kane County, 14 June 1939, 12 and 19 July 1940, and 2 May 1946. Behle (1941a:160) described nesting activities in that same locality, based partly on earlier reports by Greenhalgh, who noted as many as 30 owls present at one time. Brigham Young University has the following specimens from Utah: Provo, Utah County, 19 October 1955; Springville, Utah County, 19 March 1959; Provo, 10 April 1967; Ironton Steel Plant (now demolished), Utah County, 25 January 1969. A late nesting record was recorded by Smith et al. (1970:492) at Springville, Utah County, 4 October 1968. Frost banded a brood of six young in the attic of a school in American Fork, Utah County, 21 April 1971. Smith et al. (1974: 131–136) have described the activities of a colony near Springville, Utah County.

FAMILY STRIGIDAE

Otus asio (Linnaeus)
Screech Owl

STATUS: The Screech Owl is a fairly common resident of Utah, where it lives in the riparian communities along the streams. It occasionally occupies trees along city streets and is known to nest in such localities (Hayward field notes).

RECORDS: Presnell (1935b:201) saw a reddish brown Screech Owl at Zion National Park, Washington County, 27 January 1935. It was with a gray phased owl, and unfortunately only the gray specimen was collected. Since Peterson (1961:157) stated that the brown color phase is limited to the northern Great Basin, Presnell's report is of interest. Screech Owls have been found in many parts of the state. Collected specimens in Utah institutions represent most of the counties. The following selected published records indicate its widespread occurrence in Utah: Twomey (1942:398), two miles south of Jensen, Uintah County, 25–30 July 1935; Behle (1941b:182), Block Canyon, San Juan County, 3 and 5 April 1938; Behle (1958:19), George Creek, five miles southeast of Yost, Box Elder County, 12 July 1955; Wauer and Carter (1965:54), Zion's Canyon, 18 September 1963 and 6 January 1964. Of some 25 nesting records available to us, most of them are for the month of April.

SUBSPECIES: Specimens of Screech Owls from Utah have been variously referred to the races O. a. cineraceus, inyoensis, maxwelliae, and mychophilus. Two specimens from St. George, Washington County, were identified by H. C. Oberholser in 1942 as mychophilus, but this race was not recognized in the 1957 AOU Check-list. Behle (1948a:71), in a brief review of this species, concluded that the birds of most of the state are of the race inyoensis, although there are certain indications of a transition with cineraceus. O. a. cineraceus seems to be restricted to a small area of southeastern

Fig. 42. Mockingbird. Cedar Mountains, Tooele County, Utah, 19 June 1953. Photo by R. D. Porter and R. J. Erwin.

Utah. A specimen (Brigham Young University) from Murray, Salt Lake County, 5 June 1927, was identified years ago by Oberholser as *maxwelliae* with some question, but the specimen has been lost.

Otus flammeolus flammeolus (Kaup)
Flammulated Owl

STATUS: This is a sparse resident in Utah where it lives in forested areas especially in the mountains. It is known to nest in woodpecker holes.

RECORDS: Oberholser (1899:15) recorded a specimen taken near Salt Lake City, Salt Lake County, in the fall of 1895. Specimens (University of Utah) have been collected from near Silver City, Tooele County, 5 and 12 May 1912; near Grantsville, Tooele County, 12 June 1932; Navajo Mountain, San Juan County, 6 July 1936 (Woodbury 1939:158). The Brigham Young University collection contains a specimen from Pine Valley Mountain, Washington County, 20 October 1935, and from Mt. Timpanogos, Utah County, 3 July 1937 (Hayward 1937:

304–305). The last mentioned specimen was taken by hand from its nest in an aspen tree. The nest was located about 24 feet from the ground in a hole which had apparently been used by a Flicker since it was larger than holes used by Swallows and House Wrens. In the nest were two small young with downy white feathers. More recent records are as follows: Porter (1954: 362), specimen found dead on highway near Ogden, Weber County, 26 May 1950; Lockerbie (1951:53) reported one seen at Memory Grove, Salt Lake County, 14 October 1951; Wauer (1966a:211), four (two banded) seen in Zion Park, 8, 12, 27 May 1964, and one at Springdale, Washington County, 7 May 1965.

Bubo virginianus (Gmelin)
Great Horned Owl

STATUS: A common resident throughout the state with a wide range of distribution from lowland deserts to timbered country in the mountains. It occurs in conifer forests, streamside woodlands, and remote desert country.

RECORDS: Most of the early naturalists to visit Utah mentioned the Great Horned Owl. Stansbury sent a specimen to the U.S. National Museum of Natural History in 1850. Allen (1872b:170), Henshaw (1875: 407), and Ridgway (1877:375) all reported the species as common wherever they traveled. Numerous specimens and sets of eggs and countless observations have been made in more recent years.

SUBSPECIES: Two races occur commonly within the state, according to an account by Behle (1960b:17). A darker form, *B. v. occidentalis*, inhabits the northern part of the state, and a paler race, *B. v. pallescens*, occurs in more desert country of the south. *B. v. lagophonus* is a rare winter visitor (Behle and Ghiselin 1958:5; AOU Check-list 1957:278).

Nyctea scandiaca (Linnaeus)
Snowy Owl

STATUS: The Snowy Owl is a rare winter visitor to Utah.

RECORDS: Snowy Owls have been reported intermittently from Utah for the past 65 years. Hayward (1935b:284) reported a specimen in the Brigham Young University Life Sciences Museum collected on Provo Bench (now Orem), Utah County, December 1908. Behle (1968b:231–232) recorded the following specimens: Huntsville, Weber County, winter 1909; 15 miles northeast of Mantua, Box Elder County, 1 October 1925 (two birds that were not saved); south of Centerville, Davis County, 5 April 1953. Ferris (1954:20) recorded a sight record for Ephraim, Sanpete County, 4 January 1954. Behle (1968b:232) mentioned the sighting of a single bird on the southeastern outskirts of Salt Lake City, Salt Lake County, early January 1961. Three records are reported for 1967: Behle (1968b:232) listed an observation of one bird two miles south of Randolph, Rich County, 7 January 1967, and the collection of a decomposed body at the south end of Bear Lake, Rich County, 22 January 1967. Behle indicated that these two reports

could have been the same bird, as the two localities are only about 15 miles apart. Scott (1967:444) recorded a specimen (now in the University of Utah collection) collected 4 miles west of Syracuse, Davis County, 26 January 1967.

Glaucidium gnoma californicum Sclater
Pygmy Owl

STATUS: The Pygmy Owl is an uncommon resident of the forested sections of the state. It is more common in the coniferous forests of the mountains but also lives in woodlands and groves of dense trees along streams in the lower valleys and sometimes in cities.

RECORDS: A specimen taken in the mountains east of Ogden, Weber County, 5 October 1888, is in the US. National Museum of Natural History. Several specimens are in the Utah State University collection as follows: Oquirrh Mountains, Tooele County, 30 April 1936; Manti, Sanpete County, 24 December 1936; Logan Canyon, Cache County, 25 June 1941. The University of Utah collection has a specimen taken at the mouth of City Creek Canyon, Salt Lake City, Salt Lake County, 12 January 1941 (Behle and Ross 1945:169), and another collected near Ogden on 24 January 1943. Brigham Young University collection contains nine specimens as follows: Aspen Grove, Mt. Timpanogos, Utah County, August 1926, 30 June 1937, July 1937, 3 July 1937, 12 June 1957; near Roosevelt, Duchesne County, 22 June 1957; 22 miles south of Cannonville, Kane County, 18 June 1960 (three specimens). Wauer and Carter (1965:55) considered this species to be an uncommon winter visitor in the Zion Park area of southern Utah. Wauer (1969: 332) collected a specimen in Zion Canyon, Washington County, 5 July 1964.

Athene cunicularia hypugaea
(Bonaparte)
Burrowing Owl
Fig. 31, p. 87

STATUS: Locally rather common in

desert valleys of the state especially in prairie dog colonies. Formerly common in Salt Lake and Utah Lake valleys, but mostly driven from the more populated areas when much of the land was taken up for agriculture. Considerable numbers of migrants also appear in the state.

RECORDS: Most of the reports of the early naturalists were from Salt Lake and Utah valleys. Stansbury (Baird 1852:314) found them common in Salt Lake Valley in 1849 and 1850. Other published reports include those of Baird (1858:61) and Remy (1860 [2]:449), Salt Lake Valley; Allen (1872b: 170), Ogden, Weber County; Merriam (1873:696, 710), Salt Lake and Ogden; Henshaw (1874:9), Ogden; Ridgway (1877:368, 574), Salt Lake Valley. Oates (1902:338) reported a set of Burrowing Owl eggs from Utah in the British Museum (Natural History). This set may have been collected by Henshaw. Numerous other collections and observations of this owl have been made up to the present time. Examples are published reports of Behle (1958:19–20), Kelton, Box Elder County, 10 September 1932; Twomey (1942:399–400), 20 miles east of Vernal, Uintah County, 6 May 1937; Hardy and Higgins (1940:100), Beaverdam slope, Washington County, 16 June 1939; Behle (1955:21), 5 miles north of Ibapah, Tooele County, 22 May 1942.

Strix occidentalis lucida (Nelson)
Spotted Owl

STATUS: The Spotted Owl is a casual visitor to Utah, especially in the pinyon-juniper woodlands of southern and eastern Utah.

RECORDS: Woodbury captured an immature bird in Zion Canyon National Park in June 1928. It was photographed and released. Russell (Woodbury 1939:158) collected an immature male at the base of Navajo Mountain, San Juan County, 3 August 1936. A few sight records have been published: Behle (1960a:29) reported a bird seen in Escalante Canyon, Garfield County, August 1957, and two in Glen Canyon, Kane County, 17 July 1958. M. L. Killpack (field notes) watched one for some time at East Tavaputs Plateau, Uintah County, 6 September 1958. This occurrence was reported by Scott (1959:52) and by Hayward (1967:34). Wauer and Carter (1965: 55) reported two observations in Zion Canyon, Washington County, 9 November 1963 and 29 August 1964.

Strix nebulosa nebulosa (Forster)
Great Gray Owl

STATUS: A species of rare and accidental occurrence in Utah.

RECORDS: Oring (Scott 1960:329) reported shooting a Great Gray Owl at Logan, Cache County, 6 March 1960. According to Behle (letter 2 July 1974) this specimen is mounted and displayed in a sporting goods store in Logan, Cache County. One was observed by Derrell McCullough at Spirit Lake, Daggett County, 30 July 1962 (Behle and Perry 1975:24).

Asio otus tuftsi Godfrey
Long-eared Owl
Figs. 29, 30; pp. 85, 86

STATUS: A common resident throughout the state, breeding in pinyon-juniper forests and in woodlands along the valley streams. Old Magpie nests are frequently used as nesting and roosting sites.

RECORDS: Collections and observations of this owl were made by some of the first naturalists to visit the state. Baird (1876: 377) reported a specimen and a set of eggs taken by the Simpson expedition in Skull Valley, Tooele County, 4 May 1859. Other early collections were made by Allen (1872b: 170) near Ogden, Weber County, 8 October 1871; by Henshaw (1875:403–404) in Sevier and Millard counties in September and November 1872; and by Nelson (1875: 344) from the north slope of the Uinta Mountains in June and July 1872. Many collections and sight records have been made in recent years. Examples of published records are. Twomey (1942:400 401), near Jensen, Uintah County, 24 April and

Fig. 43. Hermit Thrush. Monte Cristo, Rich County, Utah, 15 June 1959. Photo by R. J. Erwin.

15 May 1935; Behle (1941b:182), 10 miles north of Monticello, San Juan County, 3 April 1938; Behle (1955:21), 2 miles east of Ibapah, Tooele County, 23 April 1950; Wauer and Carter (1965:55), Zion National Park, Washington County, mid-March 1965.

Asio flammeus flammeus (Pontoppidan)
Short-eared Owl
Fig. 32, p. 88

STATUS: This owl is a common resident, especially through the northern and central valleys where there are marshes and wet pasture lands. Less common in the Colorado River Basin.

RECORDS: There are a few records by early naturalists as follows: Simpson (Baird 1876:377) obtained a specimen in Wasatch County in 1859, and Henshaw collected one near Utah Lake, Utah County, in 1872. Many more recently taken specimens from Utah are in the several institutional museums within the state. Some collection and sight records are: Twomey (1942:401), Ashley Creek Marshes, Uintah County, 21 September 1937; Hardy and Higgins (1949:

100), St. George, Washington County, 5 November 1939; Behle (1958:20), east of Raft River, Box Elder County, 17 September 1941.

Aegolius acadicus acadicus (Gmelin)
Saw-whet Owl
Figs. 33, 34; pp. 89, 90

STATUS: The Saw-whet Owl is a sparse resident among aspens, pinyon-juniper, and streamside forests. It frequently winters in the valleys where it may find shelter in abandoned buildings.

RECORDS: Zion National Park, Washington County, 15 October 1933 (Presnell 1935b:202); Oquirrh Mountains, Tooele County, 30 April 1936 (Utah State University); Salt Lake City, 31 December 1934 (University of Utah); near Moab, Grand County, 15 November 1936 (Woodbury 1939:158); Beaverdam Mountains, Washington County, 17 December 1939 (specimen found dead on highway by Ross Hardy) (Hardy and Higgins 1940:100). Behle (1958:20) recorded one southwest of Standrod, Box Elder County, 8 September 1949. The following specimens are in the collection of Brigham Young University: Lehi, Utah County, 27 March 1937; two immature, Hobble Creek Canyon, Utah County, 3 August 1944; Vernal, Uintah County, 29 December 1957; Neola, Duchesne County, 4 February 1959. Wauer (1969:332) recorded the following: Zion National Park, 24 October 1964, and Springdale, Washington County, 24 December 1964.

FAMILY CAPRIMULGIDAE

Phalaenoptilus nuttallii nuttallii (Audubon) Poor-will

STATUS: The Poor-will is a fairly common summer resident throughout the state from April to October and still more common in migration. It may be found at elevations ranging from lowland deserts upward to 10,000 feet.

RECORDS: Most of the early naturalists noted the Poor-will within the state. Ridgway (1877:568), Uinta Mountains, 7 July 1869; Allen (1872b:169) near Ogden, Weber County, 7 October 1871; Henshaw (1874:8), mountains in the state in summer 1872; Merriam (1873:692, 709), Ogden, 8 and 12 June 1872; Fisher (1893:52), Escalante Desert, Iron County, 17 May 1891. Numerous collections of birds and eggs have been made in more recent years from localities throughout the state. The following examples indicate its statewide occurrence: Twomey (1942:401), two miles south of Jensen, Uintah County, 19 August 1935; Behle (1969a:29), south of Crescent Junction, Grand County, 24 June 1947; Behle (1955:21), two miles east of Ibapah, Tooele County, 4 June and 9 August 1950; Behle (1958:20), Clear Creek, Box Elder County, 29 July 1950 and 13 June 1951; Wauer and Carter (1965:56), common in Zion Canyon, Washington County, with records extending from 12 April to 18 October. Found at 10,000 feet at Cedar Breaks, Iron County, 26 August 1974 (Kingery 1975:95).

Chordeiles minor (Forster) Common Nighthawk

STATUS: The Common Nighthawk is a summer resident in lower valleys and mid-elevations throughout the state. Flocks frequently congregate around ponds, lakes, or reservoirs at dawn and dusk to feed on midges and other flying insects. Certain races appear only as migrants.

RECORDS: There are many records of nighthawks taken in Utah. The early records were reviewed by Hayward (1940: 93–96). The following are examples of collections that have been made more recently: Woodbury and Russell (1945:59), top of Navajo Mountain, San Juan County, 14 July 1936; Twomey (1942:401), Jensen, Uintah County, summer 1937; Behle (1943a: 40), junction of Virgin and Santa Clara rivers, Washington County, 9 September 1941; Behle and Selander (1952:28), mouth of Weber Canyon, Weber County, 29 May 1942; Behle (1948:71), Midway, Wasatch County, 9 June 1944; Behle (1955:21), three miles east of Ibapah, Tooele County, 4 June 1950; Wauer and Carter (1965:56), Zion National Park, Washington County, 2 September 1964.

SUBSPECIES: The breeding and migrant nighthawks of Utah are difficult to interpret subspecifically since there appears to be considerable overlapping of three races within its borders. *C. m. hesperis* seems to be dominant in the Great Basin and the mountains eastward. The breeding population of the Colorado River Basin consists of intergradient individuals having some characteristics of *C. m. howelli* in the north and *C. m. henryi* in the south (Selander 1954:57–82). A few examples of migrant *C. m. sennetti* (Twomey 1942:402; Hayward 1940:94) have been reported, but Selander (1954:78) considered these to be atypical of that race. Behle (1948a:71) obtained a specimen of *C. m. minor* at Midway, Wasatch County, 9 June 1944, and Behle and Selander (1952:28) recorded it from Ogden Canyon, Weber County, 29

May 1942. These specimens were undoubtedly migrants.

Chordeiles acutipennis texensis Lawrence
Lesser Nighthawk

STATUS: A fairly common summer resident mostly confined to the low valleys of the Virgin River and its tributaries in extreme southwestern Utah and rarely wandering into more northern counties.

RECORDS: Several specimens, all from Washington County and located in the University of Utah and Dixie College collections, were collected 14 August 1938, 6 and 7 June 1940, 15 and 17 May 1940. Merriam found this species breeding at St. George, Washington County, 31 May 1891 (Fisher 1893:53). Other published reports are: Hardy and Higgins (1940:100), St. George, 6 May 1940; Behle (1943a:41), Beaver Dam Wash, Washington County, 15 May 1940, and Santa Clara Creek, Washington County, 17 May 1940; Wauer and Carter (1965:56), Zion National Park, Washington County, 2 September 1964. Wauer (1969:332) considered this species to be a common summer resident throughout the Virgin River drainage below 2,500 feet from 24 April to 25 August. He collected one near Hurricane, Washington County, 2 June 1966. Behle et al. (1964:453) listed two specimens taken at Hanksville, Wayne County, 8 July 1961. Two northern reports are Kingery (1971:885), seen by Kashin at Vernon, Tooele County, June 1971, and Kingery (1972:97), seen by Richard Ryan at Bear River, Box Elder County, 23 September 1971.

FAMILY APODIDAE

Cypseloides niger borealis (Kennerly)
Black Swift

STATUS: The Black Swift is an uncommon summer resident in Utah where it is now known to breed in the Wasatch Mountains.

RECORDS: Knorr (1962:79) found this swift nesting at Upper Falls, Bridal Veil Falls, and near Aspen Grove on Mt. Timpanogos, Utah County, August 1959, 1960, 1961. Behle et al. (1964:453) reported a specimen found dead at Zion Canyon, Washington County, 2 August 1960. Kashin (1963a:61; 1964a:3) recorded sight records for Salt Lake City, 18 June 1963, and Red Creek near Fruitland, Duchesne County, 6 August 1963. Wauer and Carter (1965: 57) recorded Black Swifts from Zion National Park, Washington County, 2 August 1960, 11 May 1964, 25 August 1964.

Chaetura pelagica (Linneaus)
Chimney Swift

STATUS: Seemingly an accidental visitor to Utah, the Chimney Swift is of very rare and irregular occurrence in the state.

RECORDS: A specimen in the University of Utah collection was taken by Claude T. Barnes (1946:258–259) near Kaysville, Davis County, 7 May 1912. There is also a sight record (Scott 1959:391) for one reportedly seen at Utah Lake on 10 May 1959.

Chaetura vauxi vauxi (Townsend)
Vaux's Swift

STATUS: A casual visitor to the state, having been obtained or observed in both northern and southern Utah.

RECORDS: A dried mummy of this species is in the University of Utah collection. It was obtained at the bottom of a stovepipe in a cabin at Jordan Fur Farm, Davis County, 28 October 1939, and probably had been trapped in the stovepipe that spring or summer (Woodbury et al. 1949: 18). Wauer and Russell (1967:421) reported three individuals seen at Springdale Ponds, Washington County, 11 and 13 September 1965. Behle (1973b:243) reported a specimen taken at Terry Ranch, Beaver Dam Wash, in southwest Washington County, 19 May 1972. He also reported several additional sight records.

Fig. 44. Mountain Bluebird. Blacksmith Fork, Cache County, Utah, 18 July 1954. Photo by R. D. Porter and R. J. Erwin.

Aeronautes saxatalis (Woodhouse)
White-throated Swift

STATUS: This swift occurs commonly throughout the state wherever there are cliffs with crevices suitable for nesting or roosting. It lives at a wide range of elevations from desert canyonlands to the highest mountains. It may also range many miles away from its nesting site in search of food.

RECORDS: Early naturalists, including Henshaw (1874:8), Ridgway (1877:564), and Merriam (Fisher 1893:55), observed this species in the state but apparently took no specimens. Many collections and observation records have been made in recent years. Some examples are as follows: Kaiparowits Plateau, Kane County, 27 July 1937 (Woodbury and Russell 1945:61); five miles northwest of Leeds, Washington County, 11 May 1939 (Behle 1943a:41); summit of Mount Ibapah, Juab County, 3 July 1950 (Behle 1955:21); Clear Creek, Box Elder County, 18 June 1951 (Behle 1958: 20).

SUBSPECIES: Twomey (1942:403) listed the swifts of the Uinta Basin as belonging to the subspecies *A. s. sclateri* on the basis of their larger size. However, there has been some doubt that the Uinta Basin population belongs to this race. Other collectors have reported the subspecies *A. s. saxatalis* as being the common race in the state. (Hardy and Higgins 1940:100; Woodbury and Russell 1945:61; Behle 1943a:43; Behle et al. 1958:53). Behle (1973a:306) proposed that *A. s. scalteri* become a synonym of *A. s. saxatalis.*

FAMILY TROCHILIDAE

Archilochus alexandri (Bourcier and Mulsant)
Black-chinned Hummingbird

STATUS: This is a common and widespread summer resident in the state. It seems to be more common southward and in the lower valleys where it appears in April and may remain until early October or as long as there are ample flowers in bloom.

RECORDS: The earliest collections of specimens were made by Ridgway (1877:559) at Parley's Park, Summit County, June and July 1869. Henshaw (1875:374) took specimens in the Provo, Utah County, area 29 and 30 July 1872. Three specimens were collected by Merriam (1873:693) at Ogden,

Weber County, 20 June 1872. Other early collections were made by Merriam (Fisher 1893:56) in Washington County, 11–14 May 1891. In more recent years numerous collections and observations have been made within the state. Among these are the following: Stanford (1938:138), Logan, Cache County, 6 August 1931; Woodbury and Russell (1945:62), Navajo Mountain, San Juan County, 9 July 1936; Behle (1958: 20), Yost, Box Elder County, 5 August 1936; Twomey (1942:404), 10 miles west of Vernal, Uintah County, 28 May 1937. It is considered to be a common summer resident in Zion National Park, Washington County (Wauer and Carter 1965:57).

Calypte costae (Bourcier)
Costa's Hummingbird

STATUS: This species is seemingly confined to the low hot valleys of southwestern Utah and from thence southwestward. It is the most common species in its altitudinal range.

RECORDS: Costa's Hummingbird was first reported in Utah by Fisher (1893:57) when he stated that "Dr. Merriam found it common among the junipers of the eastern side of the Beaverdam Mountains, Utah May 11" (1891). Specimens have been taken at Santa Clara Creek, 15 April 1932 (University of Utah); St. George, 29 March 1936, 25 April 1940 (Dixie College, Hardy and Higgins 1940:100); Beaver Dam Wash, 8 May 1941 (University of Utah, Behle 1943a: 41); Springdale, 11 May 1940 (Utah State University, Stanford 1944:151). All of the above localities are in Washington County. Wauer and Carter (1965:57) considered this hummingbird to be less common than formerly. They recorded the following sightings: Zion National Park, Washington County, 10 May 1962, 11 April 1963, and 14 May 1964; Springdale, 11 April 1963. A northward extension of the range of this species is given by Porter and Bushman (1956:152) and Behle et al. (1958:53) for eight miles west of Boulder, Garfield County, 16 May 1953. Kingery (1975:722) reported one wintering in Salt Lake City, Salt Lake County, from October 1974 to 16 March 1975. It was at a feeder where a light kept water from freezing and vitamins and proteins fortified the food at the feeder.

Selasphorus platycercus platycercus
(Swainson)
Broad-tailed Hummingbird

STATUS: The Broad-tailed Hummingbird is the most common species in Utah and it occurs in every part of the state. It appears in the lower valleys in April and later nests, usually near streams, at higher elevations. A few individuals remain in the valleys to nest and many appear again in the summer and early fall.

RECORDS: Ridgway (1877:560–563) found this hummingbird abundant in Utah in 1869. He collected 13 specimens around Salt Lake City during his stay. Other early naturalists (Allen 1872b:169; Henshaw 1874:8; Nelson 1875:347) found it common within the state, and many collections of both birds and nests have been made more recently. The following are examples of numerous published accounts: Twomey (1942:405), Ashley Creek Marshes, Uintah County, 20 May 1937; Stanford (1938:138), Logan Canyon, Cache County, 21 May 1937; Behle (1958:20), Clear Creek, Box Elder County, 17 and 19 May 1948; Behle (1955:21), Queen of Sheba Mine, Deep Creek Mountains, Juab County, 2 July 1950. It is considered a common summer resident in Zion National Park, Washington County, by Wauer and Carter (1965: 57).

Selasphorus rufus (Gmelin)
Rufous Hummingbird

STATUS: This hummingbird is a transient species within the state of Utah. All records available to us indicate that it occurs in the state only in the summer and early fall. Nesting in the state was reported by Bee and Hutchings (1942:73), who found

a nest supposedly of this species at Lehi, Utah County, 20 June. The bird was collected and mounted by Mr. Hutchings, but the specimen has been lost and verification of this unusual record cannot be made. Based on the following collection record, Behle et al. (1964:453) also suggested the possibility of this species nesting in the state: 10 July 1961, Wasatch Plateau, north end of Fairview Reservoir, Sanpete County. This specimen had testes 2 mm long but also had a thin layer of fat suggesting it might have been a migrant. Worthen (1968:237) collected four males at the Pioneer Ranger Station, one mile north of Mount Catherine, Pavant Mountains, Millard County, 23 June 1966. These had testes 1 mm in size and may have been resident birds.

RECORDS: Early naturalists in the state did not report this species, although they found it in the neighboring states of Arizona, Colorado (Henshaw 1875:375–377), and Nevada (Ridgway 1877:559–560). Many collections and observations have been made by local ornithologists, most of them for July, August, and early September. Published records include the following: three miles northwest of Strawberry Reservoir, Wasatch County, 15 July 1934 (Behle and Ghiselin 1958:6); Navajo Mountain, San Juan County, 11 July 1936 (Woodbury and Russell 1945:63); Park Valley, Box Elder County, 12 August 1937 (Stanford 1938:138); Kanab Canyon, Kane County, 24 September 1946 (Behle et al. 1958:54).

Stellula calliope (Gould)
Calliope Hummingbird

STATUS: The Calliope Hummingbird is an uncommon summer resident in mountainous parts of the state. It is often confused with the Broad-tailed Hummingbird which occurs in the same habitats and which is much more abundant but larger. The two species have similar habits. Careful observations may reveal that it is more common than has been supposed.

Fig. 45. Blue-gray Gnatcatcher. Cedar Mountains, Tooele County, Utah, 18 June 1953. Photo by R. D. Porter and R. J. Erwin.

RECORDS: Ridgway (1875:33; 1877:372, 375) stated that it was a breeding species at Parley's Park, Summit County, in the summer of 1869. He apparently preserved no specimens. Miller (1934:160) observed one building a nest in the Escalante Mountains, Garfield County, 3 July 1931. Specimens have since been taken at Paradise, Cache County, 12 June 1932; Mantua, Box Elder County, 25 May 1933; several localities in Logan Canyon, Cache County, June and July 1941 (Utah State University); St. George and Beaver Dam Wash, Washington County, 21 June 1933 and 5 April 1941. The Brigham Young University collection contains specimens from Provo Canyon, Utah County, 19 August 1951, and from Deep Lakes, Bear Lake County, Idaho, a few miles from the Utah border. Wauer and Carter (1965:58) reported this species from the high country in Zion National Park, Washington County, 3 May 1963.

Eugenes fulgens (Swainson)
Rivoli's Hummingbird

STATUS: An uncommon species recently reported as a summer visitor in southern Utah.

RECORDS: Kingery (1971:885) reported that this species was seen repeatedly at a feeder at Springdale, Washington County, 7 July to 10 August 1971. The bird was photographed and the picture appeared in American Birds 26:98, 1972. The species has also been reported from three miles northwest of Parowan, Iron County, 24 August 1962 (Behle 1976b:42) and from Cedar City, Iron County, 24 August 1971 (Kingery 1972:97). In 1972 it was observed at Springdale from 23 May until the end of July (Kingery 1972:885). George Edmonds saw one at Salt Lake City during the last week of June and first week of July 1972 and near Brighton on 27 June 1974. Both localities are in Salt Lake County (Behle and Perry 1975:25).

FAMILY ALCEDINIDAE

Megaceryle alcyon caurina (Grinnell)
Belted Kingfisher

STATUS: The Belted Kingfisher is a resident throughout the state of Utah in the vicinity of streams and ponds. It is much less common now than formerly because of disturbance of nesting sites and persecution due to its fish-eating habits. Most common in summer but a few remain through the winter.

RECORDS: Ridgway collected specimens at Parley's Park, Summit County, 26 July and 7 August 1869 (1877:545). Allen (1872b: 169) found it common around Ogden, Weber County, and took a specimen on 7 September 1871. Henshaw found it common along the fishing streams of the state and collected a specimen at Provo, Utah County, 26 July 1872 (1875:366). Collections in the institutions of the state and elsewhere contain many specimens from various sections of Utah taken more recently.

FAMILY PICIDAE

Colaptes auratus (Linnaeus)
Common Flicker

STATUS: A common resident throughout the state where both the yellow-shafted race (rarely) and the red-shafted race (commonly) occur. It ranges from the lowland streamside woodlands and parks to the montane forests. Within the last 10 or 15 years its numbers seem to have been considerably reduced.

RECORDS: All of the early naturalist visitors to the state found the flicker to be a common bird wherever they went in the 1860s and 1870s. All of their references appear to be of the red-shafted form. Yellow-shafted Flickers, or specimens showing some features of the yellow-shafted race, have been reported more recently. Porter (1954:362) recorded a specimen from Cedar Mountains, Tooele County, 14 October 1945, and a mounted bird from Syracuse, Davis County, December 1946. Hayward (1967:36) recorded a specimen from Roosevelt, Duchesne County, 7 January 1959, and noted several specimens from that area showing signs of hybridization with the red-shafted race. Behle and Selander (1952:

28) reported specimens of hybrids from Salt Lake City, 5 April 1950. Many records of the more common Red-shafted Flicker have been published.

SUBSPECIES: A species formerly known as *Colaptes cafer* is now considered to be conspecific with *Colaptes auratus* (American Ornithologists' Union 1973:415).

The Red-shafted Flicker now becomes *C. auratus cafer* and the Yellow-shafted Flicker becomes *C. auratus auratus*. There is a sight record (Snider 1964:377) of the subspecies *C. a. chrysoides*, known as the Gilded Flicker, for Beaver Dam Wash, Washington County, 13 February and 26 March 1964.

Dryocopus pileatus picinus (Bangs)
Pileated Woodpecker

STATUS: The Pileated Woodpecker is a sparse resident in isolated sections of the state.

RECORDS: A specimen in the American Museum of Natural History was taken by C. P. Rowley at Bluff, San Juan County, 21 May 1892 (Woodbury and Russell 1945:66). Behle and Ghiselin (1958:6) recorded seeing three birds about 30 miles north of Roosevelt, Duchesne County, 10 August 1943. Behle et al. (1958:55) reported a bird near Wildcat Ranger Station, Aquarius Plateau, Garfield County, 16 August 1952, and another one 10 days later in the same general area. Hayward (1967:37) saw one near Blanding, San Juan County, 6 September 1956.

Melanerpes erythrocephalus caurinus Brodkorb
Red-headed Woodpecker

STATUS: The Red-headed Woodpecker is an uncommon resident, especially in the northern part of the state and in the Uinta Basin. Recent observations indicate that it is likely to be found nesting in the riparian woodlands of the Uinta Basin.

RECORDS: Baird (1876:377) reported a

specimen taken in Utah by McCarthy of the Simpson expedition in 1859. Ridgway (1877:554–555) observed one near Parley's Park, Summit County, in June 1869. Twomey (1942:407) found an adult male dead near Ouray, Uintah County, 28 July 1937. Williams (1942:578) collected an adult male at Bear River Migratory Bird Refuge, Box Elder County, 26 August 1941. Killpack and Hayward (1958:23) have published sight and collection records for the Uinta Basin, 27 July 1937 and 29 May 1955. Murie (Scott 1969:504) saw this species near Cedar City, Iron County, 17 February 1968.

Sphyrapicus varius nuchalis Baird
Yellow-bellied Sapsucker

STATUS: A common breeding species in the mountains of the state especially in aspen woodlands and wooded areas bordering streams. It sometimes nests along valley streams where cottonwoods and other deciduous trees occur. In winter this species tends to migrate out of the higher elevations to the southern part of its range.

RECORDS: Early naturalists observed and collected this species in Utah. Ridgway (1877:550) collected nine specimens at Parley's Park, Summit County, July 1869, and Hayden and Smith (Stevenson 1872: 463) took several specimens on the north slope of the Uinta Mountains in 1870. Henshaw (1875:393) saw it in the Wasatch Mountains and collected specimens in Washington County in October 1872. Many specimens have been observed and taken in more recent times.

Sphyrapicus thyroideus nataliae
(Malherbe)
Williamson's Sapsucker

STATUS: Williamson's Sapsucker is an uncommon summer resident in the mountains of the state. It feeds and nests primarily in conifer forests from timberline downward.

RECORDS: A few of these birds were ob-

served and collected by early naturalists. Ridgway (1877:552) collected it at Parley's Park, Summit County, in August 1869. Nelson (1875:344) found it on the north slope of the Uinta Mountains in July 1872, and Bailey (field notes) recorded a breeding record for the Bear Lake Mountains (now known as the Bear River Range, Cache County) in July 1893. Henshaw (1875:394) discovered that the unlike males and females of this bird are one and the same species. Numerous specimens from all of the mountainous counties of the state have been collected in recent years. Among them are: Stanford (1938:139), Dolomite, Tooele County, 11 September 1935, and Logan Canyon, Cache County, 10 June 1937; Behle (1960a:32), Kigalia Ranger Station, Elk Ridge, San Juan County, 28 August 1956; Wauer and Carter (1965:59), Zion National Park, Washington County, 8 December 1964.

Melanerpes lewis (Gray)
Lewis' Woodpecker

STATUS: This woodpecker is of somewhat erratic and uncommon occurrence in Utah. It sometimes appears in loose flocks, especially in late summer and fall and at such times may be rather common in certain localities. This species is also known to nest in limited areas within the state.

RECORDS: Henshaw (1875:397) considered this species to occur commonly in Utah. Specimens from almost all sections of the state have been taken, a few of which are: Tanner and Hayward (1934:227), La Sal, San Juan County, June 1927; Behle (1958: 21), Dove Creek, Box Elder County, 10 September 1932; Stanford (1938:139), Wellsville, Cache County, 22 July 1937; and Behle (1943a:42), near Leeds, Washington County, 2 May 1939. A specimen in the Brigham Young University collection was taken at Provo, Utah County, 2 December 1939. Hayward (1967:37) reported this species to be the most common woodpecker in cottonwood groves along Green River, near Ouray, Uintah County, 17 May 1958. At that time several pairs were nesting.

Picoides villosus (Linnaeus)
Hairy Woodpecker

STATUS: The Hairy Woodpecker is a permanent resident of the state in the mountains and along the wooded streamsides at lower elevations. It is known to nest in both mountain and valley woodlands but more commonly in the former.

RECORDS: The first known collection of this species in Utah was by McCarthy in 1859 (Baird 1876:377). Ridgway (1877:546) reported specimens taken at Parley's Park, Summit County, in July and August 1869. Henshaw (1875:387) collected a specimen in Grass Valley in what is now Sevier and Piute counties on 10 September 1872. Many other records and specimens are extant in various collections.

SUBSPECIES: Two subspecies have been recognized in the Utah population. A smaller race inhabiting the southern part of the state has been known as *P. v. leucothorectus*. However, Phillips et al. (1964: 74) and Rich (1967:1–130) were unable to separate this race from *P. v. orius*. Both of these races were named in the same publication (Oberholser 1911:595–622), and both Phillips and Rich elected to use the name *orius*. *P. v. orius* is especially well represented by specimens from Wayne, Garfield, Kane, and Washington counties. The larger race (*P. v. monticola*) occurs in the counties northward. Numerous examples of the intergradation between the two have been noted.

Picoides pubsecens leucurus
(Hartlaub)
Downy Woodpecker

STATUS: A rather common, widely distri-

Fig. 46. Blue-gray Gnatcatcher. Cedar Mountains, Tooele County, Utah, 18 June 1953. Photo by R. D. Porter and R. J. Erwin.

buted resident of the state breeding more commonly in aspen forests of the mountains but sometimes in streamside woods in the lower valleys. In winter the species tends to spread to lower elevations and is often seen feeding on ornamental trees around the settlements.

RECORDS: Early naturalists recorded the Downy Woodpecker from several sections of the state. Ridgway (1877:546) observed it at Parley's Park, 25 miles east of Salt Lake City, Summit County, July and August 1869. Allen (1872b:169) found it near Ogden, Weber County, in the fall of 1871, and Henshaw (1875:388) recorded it from the vicinity of Provo, Utah County. There are many records of nesting and specimens collected in more recent years.

Picoides scalaris cactophilus
(Oberholser)
Ladder-backed Woodpecker

STATUS: In Utah this woodpecker is confined to the low and hot desert areas in Washington County where it is especially common in the Joshua trees of the southern slope of the Beaver Dam Range. It also occurs in woodlands in the Beaver Dam Wash area and along the Virgin River as far as Zion National Park.

RECORDS: Bailey (field notes) found it common along Santa Clara Creek, Washington County, 17 January 1889. A few years later (14 May 1891) Merriam reported this species in the same locality (Fisher 1891:47). Behle (1943a:43) listed several collection records from Beaver Dam Wash for April and May 1932 and 1941. Brigham Young University collection contains seven specimens from St. George and vicinity, April, September, November, and December 1928 to 1934. Wauer and Carter (1965: 59) reported seeing one in Zion National Park, Washington County, 18 September 1964.

Picoides tridactylus dorsalis Baird
Northern Three-toed Woodpecker

STATUS: This species is a resident of conifer forests at higher elevations usually above 8,000 feet. It is rather common in the Uinta Mountains but more rare in the Wasatch and the higher plateaus and isolated mountains elsewhere in the area.

RECORDS: The early ornithologists seem to have missed this species, possibly because they did relatively little work at high elevations. There is one old reference (Merrill 1888:255) to specimens from Utah but no detailed information. The Brigham Young University collection contains 14 specimens mostly from Trial Lake, Uinta Mountains, Summit County. One specimen is from La Sal Mountains, Grand County, 21 July 1934, and another from Navajo Lake, Kane County, 24 August 1934. Several selected references indicate it is found occasionally in various other localities within the state: Behle (1943a:44), east of Pine Valley, Washington County, 17 June 1938; Stanford (1944:151), upper Dry Canyon, Logan, Cache County, 6 June 1940; Behle (1960a:32), Abajo Mountains, San Juan County, 24 and 25 August 1956; Worthen (1968:255–256), Big Flat Guard Station, Tusher Mountains, Beaver County, 24 July 1966.

FAMILY TYRANNIDAE

Tyrannus tyrannus (Linnaeus)
Eastern Kingbird

STATUS: A fairly common breeding species in summer in streamside woodlands in lower valleys of northern Utah. This species is less abundant than formerly and has been persecuted considerably owing to its conspicuous nesting habits. At present it seems to be most common in Cache Valley, Bear Lake Valley, and in the Uinta Basin.

RECORDS: This species was considered to be common by the early-day ornithologists, and many specimens were taken by them near Ogden, Salt Lake City, and Provo. Ridgway (1877:533) found it near Salt Lake City, Salt Lake County, in 1869. Allen (1872b:169) collected it at Ogden,

Weber County, in September 1871, and Nelson (1875:347) obtained a specimen in the summer of 1872 near Salt Lake City. Henshaw (1875:341–342) reported it as being numerous around Provo, Utah County, in late July 1872. Of the many specimens collected in recent years nearly all are from the northern and central counties of the state. Specimens taken three miles south of Kanab, Kane County, 18 June 1947 (Behle et al. 1958:56) and Zion National Park, Washington County, 13 May 1964 (Wauer and Carter 1965:59), represent the southernmost record known to us.

Tyrannus verticalis Say
Western Kingbird

STATUS: The Western Kingbird breeds in summer throughout most of the state, being most abundant in southern Utah and gradually diminishing in numbers northward. It nests in deciduous woodlands along the lower valley streams or on trees and utility poles in rural areas. This species appears to be better able to maintain its numbers in this western habitat than does the Eastern Kingbird.

RECORDS: Many records are available from the writing of early naturalists in the state, mainly from Ogden, Salt Lake, and Utah valleys. These include the reports of Allen (1872b:169), Merriam (1873:690), Henshaw (1875:343), and Ridgway (1877:532). Numerous more recent records have been published; among them are: Webster (1947: 40), three miles north of Levan, Juab County, 13 December 1945; Behle et al. (1958: 56), two miles south of Escalante, Garfield County; and Behle (1958:21), Grouse Creek, Box Elder County, 17 June 1956.

Tyrannus vociferans Swainson
Cassin's Kingbird

STATUS: A common summer resident of southern Utah and sparingly northward from late April until August. It lives in deciduous trees along streamsides, often in company with the Western Kingbird, but it is also often found in pinyon-juniper forests.

RECORDS: Mention of this species by early naturalists is lacking, presumably because they did not visit its habitat to any extent. Specimens in the Brigham Young University collection are all from San Juan, Wayne, Kane, and Grand counties. Kashin (1964:50) reported a sight record for Lofgreen, Tooele County, 20 June 1964.

Muscivora forficata (Gmelin)
Scissor-tailed Flycatcher

STATUS: This species is of accidental occurrence in Utah, and the few records available are sight records.

RECORDS: One was observed in sagebrush near Snyderville in Parley's Park, Summit County, 11 June 1948, by Guy Emerson, Charles Lockerbie, and Kenneth Tanner (Woodbury et al. 1949:20). Van den Akker (1949:25) reported this record as being at Salt Lake City. One was seen and photographed by Paul A. Pemberton at Three Lakes, near Kanab, Kane County, 11 July 1963 (Behle and Perry 1975:27). Worthen (1968:258) reported a sight record by Willard E. Ritter, Federal Game Management agent, 1.5 miles northwest of Lynndyl, Millard County, 4 September 1965.

Myiarchus tyrannulus magister Ridgway
Wied's Crested Flycatcher

STATUS: This is an uncommon summer resident of the southern part of Utah.

RECORDS: The only Utah records known to us are those published by Wauer (1968: 88). One was collected three miles above Lytle Ranch, Beaver Dam Wash, Washington County, 18 May 1966. Other observations were made by Wauer at Beaver Dam, Arizona, near the Utah border, and indicated that this species breeds in the Beaver Dam Wash area in Utah. Behle and Perry (1975:27) reported a specimen in the University of Utah collection taken at Beaver Dam Wash on 24 May 1968.

Fig. 47. Black-capped Chickadee. Rochester, Monroe County, New York, 16 October 1968. Photo by R. J. Erwin.

Myiarchus cinerascens cinerascens
(Lawrence)
Ash-throated Flycatcher

STATUS: The Ash-throated Flycatcher is a common summer resident of southern Utah and other less humid parts of the state where habitat is favorable. It is less common in northern Utah. It inhabits low trees and shrubs and is especially characteristic of pinyon-juniper woodlands.

RECORDS: Ridgway (1875:33) found it breeding at Parley's Park, 25 miles east of Salt Lake City, Summit County, in June, July, and August 1869. Henshaw (1875:346) mentioned its northward extension into Utah. Fisher (1893:61) reported that Mer-riam found the species in Washington County, 11–15 May 1891. A specimen in the American Museum of Natural History was collected by Rowley at Riverview, San Juan County, 24 April 1892. Cottam collected a female, ready to deposit an egg, south of Vernal, Uintah County, in June several years ago. Many collections and observations of both birds and nests have been made more recently from almost every county in the state. Two northern records for this species are Behle (1955:22), Deep Creek Mountains, Tooele County, 29 June 1946, and Behle (1958:22), six miles south of Grouse Creek, Box Elder County, 17 June 1956.

Sayornis phoebe (Latham)
Eastern Phoebe

STATUS: This species appears to be of somewhat irregular and casual occurrence in Utah.

RECORDS: Two specimens were collected at Springdale, Washington County, 27 March and 17 December 1965 (Wauer 1966c:519). Wauer also reported earlier sight records for Zion's Canyon and Beaver Dam Wash, Washington County, 21 October 1963 and 25 March 1965. Snider (1966: 538) reported that Wauer saw one at Beaver Dam Wash, 19 May 1966. Kashin (Scott 1970:75) reported seeing an Eastern Phoebe near the Jordan River, Salt Lake County, 11 September 1969.

Sayornis nigricans semiatra (Vigors)
Black Phoebe

STATUS: A sparse resident of the low valleys of the Virgin River drainage in Washington County and extending eastward in southern Utah to Kane and San Juan counties. It rarely occurs in northern Utah. Wauer and Carter (1965:60) considered it to be increasing in numbers in the Zion Park area in recent years.

RECORDS: The University of Utah collection contains a specimen taken by Woodbury in Washington County, 19 April 1932. Brigham Young University collection contains a specimen taken at Gunlock, Washington County, 8 April 1933, and another from St. George, Washington County, 27 April 1936. Specimens in the Dixie College collection have been taken along Santa Clara Creek, Washington County, and in the vicinity of St. George, 26 January, 25 March, and 28 April 1940 (Hardy and Higgins 1940:101). Behle et al. (1964:454) reported several records for the St. George area and from four miles north of Kanab, Kane County, 26 and 27 June 1961. They also mentioned a specimen from Newcastle, Iron County, 26 May 1962. Hayward (field notes) observed one near Bluff, San Juan

County, 13 September 1966. Behle (1966: 396) reported one entering a hole in an eave of a roof in Salt Lake City, Salt Lake County, 4 June 1963. On 16 June 1965 a badly decomposed body of a bird of this species was found in Salt Lake City.

Sayornis saya (Bonaparte)
Say's Phoebe

STATUS: Common spring, summer, and fall resident of low, open valleys and foothills or along valley streams where it lives in low brush or scattered trees. It frequently nests in abandoned buildings or in low ledges of rock. A few individuals winter in the warmer sections of the state. However, one has been reported in northern Utah near Salt Lake City, Salt Lake County, 2 February 1966 (Worthen 1972b:220).

RECORDS: Ridgway (1873:172) found this bird to be a rather common breeder in Salt Lake Valley in 1869. The U.S. National Museum of Natural History has specimens from Bear River, Box Elder County, 25 June 1872 (Merriam 1873:690), and Kanab, Kane County, 30 June 1873. Enough additional specimens and observations are available to establish the universal occurrence of this species in the state wherever there are suitable habitats. (Stanford 1938:139; Twomey 1942:411; Woodbury and Russell 1945:73–74; Behle 1955:22).

SUBSPECIES: All of the collected specimens reported above are of the race *saya*. Cottam obtained a specimen of the subspecies *yukonensis* at Johnson Creek Ranch, southwest of Yost, Box Elder County, 18 September 1941 (Behle 1958:22), and Worthen (1972b:220) recorded a specimen of this race at Saltair, 17 miles west of Salt Lake City, Salt Lake County, 2 February 1966.

Empidonax traillii (Audubon)
Willow Flycatcher
Fig. 36, p. 92

STATUS: A common breeding resident

from May to August, the Willow Flycatcher usually lives in willows and other low shrubs near water. It is for the most part confined to lower elevations but is known to breed at elevations of 7,000 feet.

RECORDS: McCarthy of Simpson's expedition collected this flycatcher at Goshiute Pass, Tooele County, in 1859 (Baird 1876: 378). Ridgway (1873:173) found it common in streamside thickets near Salt Lake City, Salt Lake County, and Merriam (1873: 691) took several specimens and three nests near Ogden, Weber County, in June 1872. These specimens are in the U.S. National Museum of Natural History. Henshaw (1875:356) found it to be common in the willows along Provo River, Utah County, in late July and early August 1872. Numerous records are available for more recent years.

SUBSPECIES: Specimens of the Willow Flycatcher are rather variable in coloration, and some problems have arisen regarding subspeciation in the group. Oberholser (1918a:85–98) named the western race, *E. t. brewsteri*, and Behle (1948a:71–72) at first considered this to be the only subspecies found in the Utah population. Later Behle and Ghiselin (1958:7–8) found the race in northeastern Utah to be *E. t. adastus*, as did Twomey (1942:412). Snyder (1953:7) considered the northeastern Utah birds to be *extimus*. However, neither *adastus* nor *extimus* was accepted in the AOU Check-list (1957:343–344). In the thirty-second supplement to the AOU Check-list (American Ornithologists' Union 1973:415–416) the flycatchers formerly grouped in the species *Empidonax traillii* are divided into two species based on a difference in vocalization. The species and subspecies found in the West are listed as *E. traillii brewsteri* under the common name of Willow Flycatcher. *Empidonax alnoram* breeds in the boreal forest areas of eastern North America, Canada, and Alaska. It could presumably appear in Utah during migration, but its occurrence in the state has not, to our knowledge, been established.

Empidonax hammondii (Xantus)
Hammond's Flycatcher

STATUS: Hammond's Flycatcher is a summer resident in the conifer and aspen forests of mountainous sections of the state, especially in the Wasatch, Uinta, and Raft River mountains. It also appears in the lower valleys in spring and fall.

RECORDS: Of the early naturalists Allen and Henshaw were the only ones to record this species in Utah. Allen (1872b:179) reported it from Ogden, Weber County, in September 1871, and Henshaw (1875:363) found it at Beaver, Beaver County, and at Cedar City, Iron County, in September and October 1872. Numerous specimens have been collected in more recent years. A few of these are from the following localities: Henry Mountains, Wayne County, September 1929 (Stanford 1931:6); 17 miles east of Kamas, Summit County, 31 May 1953 (Behle and Ghiselin 1958:8); south end of Deep Creek Mountains, Juab County, 30–31 May 1953 (Behle 1955:22); Zion National Park, Washington County, 15 May 1963 (Wauer and Carter 1965:61).

SUBSPECIES: Johnson (1966:179–200), after making measurements and other comparisons of some 545 specimens of this flycatcher, found no morphological basis for division into subspecies.

Empidonax oberholseri Phillips
Dusky Flycatcher

STATUS: This species formerly known under the name *E. wrightii* (AOU Check-list 1957:345) is a rather common flycatcher throughout the state during the summer. It nests at mid-elevations where there is considerable brush or tall shrubs. In migration it is often encountered in woodlands along the valley streams.

RECORDS: Early collectors in the state obtained a few specimens often recorded as *E. obscurus* or *E. obsecra*. Two specimens in the American Museum were taken in Utah by Drexler, 28 May 1858 and 17 May 1859. Ridgway (1877:543) reported it as being common at Parley's Park, near Salt Lake City, Summit County, during June and August 1869. Henshaw (1875: 361) found it at Provo, Utah County, 9 August 1872. Recently specimens have been taken in nearly all counties of the state from April through September, including those reported by Twomey (1942: 413), Behle (1955:22), Behle et al. (1958: 98), and Wauer and Carter (1965:61).

Empidonax wrightii Baird
Gray Flycatcher

STATUS: The Gray Flycatcher, formerly called *E. griseus* (AOU Check-list 1957: 346), is widespread as a summer resident throughout the state and is perhaps the most common of the *Empidonax* flycatchers in the area. It inhabits pinyon-juniper woodlands or tall shrubby vegetation in more desert areas.

RECORDS: Because of the confusion in separating the several species of small flycatchers of this genus, references to this species in the early literature are uncertain. In recent years many specimens have been taken from most of the counties of the state. Some of these are: Twomey (1942:413), Behle (1955:22), Wauer and Carter (1965: 62), and Hayward (1967:39–40). Nineteen specimens in the Brigham Young University collection are from San Juan, Garfield, Grand, Uintah, Utah, Juab, Emery, and Kane counties. Dates range from early April to late August.

Fig. 48. White-crowned Sparrow. Monte Cristo, Rich County, Utah, 14 July 1973. Photo by R. J. Erwin.

Empidonax difficilis hellmayri Brodkorb
Western Flycatcher

STATUS: This is a sparse breeding species
in the mountains from 7,000 to 9,000 feet
elevation. As nesting sites it often uses
rocky ledges in shaded areas where water
is nearby. It is found from late May to
early October.

RECORDS: Ridgway (1877:544) collected
two specimens at Parley's Park, east of Salt
Lake City, Summit County, 5 August 1869.
Allen (1872b:169) found it at Ogden, Weber
County, in 1871, and Henshaw considered
it to be common in cool canyons throughout the state although he collected no spec-
imens. Many specimens have been taken
in more recent years, indicating its rela-
tively widespread distribution throughout
the state where habitat is suitable: Navajo
Mountain, San Juan County, 7 August 1936
(Woodbury and Russell 1945:78); 10 miles
west of Vernal, Uintah County, 28 May
1937 (Twomey 1942:414); south end of
Deep Creek Mountains, Juab County, 31
May 1953 (Behle 1955:23); Zion National
Park, Washington County, 25 June 1962
(Wauer and Carter 1965:62). Brigham
Young University collection contains speci-
mens as follows: Salt Creek Canyon, Mt.
Nebo, Juab County, 10 July 1931; Aspen
Grove, Mt. Timpanogos, Utah County, 9
June 1934; Jerico, Juab County, 6 August
1959 (migrant); La Sal Mountains, Grand
County, 13 July 1967. Hayward (1941:3)
gives an account of nesting near Aspen
Grove, Utah County, 26 June 1937.

SUBSPECIES: Behle (1948a:72) at first
recognized two races of this species in
Utah specimens that he was able to study,
although there appeared to be considerable
overlapping of the two. The populations
from southeastern and central Utah as far
north and west as the Wasatch Mountains
are closest to the race *E. d. hellmayri*,
while those of the west desert ranges are
closer to the West Coast *E. d. difficilis*.

Later Behle (1958:23) revised his opinion
as stated above on the basis of further
study and wrote that "Western Flycatchers
from all parts of Utah are referable to *hellmayri* even though those from the mountain
ranges of the west desert section of the
state show an approach to *difficilis*."

Contopus sordidulus Sclater
Western Wood Pewee

STATUS: This is a common spring and
fall migrant and summer breeder in lower
montane forests and along valley streams.

RECORDS: All of the early ornithologists
found this species either as a migrant or
breeding bird in their travels throughout
the state, Ridgway in 1869 (1877:538), Allen
in 1871 (1872b:169), Merriam in 1872 (1873:
691), and Henshaw in 1872 (1875:356).
Many collections and observations have
been made by more recent observers.

SUBSPECIES: According to an account of
the subspecies published by Burleigh (1960:
143–144), *C. s. veliei* is the breeding subspecies in Utah. Behle (1967:133–134) has
reported the subspecies *saturatus* from a
specimen taken in the Cedar Mountains,
Tooele County, 27 May 1953; the subspecies *siccicola* from 10 specimens obtained from all parts of the state except the
Uinta Basin; and the subspecies *amplus*
from 5 specimens collected in the following localities: near Yost, Box Elder County,
7 September 1931; North Willow Canyon,
22 August 1953, and east Hickman's Canyon, 28 August 1953, both in Stansbury
Mountains, Tooele County; Flat Canyon,
13 miles east of Fairview, Sanpete County,
23 August 1950; War God Spring, Navajo
Mountain, San Juan County, 13 August
1936. Mayr and Short (1970:60–61) considered some of the subspecies as proposed
by Burleigh (1960) "unwarranted" and
recognize only the race *veliei* in the western
North American population.

Contopus[12] *borealis* (Swainson)
Olive-sided Flycatcher

STATUS: A regular but not common summer breeder in mountain coniferous forests throughout the state. In spring and fall migration it occurs in wooded areas in lower valleys.

RECORDS: A specimen in the U.S. National Museum of Natural History was taken by Ridgway at Parley's Park, Summit County, 23 June 1869 (Ridgway 1877:536). This species was also observed in the state by Merriam (1873:691), Henshaw (1875:350), Nelson (1875:344), and other early ornithologists. It has since been collected or observed in most of the counties of the state. Brigham Young University collection contains seven specimens taken in Utah as follows: La Sal, San Juan County, 12 June 1927; Lost Lake and Trial Lake, Uinta Mountains, Summit County, 12 and 29 July 1930; Pole Canyon, Utah County, 25 May 1945; Paria, Kane County, 20 May 1961; Oak Creek Camp, Garfield County, 22 June 1963; Sheep Creek Watershed, Sevier County, 27 August 1968.

Pyrocephalus rubinus flammeus
van Rossem
Vermilion Flycatcher

STATUS: A sparse resident of the low deserts of southern Utah and seemingly confined to that part of the state.

RECORDS: Woodbury (1939:159) summarized the records of this bird from southwestern Utah that were known up to that time. He listed several records from the Virgin River Valley in the vicinity of St. George, Hurricane, and near Zion Park, all located in Washington County. He also included a sight record by Clifton Greenhalgh for Kanab, Kane County, 25 April 1935. Brigham Young University collection contains one specimen from St. George, 21

December 1925, and another from the same locality, 26 April 1936. Stanford (1944: 151) obtained a pair of birds east of St. George, 10 May 1940. Wauer (1966b:351) observed one in the St. George area Christmas bird count, 28 December 1965. Wauer (Snider 1966:591) found a nest near St. George, 2 June 1966.

FAMILY ALAUDIDAE

Eremophila alpestris (Linnaeus)
Horned Lark
Fig. 35, p. 91

STATUS: A common and sometimes abundant species through the deserts of the state and occasionally in the alpine. In winter large flocks, often consisting of several subspecies, appear along roadways or on exposed ridges where the ground is bare of snow.

RECORDS: All of the early naturalists reported the Horned Lark to be common in the state. It was reported by the Stansbury expedition (Baird 1852:318), Stevenson in the Uinta Mountains (1872:464), Allen (1872b:167), Merriam (1873:685), Nelson (1875:339), Henshaw (1875:310–311), McCarthy (Baird 1876:379), Ridgway (1877: 500), and Fisher (1893:66–67). Many hundreds of collections and observations have been made in recent years.

SUBSPECIES: A strong tendency of this species toward subspeciation as well as its migratory and wandering habits during the nonbreeding season has led to considerable confusion in the subspecific identification of the Utah population. Behle (1942a:205–316) has reviewed the Horned Larks of western North America in much detail after examination of many hundreds of specimens. From his studies it would appear that two races can be identified in the breeding population in Utah. The subspecies *E. a. utahensis* is the breeding form

---

[12]Mayr and Short (1970:60) agree with Phillips et al. (1964) that the genus name *Nuttalornis* formerly used for this species "does not comprise a monotypic genus."

Fig. 49. Brewer's Sparrow. Vernon, Tooele County, Utah, 2 June 1954. Photo by R. D. Porter and R. J. Erwin.

in the Great Basin section of the state westward of the Wasatch Mountains and central plateaus, while *E. a. leucolaema* breeds in the desert lands and high alpine meadows of eastern Utah. There seems to be some intergradation between *leucolaema* and *E. a. occidentalis* in southeastern Utah (Behle 1960b:17, 19–20). Migrant and wintering birds may consist not only of breeding subspecies but also of several other subspecies such as *E. a. arcticola*, *E. a. enthymia*, *E. a. hoyti*, and *E. a. merrilli* (Behle 1943b:153–156).

FAMILY HIRUNDINIDAE

Tachycineta thalassina lepida Mearns
Violet-green Swallow

STATUS: This species is a common summer resident throughout the state where it breeds most often at higher elevations. It frequently nests in holes in aspens often in close association with Tree Swallows. The two species sometimes compete for nesting holes. Violet-green Swallows may use holes in rocky ledges for nesting sites, especially at lower elevations. From mid-April through May and again in August and September these birds appear in large migratory flocks especially near lakes and reservoirs.

RECORDS: Ridgway (1877:444) reported it from the vicinity of Salt Lake City, Salt Lake County, in May 1869. He found it nesting in cliffs. Allen (1872b:167) found it near Ogden, Weber County, 11 September 1872, and Henshaw (1875:218) considered it to be an inhabitant of high mountains. Merriam (1873:677) found it rather common in Ogden Canyon, Weber County, in June 1872. Occurrence of this species in more recent years has been recorded from every county of the state. Wauer (1969:332) reported it nesting at an extremely low elevation (1,950 feet) in Beaver Dam Wash, Washington County, 18 May 1966.

Tachycineta bicolor (Vieillot)
Tree Swallow
Fig. 37, p. 94

STATUS: A regular breeding species throughout the state, especially in the mountains where it nests in holes in aspens or other trees. In spring and late summer Tree Swallows appear in large flocks often in company with other species of swallows. Spring migration occurs from mid-March through May, and fall migration takes place through August and September.

RECORDS: Specimens were collected by the early ornithologists. Ridgway (1877: 443) obtained specimens in the vicinity of Salt Lake City, Salt Lake County, in May and July 1869. Henshaw (1875:217) found it in Utah County in August 1872. Cary (field notes 9–12 July 1907) found it nesting in aspens in the La Sal Mountains, San Juan County. Many recent records of nesting have been reported in the timbered areas of the state.

Progne subis (Linnaeus)
Purple Martin

STATUS: A sparse and localized breeding species in the mountains throughout the state where it nests in holes in aspens or dead conifers. Judging from the reports of early naturalists in the area, the martin was far more common in the early years of settlement in the state than it is at the present time. It remains in Utah from May through August. In migration it is occasionally seen with flocks of swallows.

RECORDS: Ridgway (1877:439) found it abundant in the aspens around Parley's Park, Summit County, east of Salt Lake City, during the summer of 1869. Henshaw (1875:214) reported its occurrence throughout Utah in large colonies, both in towns and cities as at Salt Lake City, Salt Lake County, where it was breeding in bird boxes. In coniferous forests of the mountains it nested in abandoned woodpecker holes. We are not aware of any such large colonies in the state at the present time, although it is found consistently in mountainous areas especially where there are aspen forests and ponds or lakes over which the birds feed. More recent records of the species have been published by Behle and Selander (1952:28) and by Hayward (1958: 406). Utah specimens in Brigham Young University collection are as follows: Aspen Grove, Mt. Timpanogos, Utah County, 22 June 1931; Skyline Drive, Sanpete County,

23 July 1960; Sheep Creek Watershed, Sevier County, 15 August 1969.

Subspecies: (Behle 1968a:166) has recognized the Utah population of Purple Martin as a new subspecies, *P. s. arboricola*, characterized by being larger than other races and with females whiter on the forehead and underparts. The type locality is given as Payson Lakes, Mt. Nebo, Utah County, elevation 8,300 feet, 10 July 1950.

Stelgidopteryx ruficollis (Vieillot)
Rough-winged Swallow

Status: The Rough-winged Swallow is a common breeding species in the lower valleys throughout the state. It nests in colonies in earthen banks along streams. It is present in the area from about mid-April to late September. In spring and fall migration it appears in large flocks.

Records: Ridgway (1877:446) found it common in the river valleys in Salt Lake Valley where it nested in earthen banks. Allen (1872b:167) considered it to be moderately common around Ogden, Weber County, in 1871. Henshaw (1875:219–220) reported finding it exceedingly abundant along the banks of the Provo River, Utah County, 26 July 1872. Fisher (1893:112) reported that Merriam considered it the commonest swallow in the Santa Clara Valley, Washington County, in May 1891. Numerous more recent records indicate that it is still a common species throughout the state.

Subspecies: The breeding subspecies found in most of Utah is *S. r. serripennis* (Behle 1958:24; Hayward 1967:41). Wauer (1969:332) obtained a female of the race *psammochroa* at Beaver Dam Wash, Washington County, 14 April 1966. This bird was flying about an earth bank with holes in it which Wauer assumed were its nesting sites. This assumption was further substantiated when he examined the ovary and found it to be 11 × 3.5 mm. If this bird was breeding at Beaver Dam Wash, the breeding range of this race would be

extended northward from Flagstaff, Arizona, about 180 miles (Phillips et al. 1964: 97). Further work needs to be carried out in southwestern Utah as Wauer (1969:332) also collected the subspecies *serripennis* in the same general locality during the breeding season.

Riparia riparia riparia (Linnaeus)
Bank Swallow

Status: A common summer resident in lowlands where it nests in colonies in vertical earthen banks. In spring and late summer Bank Swallows appear in large migrating flocks. They are especially conspicuous in late August when at dusk they fly into trees or willow patches to roost for the night.

Records: Ridgway (1877:445) found it nesting in Weber River Valley in June 1869, and Henshaw (1875:220) found it nesting in colonies with Rough-winged Swallows in July 1872. Others of the early naturalists reported it for various parts of the state. There are numerous records in more recent years. Wauer (1969:332) considered it to be an occasional visitant in the Virgin River Basin from 25 March to 19 May, and 7 to 17 September.

Hirundo rustica erythrogaster Boddaert
Barn Swallow

Status: The Barn Swallow is a widespread breeding species throughout the state where it nests in cliffs or in buildings. The birds often nest singly or in small groups, depending on the availability of nesting sites. During spring migration in April and early May and again in late summer and early fall, flocking occurs often with other species of swallows.

Records: Most of the early ornithologists doing fieldwork in the state reported it in their writings. Ridgway (1877:441) found it around Salt Lake City, Salt Lake County, and recorded its nesting in July 1869. Henshaw (1875:216) took specimens

Fig. 50. Black-throated Sparrow. Camel Back Mountain, Tooele County, Utah, no date. Photo by R. D. Porter.

at Provo in July and at Fairfield (both in Utah County) in August 1872. Many observations of birds and nesting activities have been reported in recent years.

Petrochelidon pyrrhonota (Vieillot)
Cliff Swallow
Fig. 38, p. 97

STATUS: This is perhaps the most common and widespread of the species of swallows inhabiting the state during the summer months. It nests in large colonies by attaching its mud nests to overhanging cliffs, eves of buildings, and the undersides of bridges. It is most common at lower elevations. In spring and early fall it may appear in large migrating flocks, often in company with other species of swallows.

RECORDS: Escalante (Coues 1899:359; Auerbach 1943:61) was the first to record Cliff Swallows in what is now called Deep Creek, Duchesne County, 19 September 1776. Ridgway (1877:440) considered this to be the most abundant swallow in the Great Basin where he noted nesting on cliffs and in buildings. All of the early ornithologists referred to the great num-

bers of this species, and there are numerous records for recent years.

SUBSPECIES: Behle (1960b:19) stated that two races of this species occur in Utah. According to him, *P. p. hypopolia* is found in the western part of the state and *P. p. pyrrhonota* in the eastern portion. Worthen (1968:285–287) regarded the Washington County breeding population as *P. p. tachina* and considered the birds elsewhere in the state to be intergrades between *hypopolia* and *pyrrhonota*. Behle (1976a:70), on the basis of a large sample of specimens, indicated that three races exist in Utah: *P. p. tachina* in the extreme southwestern part of the state, *P. p. hypopolia* in western Utah, *P. p. pyrrhonota* in eastern Utah, with a widespread intermediate population between *hypopolia* and *pyrrhonota* extending across Utah.

FAMILY MOTACILLIDAE

Anthus spinoletta (Linnaeus)
Water Pipit

STATUS: A fairly common breeding species in the mountains and high plateaus of the state at elevations near or above timber line. Water Pipits winter in the lower valleys near water, sometimes in large flocks.

RECORDS: All of the early ornithologists encountered the pipit in the state but chiefly during periods of migration (Stevenson 1872:463; Allen 1872:166; Henshaw 1875:187). Relatively little work was done by these observers at high elevations where the species breeds. Many specimens of both breeding and wintering birds have been taken in more recent years.

SUBSPECIES: The breeding subspecies of the state is *A. s. alticola*, and this race is also commonly found among the wintering birds. *A. s. rubescens* has been reported as a migrant to southern Utah (Behle 1943a:60; Check-list of Birds of the World 1960 [9] : 160). Porter and Bushman (1956:153) recorded two specimens of this race, one collected at Orr's Ranch, Skull Valley, 1 May 1954, and the other at Government Creek, four miles north of Camel Back Mountain, 12 May 1954, both in Tooele County. Porter (1954:363) summarized several records of *A. s. pacificus* from St. George, Washington County, and from Tooele County, taken in April, September, and December. He also reported *A. s. geophilus* collected near Simpson Mountain, Tooele County, 18 October 1952. The latter race is not recognized in the American Ornithologists' Union Check-list of North American Birds (1957:457–458) or the Check-list of Birds of the World (1960 [9] :160–162). Presumably it is a difficult race to distinguish from *A. s. pacificus* (Phillips et al. 1964:138).

FAMILY LANIIDAE

Lanius ludovicianus[13] Linnaeus
Loggerhead Shrike
Fig. 39, p. 100

STATUS: The Loggerhead Shrike is a rather common breeding species in the lower valleys and on the foothills throughout the state. It is an inhabitant of desert shrub communities and pinyon-juniper woodlands. There is some evidence that there is a general drifting southward in winter to the lower and warmer valleys of the southern part of the state.

RECORDS: Specimens of this shrike were taken or observed by several of the early naturalists. Ridgway (1877:464) found it nesting at Salt Lake City, Salt Lake County, 24 and 27 May 1869, and on Antelope Island, Great Salt Lake, 4 and 7 June 1869. He also reported it nesting at Promontory Point, Box Elder County, June 1869, and Fremont Island, 16 August 1869. Allen (1872b:167, 176) found this species "quite common" in Ogden, Weber County, during the fall of 1871 (1 September to 8 October). Merriam (1873:677) found shrikes at Salt Lake City, 11 June 1872, and Nelson (1875: 346) found them common about infrequented fields in late July and early August 1872. Henshaw (1875:235) during the same year collected a specimen at Fillmore, Millard County, 15 November. In 1891 Merriam observed them in Washington County, southwestern Utah, at Beaver Dam Mountains 10 May; Santa Clara Valley, 11-15 May; and Mountain Meadows, 17 May (Fisher 1893:115). Bailey (field notes) found it wintering along the Virgin River, Washington County, in January 1889. In more recent times numerous collection and sight records have been published, indicating that the populations are well sustained at the present time.

SUBSPECIES: There has been considerable confusion regarding the subspecific status of the shrikes occurring in Utah. The race *L. l. nevadensis,* proposed by Miller (1930: 156) as the breeding form in the Great Basin and elsewhere in the West, is placed in synonymy under *L. l. gambeli* in Check-list of Birds of the World (1960[9] :353). It

---

[13]There is evidence that *L. ludovicianus* might eventually be considered conspecific with *L. excubitor* (Mayr and Short 1970:71).

now seems that the breeding subspecies throughout most of the state is *L. l. gambeli* with a possibility that *L. l. sonoriensis* may nest in extreme southwestern Utah (Behle 1943a:61).

Lanius excubitor invictus Grinnell
Northern Shrike

STATUS: The Northern Shrike is an uncommon but regular wintering species throughout Utah. In the northern part of the state it appears to largely replace the breeding *L. ludovicianus* that drifts southward in winter.

RECORDS: McCarthy, the taxidermist with Simpson's party, collected three specimens at Camp Floyd, Utah County, in 1859 (Baird 1876:378). Henshaw (1875:233) obtained one specimen and observed others late in the fall of 1872 in southern Utah. Utah specimens in the Brigham Young University collection are as follows: Provo, Utah County, 2 November 1928, 13 February 1958, 15 December 1962; Bridgeland, Duchesne County, 31 December 1955.

FAMILY BOMBYCILLIDAE

Bombycilla garrulus pallidiceps Reichenow
Bohemian Waxwing

STATUS: An irregular but consistent winter resident throughout the state. Large flocks of the species appear in winter especially around parks or homes where there is an abundance of berries on ornamental shrubs or dried fruits left on trees. They wander from place to place wherever food is available and ordinarily do not remain long in one locality.

RECORDS: We have no records of this species in Utah until after the turn of this century when Goodwin (1905:52) noted it in Provo, Utah County, from mid-December to the first week of April. He also stated that he had seen them in Provo each winter from 1898–1899 to 1905 except 1900–1901 when none was observed. Many

collections and observation records of this species are known. Some of these are: Stanford (1938:142), Logan, Cache County, 16 March 1932; Hardy and Higgins (1940: 105), St. George, Washington County, late December; Behle (1958:29), Park Valley, Box Elder County, 29 December 1951; Wauer and Carter (1965:72), Zion National Park, Washington County, 20 December 1965. Brigham Young University collection contains some 27 specimens from the state. These specimens are mostly from the central Utah valleys with dates ranging from early November through March.

Bombycilla cedrorum Vieillot
Cedar Waxwing

STATUS: The Cedar Waxwing is a resident of Utah throughout the year, although it appears most abundantly in winter. In winter it is often seen in large flocks, sometimes in company with Bohemian Waxwings. Like the Bohemian it feeds on dried berries and fruits that remain on bushes or trees during the winter. Judging from the scarcity of reports by early naturalists in the state, the Cedar Waxwing is likely more common now than formerly owing possibly to the greater supply of food on introduced shrubs and fruit trees. In summer it nests in small numbers in woodlands along streams, canals, or in parks (Croft 1932:91).

RECORDS: Most of the early reports of this species seem to have been based on the observation of Allen (1872b:167), who regarded it as rather common around Ogden, Weber County, in September 1871. Numerous reports in more recent years indicate its continued occurrence throughout the state during all months of the year: Escalante, Garfield County, 7 June 1940 (Hayward 1967:48); four miles east of Pine Valley, Washington County, 13 September 1941 (Behle 1943a:61); Yost, Box Elder County, 21 May 1954 (Behle 1958:29). Several pairs have been known to nest on the Brigham Young University campus (Hayward field notes). Bee and Hutchings

Fig. 51. Black-throated Sparrow. Camel Back Mountain, Tooele County, Utah, 12 June 1954. Photo by R. D. Porter.

(1942:80) recorded a nest at Lehi, Utah County, 1 July.

Phainopepla nitens lepida Van Tyne
Phainopepla

STATUS: This is an uncommon resident in southwestern Utah in the Virgin River Valley. In this area it is primarily a summer resident, although some may remain throughout the year.

RECORDS: Fisher (1893:113) reported that the Phainopepla was common in the lower Santa Clara Valley, Washington County, 11-15 June 1891, and that "several pairs were breeding in the village of St. George." Behle (1943a:61) recorded three specimens taken at Anderson's Ranch, Washington County, 28 June 1932 and 5 July 1932. Brigham Young University has a specimen from St. George taken 19 June 1933 and one from Anderson's Ranch taken 18 May 1934.

Hardy and Higgins (1940:105) reported specimens from St. George, 15 November 1938 and 10 May 1939. Behle et al. (1958: 72-73) obtained six specimens two miles south of Kanab, Kane County, 18-19 June 1947. Wauer (1969:333) states that it is found in southern Utah from 1 April to 15 November.

FAMILY CINCLIDAE

Cinclus mexicanus unicolor Bonaparte
Dipper

STATUS: A common resident the year around along mountain streams and occasionally along valley streams where there is swift water.

RECORDS: This species was reported consistently by all of the early naturalists who did fieldwork along canyon streams. Ridgway (1877:407) found it nesting in Pack's

Canyon, Uinta Mountains, 7 July 1869. Allen (1872b:166) obtained 14 specimens in Ogden Canyon, Weber County, 2 October 1871, and Merriam (1873:671) noted it in the same area in June 1872. Henshaw (1875:159) reported it as being particularly numerous along Provo River, Utah County, in 1872, and Birdseye (field notes) found it near Pine Valley, Washington County, 13 October 1909. Many recent records indicate its continuing occurrence in most mountainous sections of the state. There are also a number of records from lower valley streams. Brigham Young University has specimens from near Provo, on Provo River, 4 December 1932; Escalante, Garfield County, 9 June 1936; Fruita, Wayne County, 8 June 1960. The species also occurs and nests in Zion Canyon (Wauer and Carter 1965:67).

FAMILY TROGLODYTIDAE

Campylorhynchus brunneicapillus couesi
Sharpe
Cactus Wren

STATUS: A year-round resident of the lower Virgin River Valley of southwestern Utah. It nests in thorny or spiny plants of the hot desert lands.

RECORDS: Henshaw (1875:178–179) took a specimen and saw two other birds a few miles north of St. George, Washington County, 27 October 1872. Merriam (Fisher 1893:131) found it common up to 3,800 feet on the Beaver Dam slope and in Santa Clara Valley, Washington County, May 1891. All known records are from the Washington County area. Brigham Young University has two specimens from near St. George, 27 May 1920 and 5 October 1935. Hardy and Higgins (1940:104) collected two males three miles west of the summit of the Beaver Dam Mountains on 17 February 1941. Behle (1943a:55) found this species to be common in the Joshua tree belt on the west slope of the Beaver Dam Mountains. He also noted several nests, all of which were located in cholla cactus.

Salpinctes obsoletus obsoletus (Say)
Rock Wren
Fig. 40, p. 103

STATUS: A common resident throughout Utah, breeding in rocky outcroppings at all elevations from low deserts to the alpine. In winter the Rock Wren drifts to lower elevations and southward.

RECORDS: This species was observed or collected by early naturalists in the state and reported by all of them as being very common. Ridgway (1877:419) found it in suitable localities in 1869; Allen (1872b:166) in 1871 found it abundant in the Wasatch Mountains; Henshaw (1875:180–181) recorded it in 1872 as especially common in southern Utah as did Merriam in the Virgin River Valley in 1891 (Fisher 1893:132). Many records have been published, the more recent ones being: Woodbury and Russell (1945:102), near Bluff, San Juan County, 27 October 1931; Twomey (1942:426), Green Lake, Daggett County, Uinta Mountains, 13 July 1937; Behle (1955:25), north slope of Mount Ibapah, Juab County, 2 July 1950; Wauer and Carter (1965:69), Zion National Park, Washington County, 18 June 1963.

Salpinctes mexicanus conspersus (Ridgway)
Canyon Wren

STATUS: An abundant resident of cliffs in canyon land country of southeastern Utah, becoming common to sparse in similar habitats northward. Nesting takes place in crevices in the rocky cliffs.

RECORDS: Ridgway (1873:172) regarded this wren as rare in the canyons near Salt Lake City, Salt Lake County. Henshaw (1875:181–182) found it in the cliffs and canyons of southern Utah and collected specimens in October 1872. Merriam (Fisher 1893:133) noted it breeding in the lower Virgin River Valley, Washington County, in available cliff habitats in May 1891. Loring (field notes) found it at Bluff, San Juan County, in November 1893.

Brigham Young University has specimens taken in canyons east of Provo, Utah County, 4 February 1933, 27 July 1944, and 4 October 1946.

Cistothorus palustris (Wilson)
Long-billed Marsh Wren
Fig. 54, p. 142

STATUS: An abundant species in the marshlands around Great Salt Lake and Utah Lake and present in other lowland areas of the state in lesser numbers.

RECORDS: Early records of this species in the state include those of Allen (1872b:166), at Ogden, Weber County; Henshaw (1874: 3), who considered it exceedingly abundant in marshy areas in the state; and Ridgway (1877:425–426) at various localities in Utah. Many records of more recent years have been published. Presnell (1935b:204) did not report this species from Zion National Park, Washington County, but Henshaw (1875:186) collected a specimen at Toquerville, Washington County, a few miles west of Zion, 15 October 1872. More recently Wauer and Carter (1965:68) considered it to be a fairly common migrant in areas near Zion Canyon below the high country and believed that it has increased in recent years.

SUBSPECIES: The race *C. p. plesius* appears to be the breeding form throughout most of the state, but Behle (1948a:75–76) considered some of his specimens from St. George, Washington County, and Kanab, Kane County, to be of the subspecies *C. p. aestuarinus*. The latter race may range northward along the Colorado River an unknown distance from its more usual range in southern California and Arizona.

Thryomanes bewickii eremophilus
Oberholser
Bewick's Wren

STATUS: This wren is primarily an inhabitant of pinyon-juniper forests, particularly of southern and eastern Utah, extending its breeding range as far north in the state as the Uinta Basin.

RECORDS: Henshaw (1875:183) found the wren at Iron City, Iron County, 6 October 1872, and at several localities in Washington County about the same time. Merriam (Fisher 1893:134) and Birdseye (field notes) also reported this species from Washington County in 1891 and 1909. More recent fieldwork has resulted in many records from the pinyon-juniper areas of eastern Utah (Killpack and Hayward 1958:23; Hayward 1967:45). The species appears to be less common in the Great Basin. A specimen at the University of Utah was taken at Benmore, Tooele County, 10 June 1934, and another in Utah State University was collected at Vernon, Tooele County, 2 May 1936 (Stanford 1938: 141).

Troglodytes troglodytes (Linnaeus)
Winter Wren

STATUS: A sparse winter resident of the state and occasionally reported breeding (Treganza, near Boulter, Juab County, 11 June 1911).

RECORDS: Collection records of the species are scattered and few. There is a specimen in the U.S. National Museum of Natural History from Provo, Utah County, 6 November 1888, collected by Vernon Bailey. Brigham Young University has a specimen taken by C. Cottam in Rock Canyon, near Provo, Utah County, 26 December 1927. Other records are as follows: Boulter, Juab County, 11 June 1909 (Treganza); Santa Clara Creek, Washington County, 16 March 1940 (Hardy and Higgins 1940:103); Capitol Reef Monument, Wayne County, 5 November 1941 (Behle et al. 1958:67). Several sight records have been published: Behle (1958:27), Clear Creek Canyon, Raft River Mountains, Box Elder County, 5 August 1936; Grater (1943:76), Zion National Park, Washington County, 1 February 1942; Utah Audubon News (1964:2), Salt Lake City, Salt Lake County, 22 December 1963. Winter wrens were reported by Kingery (1976:103) for Logan, Cache County, and Zion National Park in the fall of 1975.

SUBSPECIES: Owing no doubt to the paucity of specimens, there has been no careful study of the subspecific status of the Utah population of winter wrens. According to Check-list of Birds of the World (1960[9]:416), Utah would most likely fall within the range of *T. t. pacificus*.

Troglodytes aedon parkmanii Audubon
House Wren
Fig. 41, p. 106

STATUS: The House Wren is a common summer resident in wooded areas of both mountains and lowlands. It is present from late April through October over most of the state, and a few remain over winter in the low Virgin River Valley (Wauer and Carter 1965:68). This species nests in holes in trees or under loose bark and frequently in abandoned buildings.

RECORDS: Ridgway (1877:422–4) took five nests in Parley's Park, Summit County,

east of Salt Lake City, 23–27 June 1869. Henshaw (1875:184–185) noted that it was common at elevations up to 10,000 feet in the areas of the state visited by him. In more recent times many additional records have been obtained.

FAMILY MIMIDAE

Dumetella carolinensis (Linnaeus)
Gray Catbird

STATUS: The Gray Catbird is a common summer resident throughout the state where it lives in thickets along the lower valley streams or ditch banks and in similar habitats around dwellings and parks. The bulk of the population arrives in late May or early June and remains until October. A few may winter here. Kashin (1974:488) reported one at Salt Lake City, Salt Lake County, 16 December 1973.

RECORDS: During his observations of 1869, Ridgway (1877:399) found this species to be one of the most abundant birds in the Wasatch region. Allen (1872b:165) reported

Fig. 52. Sage Sparrow. Rush Valley, Tooele County, Utah, 31 May 1954. Photo by R. D. Porter and R. J. Erwin.

it as common along the Weber River, Weber County, 1 September to 8 October 1871. Other early records for Utah were made by Merriam (1873:670, 705), Henshaw (1875:153), and Vernon Bailey (field notes). Additional notations of this species are continuously being made to the present time.

Mimus polyglottos leucopterus (Vigors)
Mockingbird
Fig. 42, p. 109

STATUS: A summer breeding inhabitant of tall semidesert brushlands throughout most of the state. Most common in the lower valleys of the Virgin River and Colorado River and becoming less common northward.

RECORDS: The early naturalist explorers did not report the Mockingbird from the northern part of the state. However, Merriam (Fisher 1893:127) found it to be common in Washington County in May 1891. Rowley collected specimens for the American Museum of Natural History at Bluff, San Juan County, in May 1892 (Woodbury and Russell 1945:103). Birdseye (field notes) reported it from St. George, Washington County, in 1892. Numerous more recent records have been reported including Tanner (1936:185–187), who summarized Utah records to that date; Stanford (1944:151), Ouray Valley, Uintah County, 6 June 1940; Behle (1960a:41), Moab, Grand County, 8 June 1956; Wauer and Carter (1965:69), Zion National Park, 24 November 1964. More northern breeding records include those of Bee and Hutchings (1942:78), who found them nesting in tall greasewood west of Lehi, Utah County, in late May and June.

Oreoscoptes montanus (Townsend)
Sage Thrasher

STATUS: The Sage Thrasher is a common summer resident of the lower desertlands where it nests in greasewood or tall sage-

brush communities. It is found in Utah from March through October.

RECORDS: The former abundance of the Sage Thrasher in Utah is indicated by the numerous collection and observation records of all of the early naturalist explorers. Ridgway (1877:402) seems to be the first to have recorded it and took nests and birds from Antelope and other islands of Great Salt Lake in June 1869. Other early reports include Allen (1872b:166), Ogden, Weber County, September 1871; Merriam (1873:670), Ogden, 11 June 1872; Henshaw (1875:149), central and southern Utah, fall of 1872. Hundreds of additional records have accumulated from every county of the state in recent years.

Toxostoma rufum longicauda (Baird)
Brown Thrasher

STATUS: The Brown Thrasher seems to be of casual occurrence in Utah. Surely it is rare, although there is some evidence that it may nest within the state.

RECORDS: Grantham (1936:85) banded a specimen at Zion Canyon, Washington County, 7 December 1935. It was later preserved as a specimen. Wauer and Carter (1965:69) reported that Presnell observed one in Zion Canyon in late March 1936. Behle (1954b:313) reported a specimen taken in Salt Lake City (Tracy Aviary), Salt Lake County, 25 June 1953. Brigham Young University has a specimen from Roosevelt, Duchesne County, 29 December 1954. Hayward (1967:45) erroneously recorded this specimen as 29 December 1955. Hayward (1967:45) saw one at the junction of the San Rafael and Green Rivers, Emery County, 4 June 1957. Behle et al. (1964:454) found it at Fish Springs, Juab County, 9 June 1961. Carter (1967 mimeographed list) recorded a sight record from Arches National Monument, Grand County, 25 September 1967. Kingery (1973:94) reported one observed at Fish Springs, Juab County, 27 October 1972. Kingery

(1975:96) reported them at Salt Lake City in early September 1974; Bear River, Box Elder County, 27 October to 12 November 1974; Canyonlands National Park, San Juan County, 4 December 1974.

Toxostoma bendirei bendirei (Coues)
Bendire's Thrasher

STATUS: A sparse summer resident in southern Utah.

RECORDS: Early naturalists who visited southern Utah did not record Bendire's Thrasher in their lists. Brigham Young University has a specimen from Monument Valley, San Juan County, 4 July 1927. Cottam, who collected the specimen, reported seeing several birds in that area. A specimen in the University of Utah collection was taken near Escalante, Garfield County, 9 May 1937 (Woodbury 1939:159). Behle (1960a:41) recorded a sight record at the top of Lake Canyon, San Juan County, 14 July 1958. Kingery (1971:886) reported a Bendire's Thrasher seen twice during the breeding season of 1971 at Vernon, Tooele

County. Three were observed at the same locality on 24 May 1975 (Kingery 1975:888).

Toxostoma lecontei lecontei Lawrence
Le Conte's Thrasher

STATUS: Le Conte's Thrasher appears to be confined in Utah to the Virgin River Valley and the south slope of the Beaver Dam Mountains in Washington County. It has been reported rarely from Utah, although it is rather common in southern Nevada.

RECORDS: Fisher (1893:130) listed a specimen in the U.S. National Museum of Natural History taken in Beaver Dam Mountains, Washington County, 10 May 1891, by C. H. Merriam. Merriam in his notes indicated that it was rather common on the west side of this mountain range where it lived in close association with the Cactus Wren. Presnell (1935b:205) reported it as having been observed near Shunes Creek, Zion National Park, Washington County (no date given). Wauer (1964:292) saw two at St. George on 19 December 1963.

Fig. 53. Sage Sparrow. Rush Valley, Tooele County, Utah, 31 May 1954. Photo by R. D. Porter and R. J. Erwin.

Fig. 54. Long-billed Marsh Wren. Ogden Bay, Weber County, Utah, 1 July 1969. Photo by R. J. Erwin.

Toxostoma dorsale coloradense van Rossem
Crissal Thrasher

STATUS: An uncommon resident of the Virgin River Valley in southwestern Utah. Also reported from Kanab, Kane County. Judging from available records, it is the most common of the four representatives of the genus found in southern Utah.

RECORDS: Early records of this species include a specimen in the U.S. National Museum of Natural History taken by Palmer at St. George, Washington County, 9 June 1870. Henshaw (1874:2) saw this species in St. George in 1872. Yarrow and Henshaw (field notes) reported it there in January 1889 (specimen in U.S. National Museum of Natural History). Merriam (Fisher 1893:130) found it breeding in the lower Santa Clara Valley, Washington County, 16 May 1891. Brigham Young University has four specimens taken at St. George in late December 1926 and 8 April 1933. Behle et al. (1964:454) obtained seven specimens from City Springs area, St. George, 31 December 1960, 20 June 1961, 25–26 May 1962. Wauer (1964:292) reported seeing four at St. George, 19 December 1963. Lund (1968a:360) observed a Crissal Thrasher at Kanab, Kane County, 20 December 1967. One was also seen at St. George, 25 September 1974 (Kingery 1975:96).

FAMILY MUSCICAPIDAE

Sialia mexicana Swainson
Western Bluebird

STATUS: The Western Bluebird is a species common to central and southern Utah where it lives in lower mountain and pinyon-juniper communities. There is some altitudinal migration in spring and autumn, and the species winters at lower elevations in flocks. Several pairs were found nesting in a grove of aspens near the Kanab Sand Dunes, Kane County, 7 May 1957 (Hayward 1967:46).

RECORDS: Early naturalists in Utah did not mention this species in Utah. A specimen in the U.S. National Museum of Natural History was taken by Bailey near Kanab, Kane County, 26 December 1888. Sight records were reported by Cary on the lower eastern slope of the La Sal Mountains, Grand or San Juan counties, July 1907 (field notes). Nelson and Birdseye (field notes) observed it near Kanab and in Washington County in 1909. There are numerous more recent records and collections.

SUBSPECIES: Both the race *S. m. occi-*

dentalis and *S. m. bairdi* appear in the Utah population. The former seems to be a wintering and transient race, while *bairdi* is the breeding subspecies. Several of the earlier records of *occidentalis*, especially nesting records, may be questioned. Behle (1941b:183) reported a specimen of *occidentalis* (transient) taken near Moab, Grand County, 6 April 1938, and Twomey (1944a:89) collected one on 21 October 1937 at Kanab, Kane County, in a flock of seven *bairdi*. A series of eight specimens in the Brigham Young University collection taken near the Kanab Sand Dunes, Kane County, early May 1955, are all of the race *bairdi*. These birds were in breeding condition.

Sialia currucoides (Bechstein)
Mountain Bluebird
Fig. 44, p. 115

STATUS: Formerly a common summer resident in valleys and mountains throughout the state. Now, less common and mostly confined to mountains and high valleys as a breeding species but frequently appearing in flocks in the lower valleys during spring and fall migration. A few winter in central and southern Utah (Wauer and Carter 1965:70).

RECORDS: In the accounts of early explorations in Utah the Mountain Bluebird was frequently mentioned. The Stansbury party (Baird 1852:307, 314–315, 328) reported it in Salt Lake Valley in 1849 and collected specimens for the U.S. National Museum of Natural History. Remy (1860[2]:450) reported this species in 1855. Ridgway (1877:405–406) found it in several localities in Utah in June and August 1869, and Henshaw (1875:162–163) also reported it from various areas of the state visited by him in September, October, and November 1872. Numerous collections and observations have been made in more recent years.

Myadestes townsendi townsendi
(Audubon)
Townsend's Solitaire

STATUS: A widespread but not common species that nests in the mountains and winters at lower elevations in foothills and valleys.

RECORDS: Of the early naturalists in Utah, Henshaw (1875:231–232) collected two specimens, one at Pine Valley, Washington County, and the other in Millard County in October and November 1872. Vernon Bailey (field notes) found a specimen killed at Provo, Utah County, 14 November 1888, and noted that it was common in canyons near Manti, Sanpete County, 3 December. In more recent years records have been obtained from most of the counties of the state.

Zoothera naevia (Gmelin)
Varied Thrush

STATUS: This is a rare and possibly accidental visitor in Utah.

RECORDS: The only collection record available for Utah is a specimen at Brigham Young University taken at Cedar City, Iron County, 4 December 1967. Merlin L. Killpack (letter) captured a Varied Thrush in a banding operation at Ogden, Weber County, 22 December 1973. The specimen was photographed but was unfortunately destroyed by a house cat before it could be studied further. The first sight record was recorded from Jordan River Park, Salt Lake City, Salt Lake County, 22 and 29 December 1946 and 1 January 1947, by Kenneth Tanner, Mr. and Mrs. C. W. Lockerbie, and several other observers. The bird was feeding on the fruit of the Russian olive (Lockerbie 1947a:17; Bader 1947:107). Keith (1968:245–276) summarized the eight records for this species in Utah up to and including May 1966. Since then, five more sight records have been reported: Kashin (1967:347) reported one observed sometime between 21 December 1966 and 2 January

1967 in the Salt Lake area. Kingery (1973: 94) stated that one was seen 30 October 1972 at Bryce Canyon, Garfield County, and listed another Salt Lake record on 6 November 1972. Mitchell (letter 1974) observed a male and female, 16, 18, 19 May 1974, at Glen Canyon City, Kane County. A single bird was seen at Zion National Park, Washington County, 28 April 1975 (Kingery 1975:888).

SUBSPECIES: The races *naevia* and *meruloides* are found along the Pacific coast north to Alaska. The one collected specimen mentioned above has been identified as *meruloides* by M. R. Browning of the U.S. National Museum of Natural History.

Catharus fuscescens salicicola (Ridgway)
Veery

STATUS: The Veery, also sometimes called Willow Thrush, is a summer inhabitant of streamside woodlands especially in the lower valleys. From available records it would appear that this species was much more common in the early days of settlement than it is at present. Apparently it has not been able to adjust to the pressures of human population.

RECORDS: Ridgway (1877:398) found this thrush very abundant along the lower portions of the Provo River, Utah County, 10–11 July 1869. He also found it along the Weber and Bear rivers. Henshaw (1875: 148) considered it to be an abundant summer resident in Utah. Strangely enough, neither of these workers obtained specimens. A specimen was taken northeast of Wellsville, Cache County, 21 July 1927 (Stanford 1938:141). There is a specimen in the Royal Ontario Museum collected near Jensen, Uintah County, in July 1935. Stanford (1931:8) reported a specimen taken near Salina, Sevier County, 10 April 1929, but the location of this specimen is not known. Behle and Selander (1952:29) recorded a male specimen collected along Clear Creek, Raft River Mountains, Box Elder County, 14 June 1951. This specimen had enlarged testes and was suspected of breeding. Several sight records have been recorded, including a more recent one by Kashin (1964:50) for American Fork Canyon, Utah County, 13 June 1964. Hayward (field notes) regarded this thrush as common in woodlands along Provo River, Utah County, in the 1930s, but no specimens were taken. Several instances of nesting have been recorded. Brigham Young University collection contains three sets of eggs as follows: Provo River near Provo, Utah County, 29 June 1933, set of two with one cowbird egg collected by R. G. Bee; City Creek, Salt Lake County, 1 June 1934, set of four collected by A. D. Boyle; Provo, 4 June 1934, set of four collected by D. E. Johnson. The sets of Veery eggs are decidedly darker blue than a series of Audubon's Hermit Thrush eggs from the Wasatch Mountains. Kashin found one in Salt Lake City, Salt Lake County, 13–14 January 1972 (Kingery 1972: 636).

Catharus ustulatus (Nuttall)
Swainson's Thrush

STATUS: This is a fairly common summer resident in the mountains of northern and central Utah. It appears to be less common southward. It inhabits approximately the same altitude zone as the Hermit Thrush but tends to live closer to water where it nests in tall shrubs, conifers, and aspens. It is less common than the Hermit Thrush.

RECORDS: The earliest published record for the state is that of Ridgway (1877:397–398), who considered it a common breeder in streamside thickets. He collected specimens, nests, and eggs, 23 and 27 June 1869, at Parley's Park, Summit County. Osgood (field notes) found it at Puffer Lake, Beaver County, and Brian Head, Iron County, August and September 1908. Brigham Young University collection contains specimens as follows: Strawberry Reservoir, Wasatch County, 7 July 1926; Kamas, Summit County, 21 August 1930;

Yost, Box Elder County, 7 September 1957; Strawberry River, Duchesne County, 19 June 1961; Sheep Creek Watershed, Sevier County, 16 July 1968 and 8 July 1969.

SUBSPECIES: According to Bond (1963: 373–387), the subspecies occurring in Utah is C. u. almae, although he appears to have examined few specimens from the area. Ripley (Checklist of Birds of the World 1964[10]:171–173) also considered almae to be found in Utah. Wauer (1969:333) obtained a specimen of the race swainsoni in Zion National Park, Washington County, 27 May 1966.

Catharus guttatus (Pallas)
Hermit Thrush
Fig. 43, p. 112

STATUS: The Hermit Thrush is a common breeding species in mountains throughout the state. It is also a frequent migrant in spring and autumn when it may be found in woodlands and thickets along valley streams and occasionally in semidesert country.

RECORDS: Ridgway (1877:394–395) found this species in the Wasatch Mountains in May and August 1869. Allen (1872b:173) reported it for Ogden, Weber County, and Henshaw (1875:144) also recorded it for Utah. In more recent years many additional records have been published.

SUBSPECIES: C. g. auduboni appears to be the common nesting subspecies in the mountain ranges of northern and eastern Utah. Behle (1948a:76) regarded the breeding thrushes of southern and southwestern Utah as C. g. polionotus. This view is also indicated in Checklist of Birds of the World (1964[10]:174). However, the status of the subspecies of C. guttatus is still somewhat unsettled (Aldrich 1968: 1–33; AOU Supplement 1973:416).

Hylocichla mustelina (Gmelin)
Wood Thrush

STATUS: The Wood Thrush is of rare and

accidental occurrence in Utah.

RECORDS: Behle (1966:396) reported that a specimen was captured after flying into a wire at Tracy Aviary, Liberty Park, Salt Lake City, Salt Lake County, 14 October 1963. The bird later died and was preserved as a specimen. Kashin observed one at American Fork, Utah County, May 1964 (Behle and Perry 1975:32).

Turdus migratorius propinquus Ridgway
American Robin

STATUS: A common resident throughout the state. Originally probably an inhabitant of streamside woodlands and mountain forests but spreading into farmlands, parks, cities, and towns following settlement by white man. Although its numbers seem to have diminished somewhat in the past

Fig. 55. Dark-eyed Junco. Monte Cristo, Rich County, Utah, 27 June 1973. Photo by R. J. Erwin.

decade, the robin is still a rather common summer inhabitant of valleys and mountains up to timberline. In winter it is of erratic occurrence depending upon the presence of food. In canyons it is often found in large flocks where wild berries are available, and it frequently occurs around settlements where berries of ornamental shrubs or fruits are left on the trees.

RECORDS: McCarthy (Baird 1876:378) collected a specimen at Camp Floyd (now Fairfield, Utah County) in 1859. All of the early naturalists to visit Utah reported it. Ridgway (1877:393) collected a number of specimens in the Wasatch and Uinta mountains in June and July of 1869, but he collected none in the valley. Henshaw (1875: 143) observed that in September 1872 it was very common in Provo, Utah County,

Fig. 56. Chipping Sparrow. North Fork Ogden River, Weber County, Utah, 30 June 1930. Photo by R. J. Erwin.

where a few years before it was unknown. Most of the early observations indicate that it was not an abundant species in the early days of settlement. In recent years numerous observations and collections have been made both in the valleys and in the mountains.

Polioptila caerulea amoenissima Grinnell
Blue-gray Gnatcatcher
Figs. 45, 46; pp. 118, 121

STATUS: A summer resident, less common north to the Great Salt Lake and the Uinta Basin. Its distribution in the state

Fig. 57. Yellow Warbler. Rochester, Monroe County, New York, 9 July 1967. Photo by R. J. Erwin.

seems to depend somewhat on the presence of pinyon-juniper forests in which it most frequently nests. However, it is also found in willows or brush. It has been reported from early April to mid-September.

RECORDS: Early naturalists in the state reported the species only from the southern-

most counties. In 1891 Merriam and Bailey (Fisher 1893:143–144) found it breeding commonly in Santa Clara Valley, 11 to 15 May, and in junipers on Beaver Dam Mountains, both localities in Washington County. Osgood (field notes) found it in scrub oak at the base of Beaver Mountains, Beaver

Fig. 58. Yellow-rumped Warbler. Monte Cristo, Rich County, Utah, 7 July 1973. Photo by R. J. Erwin.

Fig. 59. Solitary Vireo. North Fork Ogden River, Weber County, Utah, 8 July 1956. Photo by R. J. Erwin.

County, 25 August 1908. Nelson and Birds-eye (field notes) saw some near Kanab, Kane County, 3 September 1909. Reports of occurrence in more northern counties have been made in recent years. Treganza (field notes) found it nesting in the West Tintic Mountains, Juab County, in 1912 and 1914. One from Skull Valley, Tooele County, taken 22 July 1935, is in the University of Utah collection. A specimen from Antelope Island, Davis County, collected 24 June 1938, is in the U.S. National Museum of Natural History. Brigham Young University has specimens from Provo Bay, Utah County, 10 May 1942, and from Cedar Valley, Utah County, April 1946. Bee and Hutchings (1942:80) reported it nesting in Cedar Valley, Utah

County, in late June and early July. Hayward (field notes) found it to be very common near Bonanza, Uintah County, in June 1954.

FAMILY SYLVIIDAE

Regulus satrapa Lichtenstein
Golden-crowned Kinglet

STATUS: This species is a rather common breeding species in coniferous forests of mountainous areas throughout most of the state. In winter it tends to move down to lower elevations where it occurs in small flocks in brush or pinyon-juniper woodlands. The Golden-crowned Kinglet seems to be less common than the Ruby-crowned

Kinglet, but it is more secretive and less conspicuous in song so that it is more likely to be overlooked.

RECORDS: The earliest records for the state appear to be those of Osgood (field notes), who found it at Fish Lake Park, Sevier County; Rabbit Valley, Wayne County; and in the Henry Mountains, Garfield County. His observations were made in September and October 1908. Treganza (field notes) noted that they were common in the Wasatch and Uinta mountains where

Fig. 60. Warbling Vireo. Snow Basin, Weber County, Utah, 30 June 1959. Photo by R. J. Erwin.

he located 27 nests. Nearly all the numerous collection records are for fall, winter, or early spring. Woodbury (1939:159–160) and Behle and Ross (1945:169) summarized collection and sight records of this species.

SUBSPECIES: The Utah population of Golden-crowned Kinglets has been variously referred to the races *olivaceus* or *amoenus*. The AOU Check-list (1957:453) includes Utah within the range of *R. s. amoenus* named by Van Rossem (1945:77–78). Behle (1955:26; 1958:29; Behle et al. 1958:71) used *R. s. olivaceus* in lists of birds from the Deep Creek Mountains, the Raft River Mountains, and the Kanab area. Later Behle referred to them as *R. s. amoenus* in his treatise on birds of southeastern Utah (1960a:43). A series of eight specimens at Brigham Young University, all taken in fall, winter, or early spring, came within the larger size range of *R. s. amoenus* with the exception of one specimen. It would seem that there is a need to assemble a collection of breeding as well as wintering birds to clarify the subspecific relations of the Utah population.

Regulus calendula cineraceus Grinnell
Ruby-crowned Kinglet

STATUS: This is a common breeding species in coniferous forests throughout the mountain ranges of the state. In fall, winter, and spring it occurs in small flocks or individually in lowland areas wherever there are streamside woodlands or ornamental trees. During the nonbreeding season it is more common southward.

RECORDS: This kinglet was reported by most of the early naturalists who visited Utah. Ridgway (1875:33) considered it a common breeding species at Parley's Park, Summit County, during the summer of 1869. Most of the other early observations or collections were made in fall, winter, and early spring when the birds were migrating or on their wintering ground. Henshaw (1875:165) took a specimen near St. George, Washington County, 26 September 1872. A specimen in the American Museum was

taken by Rowley, near Four Corners, on the San Juan River, 20 April 1892. The Museum of Comparative Zoology contains specimens collected by Allen near Ogden, Weber County, in September 1871. Many collections have been made and reported in recent years.

FAMILY PARIDAE

Parus atricapillus Linnaeus
Black-capped Chickadee
Fig. 47, p. 124

STATUS: The Black-capped Chickadee is a rather common permanent resident throughout the state, being somewhat more common northward. In winter it inhabits woodlands along the streams of the valleys but in summer tends to move upwards into the mountains where it breeds. This active species almost invariably appears in pairs or small flocks of two or three pairs.

RECORDS: Reports of the early naturalists vary as to the numbers of these chickadees. Baird (1852:316) reported one specimen taken in Utah by Stansbury in 1849 or 1850. He called it rare. Ridgway (1877:412) stated that it was probably wanting in the western Great Basin and extremely rare on the eastern side in 1869. Allen (1872b:166) called it abundant around Ogden, Weber County, in September 1871. Neither Merriam nor Nelson found it in 1872. Henshaw (1875:171) reported it as common in cottonwood groves near Provo River, Utah County, in July and November 1872, but did not see it elsewhere in his travels. Vernon Bailey (field notes) considered it to be common to abundant from Salt Lake City, Salt Lake County, all the way to southern Utah during October, November, and December in 1888. The variable observations by these early travelers reflect the erratic nature of these chickadees in their search for food, especially in winter, and would probably be no indication that they were less common than they are at present.

SUBSPECIES: The Utah population appears to contain two recognizable subspecies, although many specimens seem to be intergrades between the two. A race known as *P. a. septentrionalis,* typical of west central Canada and central United States, intergrades in eastern Utah with *P. a. nevadensis* which occurs in the Wasatch Mountains and Great Basin sections of Utah. *P. a. garrinus,* described by Behle (1951:75–79), was placed in synonomy with *P. a. septentrionalis* in Checklist of Birds of the World (1967 [12] :81). Wauer (1969: 332) reported a specimen of the race *nevadensis* at Springdale, Washington County, 20 March 1965, as being the first for the Virgin River Valley.

Parus gambeli Ridgway
Mountain Chickadee

STATUS: A permanent resident with considerable altitudinal migration. In summer it inhabits coniferous forests where it breeds, but in winter it spreads into streamside woodlands at lower elevations.

RECORDS: Several of the early naturalists made note of this chickadee in Utah. Ridgway (1877:411) found it in the Wasatch and Uinta mountains in 1869. Stevenson (1872:464) recorded it from the Uinta Mountains, Summit County, September 1870. Henshaw (1875:170) regarded it as a common resident in coniferous forests and found it also in lower valleys in November 1872. He collected several specimens at Fillmore, Millard County, 17 November 1872. Many records are available from more recent collections and observations.

SUBSPECIES: *P. g. inyoensis* appears to be the only clear-cut subspecies inhabiting Utah. In eastern and southern Utah it intergrades with *P. g. gambeli,* a race typical of the Rocky Mountains. A population named *P. g. wasatchensis* by Behle (1950b:273–274), which he supposed inhabited Utah,

was considered by Snow in Check-list of Birds of the World (1967 [12] :84–85) to be a synonym of *P. g. inyoensis.*

Parus inornatus ridgwayi Richmond
Plain Titmouse

STATUS: A common resident found throughout the state but especially characteristic of pinyon-juniper woodlands.

RECORDS: The type of this subspecies named by Richmond (1902:155) was collected by Henry W. Henshaw at a locality then known as "Iron City," Iron County, 8 October 1872 (Henshaw 1875:168). This specimen is now in the U.S. National Museum of Natural History. Numerous collection and sight records are available from all sections of the state, especially where pinyon-juniper forests are present.

Auriparus flaviceps acaciarum[14] Grinnell
Verdin

STATUS: A breeding species of hot deserts along the Virgin River of southwestern Utah.

RECORDS: Merriam (Fisher 1893:142) found several nests of Verdin on Beaver Dam Creek, Arizona (near Utah), 9–10 May 1891, and a single nest near the junction of Santa Clara Creek with the Virgin River, Washington County, 14 May 1891. Two specimens at the University of Utah were collected near the Utah-Arizona border, one in Arizona, 28 October 1938, and the other in Utah, 9 May 1941 (Behle 1943a:53). There is a sight record (Wauer and Carter 1965:66) from Zion National Park, Washington County, 20 December 1962.

Psaltriparus minimus[15] (Townsend)
Bushtit

STATUS: A permanent breeding resident of the state where it occurs most commonly in pinyon-juniper forests or in brushlands

---

[14]Snow (Check-list of Birds of the World 1967 [12] :69) has placed this species in the family Remizidae rather than Paridae.

[15]Snow (Check-list of Birds of the World 1967 [12] :59) places this species in the family Aegithalidae rather than Paridae.

Fig. 61.   Northern Oriole.   Ogden, Weber County, Utah, 18 June 1973.   Photo by R. J. Erwin.

Fig. 62. Brewer's Blackbird. Tremonton, Box Elder County, Utah, 9 June 1974. Photo by R. J. Erwin.

at mid elevations. It has been reported from most of the counties, although it is more abundant southward.

RECORDS: Early records for the state include those of Ridgway (1877:413–414), who observed a few near Salt Lake City, Salt Lake County, in 1869. It was taken by Stevenson (1872:464) on Green River, Daggett County, 10 October 1870. Henshaw (1875:172) reported large flocks in several localities of the state in fall and winter. He noted it in pinyon-juniper and streamside thickets and collected specimens at Iron City, Iron County, 5 October

1872, and at Beaver, Beaver County, 10 November 1872. Numerous additional records are available in recent years.

SUBSPECIES: The race *P. m. plumbeus* appears to be found in Utah except for the southwestern and south central areas. Here many specimens are intergrades between *P. m. plumbeus* and *P. m. providentalis*, the latter being a race described by Avery (1941:74–75) from Providence Mountains of southeastern California. Behle (1948a:45) regarded two specimens from Kanab, Kane County, as being well-defined *P. m. providentalis*.

FAMILY SITTIDAE

Sitta pusilla [16] Latham
Pigmy Nuthatch

STATUS: The Pigmy Nuthatch is present as a permanent resident throughout Utah wherever there are forests of ponderosa pine. While not strictly confined to the ponderosa pine, it seems to be more at home there and is often rather common in such forests.

RECORDS: This nuthatch was observed rarely by early naturalists in the state, owing perhaps to its limited habitat. Neither Henshaw (1874:3) nor Ridgway (1877:373) reported taking any specimens, but Henshaw did mention that it occurred in the state. Vernon Bailey (field notes) found it in ponderosa pine between Garfield and Kane Counties, 18 December 1888. Cottam took one from a juniper near Lynndyl, Millard County, 18 September 1926. Twomey (1942:424) took specimens at Green Lake, Daggett County, 30 June 1937. A few records are available from the Henry Mountains and high plateaus of Garfield County (University of Utah and Brigham Young University). Specimens have also been taken principally from ponderosa pines in Pine Valley Mountains of Washington County (Behle 1943a:54; Hardy 1941b:236). Wauer and Carter (1965:67) reported them from localities in Zion National Park, Washington County. Most of the available records for the species are from the La Sal and Blue mountains of San Juan County where they seem to be most common.

SUBSPECIES: Birds inhabiting the Utah area are of the subspecies *S. p. melanotis.* Hardy (1941b:236) regarded specimens of the Pine Valley Mountains as *S. p. canescens,* but Behle (1943a:54) cast some doubts upon the identification. Worthen (1968: 320–322) concluded that the subspecies

canescens does not occur in Utah. Furthermore, Greenway in Check-list of Birds of the World (1967[12]:135) stated that S. *p. canescens* is "perhaps not separable from *melanotis.*"

Sitta canadensis Linnaeus
Red-breasted Nuthatch

STATUS: A common summer resident and breeding species principally in coniferous forests throughout the mountains and high plateaus of the state. It may sometimes be found as a migrant in the lower valleys.

RECORDS: Ridgway (1877:416) regarded this species as being less common than the Pigmy and White-breasted Nuthatch in the summer of 1869 in coniferous forests of the Wasatch Mountains. It was missed by most of the other early naturalists, presumably because they did relatively little work in the mountains. Where suitable habitat occurs, this species has been reported in recent years from most parts of the state.

Sitta carolinensis Latham
White-breasted Nuthatch

STATUS: A permanent resident of pinyon-juniper forests, coniferous forests, and streamside woodland throughout the state. While it may not be regarded as a common species in Utah, this nuthatch is rather widespread and not so restricted to particular habitats as the other two species. Sometimes it occurs in small loose colonies, especially in less disturbed woodlands along the valley streams.

RECORDS: Some of the early naturalists who visited in Utah missed this species entirely, and all considered it to be rare. Ridgway (1875:32) found it breeding in Parkley's Park, Summit County, in 1869, and Henshaw (1874:3) reported a single specimen from the Wasatch Mountains. This species has been reported often in more

---

[16]Phillips et al. (1964:114–115) and Mayr and Short (1970:66) consider S. *pygmaea* to be conspecific with S. *pusilla.*

recent years from most of the counties of the state where suitable habitat occurs.

SUBSPECIES: Greenway in Check-list of Birds of the World (1967[12]:138–139) included *S. c. tenuissima* and *S. c. nelsoni* in the Utah population. However, his description of their distribution is not clear and indicates that the ranges of the two races overlap. It seems evident that *S. c. nelsoni* inhabits most, if not all, of the state. If *S. c. tenuissima* occurs at all, it should be looked for in the mountains of western Utah. Behle (1943a:54) found one specimen from Pine Valley Mountains, Washington County, that approached *tenuissima* in bill length, but other specimens from that area appeared to be typical *nelsoni*. A race described by Twomey (1942:422–424) as *S. c. uintaensis* has not been accepted by other ornithologists. This race is considered a synonym for *S. c. nelsoni* (Checklist of Birds of the World 1967[12]:138–139).

FAMILY CERTHIIDAE

Certhia familiaris Linnaeus
Brown Creeper

STATUS: A widespread but not common resident throughout the state where it lives in summer principally in montane coniferous forests and tends to migrate to lower elevations in winter. It is a quiet bird and often solitary so that its presence may be easily overlooked.

RECORDS: Some of the early-day naturalists considered the Brown Creeper to be rather common or even abundant (Nelson 1875:343; Ridgway 1877:418). It was missed by other observers such as Allen, Merriam, and Henshaw. Numerous records and observations have been made more recently.

SUBSPECIES: Behle (1948a:75) has reviewed the subspecific status of the Brown Creeper in Utah. It appears that the birds of the Kane County area and presumably those of Washington County belong to *C.*

f. leucosticta, while *C. f. montana* occurs elsewhere in the state.

FAMILY EMBERIZIDAE

Calcarius lapponicus (Linnaeus)
Lapland Longspur

STATUS: The Lapland Longspur is an uncommon but apparently consistent visitor in Utah most likely to be found in winter, late fall, and early spring. It associates often with flocks of Horned Larks and seems to be more common in the Colorado River Basin.

RECORDS: Several records have been reported for the Uinta Basin (Killpack 1953: 152; Killpack and Hayward 1958:25). Specimens from that area in the Brigham Young University collection are as follows: one, Roosevelt, Duchesne County, 1 January 1952; five, Myton, Duchesne County, 17 December 1955, 28 January 1956, 15 January 1957, February 1958. Porter (1954:364) reported specimens from four miles north of Camel Back Mountain, Tooele County, 13 April 1953, and near the same locality on 3 November 1953. Behle et al. (1964: 456) reported specimens from Farmington Bay Waterfowl Management area, Davis County, 5 November 1955, and three miles east of Camel Back Mountain, Tooele County, 9 October 1957. A large flock (120) was reported at Bear River Migratory Bird Refuge, Box Elder County, 18 February 1975, by Kingery (1975:724).

SUBSPECIES: Judging from the specimens collected to date, *C. l. alascensis* appears to be the most common race found in Utah. A specimen of *C. l. lapponicus* from near Camel Back Mountain, taken 13 April 1953, was reported by Porter (1954:364).

Calcarius ornatus (Townsend)
Chestnut-collared Longspur

STATUS: A rare, seemingly accidental, visitor in Utah.

RECORDS: Porter (1954:364) recorded a

specimen taken near Government Creek, four miles north of Camel Back Mountain, Tooele County, 14 October 1953. One was observed by Stewart Murie in Cedar Valley, Iron County, 25 November 1966 (Behle and Perry 1975:45). Kertell reported one at Zion National Park, Washington County, 10 October 1974 (Kingery 1975:97). Three were observed at Farmington Bay, Davis County, 20 April 1975 (Kingery (1975:889).

Plectrophenax nivalis nivalis (Linnaeus)
Snow Bunting

STATUS: The Snow Bunting is a regular although uncommon winter visitor in Utah. It is known to occur only in the northern part of the state.

RECORDS: At the Bear River Migratory Bird Refuge, Box Elder County, it was reported to be common in the winter of 1930–31, and three specimens were taken there 13 October 1932 (Behle and Ross 1945:170). One of these specimens is in the University of Utah collection. Another specimen in the University of Utah collection was taken near Centerville, Davis County, 29 November 1939 (Behle and Ross 1945:170). Three specimens from Utah at Brigham Young University are as follows: near Provo, Utah County, 25 February 1934 (Johnson 1935a: 160), and 9 February 1935 (Johnson 1935b: 294); Fort Duchesne, Uintah County, 14 January 1952 (Killpack 1953:152). Lockerbie and Behle (1952a:17) reported that Floyd Thompson saw a flock of 25 at Rock Island, Utah Lake, Utah County, 5 November 1951. One specimen was found dead on the island. Behle (1958:37) reported one observed at Stanrod, Box Elder County, 30 December 1951.

Calamospiza melanocorys Stejneger
Lark Bunting

STATUS: The Lark Bunting is a sparse but regular summer resident and migrant especially in the northern part of the state. It is primarily a grassland species but also inhabits semideserts where sagebrush and other low-growing shrubs are predominant. During migration it appears sporadically in small numbers in pasture lands and fields.

RECORDS: The earliest record of the species in Utah was a specimen taken by the Simpson Expedition presumably in Cedar Valley, Utah County, in 1859 (Baird 1876:379). At Parley's Park, Summit County, Ridgway (1877:487) collected a juvenile specimen and regarded the species as a straggler from the Great Plains. Specimens in the U.S. National Museum of Natural History were taken at Bear River Migratory Bird Refuge, Box Elder County, 1 June 1916. In recent years several collections have been made in Salt Lake, Utah, Juab, Millard, Sanpete, and Washington counties. Recent published reports include those of Killpack (1951:99) and Behle and Ghiselin (1958:19) for the Uinta Basin and Behle et al. (1964:455) for Tooele County. Treganza (field notes) reportedly found two nests and noted several birds on the flat between Garfield and Saltair, Salt Lake County, but the dates are not available. Another record of breeding at Murray (AOU Check-list 1957:585) was apparently based on a report by Behle and Selander (1952:31), who took a male in breeding condition at that locality on 11 June 1950. Porter and Egoscue (1954:219–221) gave a very complete account (28 specimens, 98 observations) of this species in Utah.

Zonotrichia iliaca (Merrem)
Fox Sparrow

STATUS: The Fox Sparrow is a sparse breeding species particularly in the northern part of the state. It is also a migrant, but a few possibly winter here. It inhabits thickets usually near running water or springs and ranges from the lower valleys well into the mountains. In the 1930s it was rather common in Utah Valley especially along Provo River, but in recent years it has become very scarce (Hayward field notes).

RECORDS: Ridgway (1877:486–487) found it to be an abundant breeder in Parley's Park, 25 miles east of Salt Lake City, in the summer of 1869. Allen (1872b:168) observed it near Ogden, Weber County, 10 September 1871. Henshaw (1875:293) took a specimen near Provo, Utah County. There have since been numerous records, mostly from northern Utah. Brigham Young University has the following specimens from Utah: Long Lake, Uinta Mountains, 21 July 1930; Provo, Utah County, 18 March 1932, 25 June 1932, 4 April 1935, 3 March 1958; Sheep Creek Watershed, Sevier County, 3 May 1969.

SUBSPECIES: The Utah population was referred to the race Z. i. swarthi by Behle and Selander on the basis of the "decided gray color to the head and back" (1951a: 364). However, Ridgway (1901:395) has used this same character to distinguish the race Z. i. schistacea. Phillips et al. (1964: 24) considered swarthi to be a synonym of schistacea, but Paynter, in Check-list of Birds of the World (1970[13]:44–45), has recognized Z. i. swarthi as the race found in Utah.

Zonotrichia melodia (Wilson)
Song Sparrow

STATUS: The Song Sparrow is a common resident species throughout the state. It is confined mainly to thickets along valley streams or irrigation canals or occurs around the borders of lakes and ponds wherever there are thickets or emergent vegetation providing ample cover for nesting and feeding.

RECORDS: All of the early naturalists including Allen (1872a:168), Merriam (1873: 682), Henshaw (1874:6), Ridgway (1877:482–483), and others found this bird in abundance throughout the state and collected many specimens as well as their nests and eggs. Numerous specimens taken more recently are in the collections of the various institutions of the state.

SUBSPECIES: The race now known as Z. m. montana is the breeding and also wintering form throughout most of the state of Utah. Z. m. fallax, at one time named Melospiza melodia virginis (Marshall and Behle 1942:123), occurs in a limited area of the lower Virgin River drainage in Washington County. Intergradation between fallax and montana seems to occur in south central and southeastern Utah (Behle 1948a:79–80). However, Wauer (1969:334) collected a female of the race montana on a nest at St. George, Washington County, 17 June 1966. Two specimens in the Brigham Young University from Bear Lake Valley near the Utah-Idaho border show some features of Z. m. merrilli and indicate intergradation with montana. Behle and Ross (1945:170) reported a specimen taken in the winter near Hooper, Weber County, which also showed characteristics of merrilli. Worthen (1968:465) recorded two specimens of Z. m. merrilli in the University of Utah collection from Delta, Millard County, 18 December 1965. Fisher (1893: 100) reported that Bailey collected a specimen of the subspecies guttata at Santa Clara, Washington County, 13 January 1889. Later Ridgway (1901:361) considered this specimen to be a representative of the race merrilli, which seems to be valid in that the American Ornithologists Union Check-list (1957:632–633) lists merrilli as wintering in southern Utah at Santa Clara. Four specimens in the Royal Ontario Museum taken near Jensen, Uintah County, in the spring of 1935, were identified by P. A. Taverner as Z. m. juddi (Twomey 1942: 476). Behle (1958:37) reported five specimens of the subspecies fisherella taken at Yost, Raft River, and Grouse Creek, Box Elder County, 18–19 September 1941. Since there seems to be some latitudinal migration among song sparrows, it is likely that individuals of these several races may appear in the winter population or as migrants out of their breeding range.

Zonotrichia lincolnii (Audubon)
Lincoln's Sparrow

STATUS: A rather common summer bird of the mountains of the state where it nests in boggy areas, especially where there is a growth of willows or other low-growing shrubs. In spring and fall it appears as a migrant near water in the lower valleys. Most of the migration takes place during April-May and September-October.

RECORDS: The first specimen was taken by the Stansbury expedition to Great Salt Lake, 21 March 1850 (Baird 1852:317). This was most likely a migrating bird. Remy (1860[2]:450) included it in his list of Utah birds in 1855. Ridgway (1877:485) found it plentiful as a migrant in the lower valleys and nesting at Parley's Park, Summit County, in 1868–69. Stevenson (1872:465) collected a specimen at the head of Henry's Fork, Summit County, in 1870. Allen (1872b:168) found it to be exceedingly abundant at Ogden, Weber County, in 1871. Henshaw (1874:6) considered it to be rather uncommon. He collected a specimen in Grass Valley, Sevier County, 10 October 1872 (Henshaw 1875:283–284). Numerous records and collections of both migrating and breeding birds have been made in more recent years.

SUBSPECIES: Most of the birds taken in Utah, whether breeding or migrating, seem to belong to the race *Z. l. alticola*, a larger race proposed by Miller and McCabe (1935:156). All of the specimens in Brigham Young University fall within the size range of that subspecies. The subspecies *Z. l. lincolnii* may also be found in the migrating population. Behle (1941b:184) reported a specimen from Moab, Grand County, 9 April 1938. It has also been collected at the junction of the Virgin River and Santa Clara Creek, Washington County, 9 September 1941 (Behle 1943a:78), and near Vernal and Jenson, Uintah County, in May and September 1937 (Twomey 1942:475). Early records of *Z. l. lincolnii* prior to the naming of *Z. l. alticola* are somewhat

doubtful. Worthen (1968:461) obtained a specimen of the race *lincolnii* from Clear Lake, Millard County, 20 March 1965.

Zonotrichia georgiana ericrypta
(Oberholser)
Swamp Sparrow

STATUS: An uncommon winter visitor in Utah to be looked for in large flocks of White-crowned Sparrows.

RECORDS: Henshaw (1875:285) collected a specimen near Washington, Washington County, 23 October 1872. Behle (1954b:313) reported a specimen taken in Salt Lake City, Salt Lake County, by Boyd Shaffer, 20 February 1952. The specimen was placed in the Tracy Aviary of that city. Wauer and Russell (1967:423) gave two more records of this species in the Virgin River Valley. One specimen was collected at Springdale Ponds, Washington County, 2 March 1965, and is in the Zion Park collection. There is also a sight record on 9 February 1966 near the confluence of the Virgin and Santa Clara rivers, Washington County. Carter (Scott 1965:501) recorded a specimen taken at Arches National Monument, Grand County, 19 May 1965.

Zonotrichia querula (Nuttall)
Harris' Sparrow

STATUS: A regular but uncommon winter resident in most parts of Utah. Wauer (1969:334) considered this species to be a regular winter visitor in the Virgin River Valley of southwestern Utah. It is usually found in company with flocks of White-crowned Sparrows or juncos living in lower and warmer valleys.

RECORDS: This species was not reported by early naturalist visitors to the state but could have easily been overlooked because of its casual association with flocks of more common sparrows. Published collection records of more recent years are as follows: Linwood, Daggett County, 26 November 1916 (Cottam 1942b:255); Centerville,

Davis County, 9 February 1937 (Woodbury 1939:162); Wellsville, Cache County, 17 April 1937 (Stanford 1938:145); Price, Carbon County, 28 December 1941 (Behle and Higgins 1942:54); Nephi, Juab County, 15 March 1942 (Long 1943:39); Mt. Pleasant, Sanpete County, 4 February 1951 (Behle and Selander 1952:31); Government Well, Tooele County, 21 October 1953 (Porter 1954:363); Santa Clara, Washington County, 16 December 1939 (Behle and Higgins 1942:54). Brigham Young University has the following specimens from Utah: Myton, Duchesne County, 4 and 29 December 1955; two specimens, near Magna, Salt Lake County, 7 January 1971. Several sight records have also been published (Kashin 1964b:293, 1966:351, 1967:347; Wauer 1965a:311).

Zonotrichia leucophrys (Forster)
White-crowned Sparrow
Fig. 48, p. 127

STATUS: A common year-round resident in Utah with one race breeding in the mountains throughout the state and another wintering in large flocks in the foothills and valleys.

RECORDS: Specimens of this sparrow were taken by most of the early ornithologists who visited Utah. Ridgway (1877:470–471) found it nesting in the Wasatch Mountains in June and July 1869. Stevenson (1872:464) reported specimens taken by the Hayden expedition on Green River in October 1870. Allen (1872b:177) collected specimens from near Ogden, Weber County, in September 1871. Henshaw (1875:260–263) collected it from several localities in the state in the fall of 1872 and thought that it bred in the Wasatch Mountains. Many records from all of the counties of the state have since been recorded.

SUBSPECIES: The race breeding within the state has been called Z. l. oriantha, named originally from the Warner Mountains near Adel, Oregon (Oberholser 1932. 12). This name was extended by Miller (1941:262) to include the Utah breeding population. Banks (1964:114) was unable to separate Z. l. oriantha from Z. l. leucophrys from eastern North America and considered the former to be a synonym of the latter. Paynter in Check-list of Birds of the World (1970[13]:60–61) feels justified in retaining the name oriantha, however. The race Z. l. gambelii, distinguished on the basis of white rather than black lories, seems to be quite distinct. It is the common wintering subspecies in Utah, although lesser numbers of Z. l. oriantha may also appear in the wintering flocks.

Zonotrichia albicollis (Gmelin)
White-throated Sparrow

STATUS: The White-throated Sparrow appears to be a sparse winter resident or migrant in Utah. It should be looked for in flocks of wintering White-crowned Sparrows or juncos.

RECORDS: Porter (1954:364) reported collecting one specimen at Orr's Ranch, Tooele County, 12 October 1953. Wauer and Russell (1967:423) collected a female at Oak Creek Canyon, Zion National Park, Washington County, 29 October 1965. Merlin L. Killpack (pers. comm.) captured one in a banding operation at Ogden, Weber County, 15 December 1963. The specimen was banded and released. Other records from Utah that we have been able to find are sight records. They are as follows: Box Elder, Salt Lake and Utah counties, between 14 October and 15 May (no years) (Woodbury et al. 1949:35); Springdale, Washington County, 20 November 1964 (Wauer and Carter 1965:85); Terry Ranch, Beaver Dam Wash, Washington County, 15 May 1965, and near St. George, Washington County, 11 January 1966 (Wauer and Russell 1967:423); near Cedar City, Iron County, 5 October 1966 (Scott 1967:64); Arches National Monument, Grand County, 30 December 1966 (Carter 1967b:345); Arrowhead Mine, southern Utah, fall 1969 (Scott 1970:75); Stansbury Mountains,

Tooele County, 18 October 1972 (Kingery 1973:96); Zion National Park, early May 1973 (Kingery 1973:802).

Zonotrichia atricapilla (Gmelin)
Golden-crowned Sparrow

STATUS: A rare but seemingly regular winter resident in lower and warmer valleys throughout the state. It is likely to be found with flocks of White-crowned Sparrows.

RECORDS: In Zion Canyon, Washington County, a bird was captured on 16 January 1936 and eventually made into a study skin (Long 1936:89–90). One was also taken at Standrod, Box Elder County, 4 October 1947 (Greenhalgh 1948:46). Porter (1954: 364) reported collecting a specimen at Cane Springs, west side of Cedar Mountains, Tooele County, 13 October 1952. A number of sight records are also available. These include: Zion National Park, 7 March 1942 (Woodbury et al. 1949:35); Zion National Park, 22 April 1963, and Springdale Ponds, Washington County, 13 April 1964 and March 1965 (Wauer and Carter 1965: 85); Santa Clara, Washington County, 28 December 1965 (Wauer and Russell 1967: 423); St. George, Washington County, 29 December 1969 (Lund 1970:416); Zion National Park, 27 January 1974 (Kingery 1974: 672); Logan, Cache County, 25 April 1975 (Kingery 1975:889). A Golden-crowned Sparrow was trapped, banded, and observed at Logan from 26 March until 3 May 1976 by Balph (1976:67). She thought this bird might have wintered in the Logan area.

Junco hyemalis (Linnaeus)
Dark-eyed Junco
Fig. 55, p. 146

STATUS: A common year-round resident of the state composed of two subspecies that breed in the mountains and several subspecies that winter in the area. In summer the nesting birds are confined almost entirely to montane forest communities. In winter large flocks occur, especially in lower valleys and foothills, but they may be found at almost any elevation where ground food is available.

RECORDS: Collections and observations of this abundant species by early collectors in the state as well as by more recent observers are numerous for all parts of the area. No attempt will be made to list them here.

SUBSPECIES: Several forms of the Junco in the United States previously considered to be separate species are now regarded as subspecies of *Junco hyemalis.* (Mayr and Short 1970:86; AOU Check-list 1973: 418). This is because more field work has indicated that there is a general overlapping and hybridization wherever the breeding populations of the several forms meet. *J. h. caniceps* appears to be the breeding subspecies in the mountains through most of Utah. However, *J. h. mearnsi* breeds in the Wasatch Mountains of extreme northern Utah. In this area the two breeding forms hybridize commonly. Wintering juncos in Utah are primarily of the race *J. h. montanus,* which is of an extremely variable group somewhat confused with *J. h. shufeldti,* which may also occur in the wintering populations. Smaller numbers of *J. h. hyemalis* (Behle and Higgins 1942:54–55) — *J. h. mearnsi, J. h. caniceps, J. h. cismontanus* (Behle 1941b:184), and possibly other races — also appear in winter, usually in mixed flocks.

Ammodramus sandwichensis (Gmelin)
Savannah Sparrow

STATUS: A common summer resident March through September throughout most of the state except in the warmer desert areas of southwestern Utah where it occurs mainly in winter. It lives in salt grass meadows and open pasture lands around the borders of lakes and ponds.

RECORDS: Ridgway (1877:464–465) collected specimens, nests, and eggs from several localities near Salt Lake City, Salt

Lake County, in May, June, and July 1869. Henshaw (1875:254–255) took six specimens near Provo, Utah County, in July and August 1872. Nelson (1875:346) collected a specimen near Salt Lake City on 7 July 1872. During the years 1888 to 1893, Bailey (field notes) recorded several collections and observations in Utah as follows: Ogden, Weber County, 8 October; Kanab, Kane County, 21 December; Virgin River Valley, Washington County, January; Fairfield, Utah County, abundant in meadows, 20–30 July; Laketown, Rich County, 25 July. Many records of birds and nesting activities have been recorded recently.

SUBSPECIES: The common and apparently only breeding subspecies within the state is A. s. nevadensis. A specimen taken by Vernon Bailey and now in the U.S. National Museum of Natural History was collected at Ogden, Weber County, 8 October 1888, and is considered to belong to the race A. s. anthinus (Woodbury et al. 1949:33). A second specimen of this race now in the University of Utah was taken by Behle (1943a:74) at Santa Clara, Washington County, 19 December 1939. Porter and Bushman (1956:153) have reported three specimens of anthinus from Orr's Ranch, Skull Valley, Tooele County, 13, 14, 21 April 1954. Wauer (1969:334) reported three specimens from Washington County: a female taken at Washington on 14 January 1966, a male at the same locality on 18 February 1966, and another male at St. George on 4 March 1966. Worthen (1968: 437) recorded a male anthinus from Wah Wah Spring, Beaver County, 24 May 1962.

Ammodramus leconteii (Audubon)
Le Conte's Sparrow

STATUS: This is a species of rare or accidental occurrence in Utah. The only known specimens were noted in winter and spring.

RECORDS: A specimen at Brigham Young University was taken two miles southwest of Provo, Utah County, 24 December 1927,

by Cottam (1941a:116). Three others were seen near the same locality on 10 March 1928 (Woodbury et al. 1949:33). Carter (Scott 1966:537) observed one at Moab, Grand County, 19 April 1966.

Ammodramus savannarum perpallidus
(Coues)
Grasshopper Sparrow

STATUS: Formerly a common breeder in the valleys of northern Utah; now very rare. Early observers reported that this bird lived in the dry grassy plains. Since most of the dry grasslands in Utah were soon taken up for farmlands or else were heavily overgrazed, it is likely that the species' disappearance was a result of the loss of its native habitat. By the restoration of much of this grassland in recent years it is possible that the Grasshopper Sparrow might become reestablished.

RECORDS: Ridgway (1877:467) obtained the type specimen of this bird from Antelope Island, Great Salt Lake, 4 June 1869, and considered it to be abundant. Allen (1872b:167) found it common in September 1871 near Ogden, Weber County, and Merriam (1873:706) found it nesting there on 5 June 1872. Henshaw (1875:257–258) took a specimen near Gunnison, Sanpete County, 7 September 1872. Nelson (1875: 346) found it common in the fields near Bountiful, Davis County, in 1872. Bailey (field notes) reported sighting a specimen north of Ogden in July 1893 and stated that they were common. Pearson (1927:381) referred to it at Currant Creek, Wasatch County, and Cottam and Williams observed one near Stewart's Lake, Jensen, Uintah County, 21 September 1941. Behle and Ross (1945:169) obtained a specimen 10 miles west of Salt Lake City, Salt Lake County, 20 September 1942. Behle et al. (1964:455–456) reported one taken near Camel Back Mountain, Tooele County, 19 September 1961.

Spizella arborea ochracae Brewster
Tree Sparrow

STATUS: A rather common winter resident in the central valleys of the state from late September to early May. It is more common in northern Utah than it is farther southward. Its wintering habitat includes brushy areas where it is often found with Song Sparrows and White-crowned Sparrows.

RECORDS: Stevenson (1872:465) reported collecting specimens on Green River and Henry's Fork near the Utah-Wyoming border, 11 October 1870. Henshaw (1875: 277) found it to be common at Provo, Utah County, in December 1872, and a few were observed around Beaver, Beaver County, during the first part of November 1872. Bailey and Loring (field notes) reported them from Manti and Gunnison, Sanpete County, in December 1888, and from Bluff, San Juan County, in November 1893. There are many recent records from nearly all the counties of the state.

Spizella passerina arizonae Coues
Chipping Sparrow
Fig. 56, p. 147

STATUS: A common summer resident throughout the state from April into October. This species ranges in altitudinal distribution from montane coniferous forests to valley woodlands and brushlands. It is less common in very dry deserts. During migration it often appears in sizable flocks, especially in sagebrush communities.

RECORDS: Early ornithological work in Utah including that done by Allen (1872b: 168), Henshaw (1875:277–278), and Ridgway (1877:479) all commented on the abundance of the Chipping Sparrow in Utah. Several hundred records, representing all sections of the state, have more lately accumulated.

Spizella atrogularis evura Coues
Black-chinned Sparrow

STATUS: A rather common species of the Virgin River Valley in southwestern Utah. It lives in brushy areas in canyons and apparently breeds there. There is some indication that it may have increased in numbers in more recent years (Wauer and Carter 1965:84).

RECORDS: The earliest record of this species for Utah seems to be that of Hardy and Higgins (1940:110), who observed them on 8 April 1939 and collected them near the summit of Beaver Dam Mountains, Washington County, 20 May 1939 and 16 June 1939. Behle (1940:224) obtained four specimens at Danish Ranch, near Leeds, Washington County, 20-30 April 1939. Wauer and Carter (1965:84) reported this species as being a "fairly common summer resident" in Zion National Park, Washington County. Their records range from 22 April to 14 September.

Spizella pallida (Swainson)
Clay-colored Sparrow

STATUS: A rare and probably accidental visitor in Utah.

RECORDS: Knowlton (1937:165) collected a specimen at Dolomite, Tooele County, 21 September 1934. Behle and Perry (1975:44) report that Gleb Kashin saw one at Spirit Lake, Daggett County, late August 1961, and that Stewart Murie saw this species many times in the area of Cedar City, Iron County, in the spring and fall of 1963, 1964, and 1965.

Spizella breweri breweri Cassin
Brewer's Sparrow
Fig. 49, p. 130

STATUS: A very common summer resident of Utah where it is known to occur from mid-April to mid-October. It lives primarily in sagebrush lands or in mixed sage and grasslands. In late summer and fall it gathers in large flocks where it may be seen along roadways or on its breeding grounds.

RECORDS: Baird (1876:379) reported specimens taken by McCarthy of the Simpson explorations in areas of uncertain location in western Utah, 9 May 1859. Ridgway (1877:481) found it nesting in abundance in sagebrush near Salt Lake City, Salt Lake County, and collected 22 sets of eggs in May and June 1869. Allen (1872b:168) apparently confused it with the Clay-colored Sparrow but considered it to be common around Ogden, Weber County, in September 1871. Bailey (field notes 1893), after much travel in the state, concluded that it was common all through the sagebrush communities. In more recent years there have been many hundreds of records from every county.

Pooecetes gramineus (Gmelin)
Vesper Sparrow

STATUS: A common breeding bird of sagebrush areas throughout the state. It appears to be most abundant in higher valleys where it occupies the same habitat as the equally common Brewer's Sparrow. Like the latter species, it often appears in flocks during spring and fall migrations in March, April, and September.

RECORDS: Abundant records of occurrence are available from early collectors in the state as well as from more recent observers. Ridgway (1877:466) found it breeding at Parley's Park, Summit County, in June and July 1869. Four specimens now in the U.S. National Museum of Natural History were taken by the Hayden expedition on the north slope of the Uinta Mountains in September 1870 (Stevenson 1872:464). Henshaw (1875:256) considered the Vesper Sparrow and Savannah Sparrow to be the most common species of sparrows in the state. It is still an abundant species.

SUBSPECIES: *P. g. confinis* is the common breeding and migrant subspecies found in Utah. *P. g. affinis*, which is a smaller and more brownish race, appears to be an uncommon migrant. A specimen of this race in the University of Utah collection was taken at King's Ranch, Henry Mountains,

Garfield County, 9 September 1929 (Stanford 1931:10). Another specimen at Brigham Young University is from Panguitch, Garfield County, 20 August 1934. More recently Behle and Selander (1952:31) have reported specimens from St. George, Washington County, 11 September 1941, and from Farmington Bay Refuge, Davis County, 1 September 1949. Behle (1959:34) reported a specimen collected by Cottam at Yost, Box Elder County, 18 September 1941.

Chondestes grammacus strigatus
Swainson
Lark Sparrow

STATUS: A summer resident breeder found throughout the state from April through September. It may winter in southern Utah where Wauer and Carter (1965:82) saw three birds near Rockville, Washington County, 29 December 1964. It inhabits open brush communities mainly in the lower foothills and valleys. Areas of scattered sagebrush seem to provide the most favorable nesting habitat.

RECORDS: Ridgway (1877:470) found this species nesting under sagebrush around Salt Lake City, Salt Lake County, and collected several specimens in May and June 1869. Nelson (1875:346) found it abundant in flocks near Bountiful, Davis County, in July and August 1872. Henshaw (1875:259–260) encountered it in many localities and took six specimens near Provo, Utah County. Bailey (field notes) found it common during his travels in Utah in 1890, 1891, and 1893. In recent years many reports have listed it as a common species in suitable habitat.

Aimophila[17] bilineata deserticola
(Ridgway)
Black-throated Sparrow
Figs. 50, 51; pp. 133, 136

STATUS: A summer resident throughout

---

[17]Phillips et al. (1964:202) and Mayr and Short (1970:84) concur in merging the former genus *Amphispiza* into *Aimophila*.

much of the state from late April to September. This sparrow is more common to the drier desert country, especially the more saline communities where shadscale, greasewood, and other low shrubs are found. It is more abundant southward, and a few may winter in the Virgin River Valley of southwestern Utah (Hardy and Higgins 1940:109).

RECORDS: This sparrow seems not to have been noted by a number of the early ornithologists who visited Utah. However, Ridgway (1877:475–476) collected specimens and nests around the Great Salt Lake and on Antelope Island in May and June 1869, and Merriam (Fisher 1893:96) found it in 1891 on both slopes of the Beaver Dam Mountains and in the lower Santa Clara Valley, both localities in Washington County. He found several nests with eggs and considered it an abundant breeding bird. Among the more northern records are three specimens in the Brigham Young University collection from Cedar Valley, Utah County, 3 May 1936. Other northern records for the state are: Behle (1955:30) Fish Springs, Juab County, 25 June 1946; Behle (1958:34) Standrod, Box Elder County, 19 May 1948. There are numerous records from the southern counties of the state.

Aimophila belli nevadensis (Ridgway)
Sage Sparrow
Figs. 52, 53; pp. 139, 141

STATUS: A rather sparse summer resident throughout much of the state confined to sagebrush, greasewood, and other shrubs of the open valleys. In the northern part of the state it occurs on the nesting grounds from late March into October. Wintering birds may be found in the Virgin River Valley in southwestern Utah (Wauer and Carter 1965:83) and in southern Nevada (Phillips et al. 1964:201–202).

RECORDS: Ridgway (1877:476) found this sparrow less abundant than the Black-throated Sparrow in the deserts around

Great Salt Lake in 1869. Stevenson (1872:465) made records of specimens collected on the north slope of the Uinta Mountains and Green River (Wyoming?) in early October 1870. Allen (1872b:168) found it common in sagebrush near Ogden, Weber County, in September 1871. Henshaw (1875:276) reported collecting specimens in Iron and Washington counties in October 1872. Bailey (field notes) found it wintering around St. George, Washington County, January 1889. More recently many collection and sight records have come from most of the counties of the state.

Aimophila ruficeps scottii (Sennett)
Rufous-crowned Sparrow

STATUS: An uncommon resident of southwestern Utah where it has been found in the warmer canyons in Zion National Park. Scanty records indicate that it is both a wintering and breeding species in that area.

RECORDS: There is some question as to when this species was first observed in Utah. Scott (1964:60) indicated that a specimen was collected in Oak Creek Canyon, Zion National Park, Washington County, 25 October 1963. Wauer and Carter (1965:82) mentioned the first record of this species as being collected 25 October 1964. Wauer (1965:447), in his summary of the Rufous-crowned Sparrow in Utah, indicated the first bird collected was on 5 November 1963 and that the first bird recorded was one banded 3 November 1963. This bird banded in November was recaptured 2 December 1963 and 4 March 1964, indicating that it wintered in Zion National Park during 1963–64. Wauer in this same report indicated different sightings, collections, or bandings between 3 November 1963 and 30 January 1965. There is also a report of nesting at Zion National Park, 28 June 1966 (Scott 1966:589). Lund (1968b:361) noted a sight record for Zion National Park, 27 December 1968, and Scott (1974:489) reported another at Zion, 17 December 1973.

Fig. 63. House Finch. Cedar Mountain, Tooele County, Utah, 30 June 1953. Photo by R. D. Porter and R. J. Erwin.

Pipilo chlorurus (Audubon)
Green-tailed Towhee

STATUS: A common summer resident and breeder in foothills and mountains throughout the state. It may occur rarely in winter (Bader 1948:109). It nests in shrubby communities where there is rather dense cover from 5,000 feet to timberline and frequently wanders into the alpine when the young are grown. During migration it may also appear in shrubs or streamside thickets in lower valleys.

RECORDS: This species was included in most of the early lists of Utah birds. Ridgway (1877:496–497) considered it to be common in various localities around Salt Lake City in 1869. Two specimens in the U.S. National Museum of Natural History were taken by the Hayden Expedition to the Uinta Mountains, 20 September 1870. Allen (1872b:168) found it common around

Ogden, Weber County, after 20 September 1871. Henshaw (1875:309) collected specimens in central Utah in August and September 1872. Such travelers through the state as Merriam, Bailey, Preble, and Osgood all recorded the Green-tailed Towhee in their field notes. Many records of birds and nests have been reported more recently from all the counties of the state.

Pipilo erythrophthalmus (Linnaeus)
Rufous-sided Towhee

STATUS: This towhee is a common inhabitant of shrubby lower slopes of the mountains throughout most of the state. It is especially common in the oakbrush community of the Wasatch Front where it lives the year around. A few individuals also breed in thickets along the valley streams. In winter there is some altitudinal as well as latitudinal migration, particularly of those birds breeding at higher elevations or farther north.

RECORDS: Ridgway (1877:494–495) considered this species to be common around Salt Lake City, Salt Lake County, and took several specimens as well as six nests with eggs between 20 May and 18 June 1869. Allen (1872b:168) found it at Ogden, Weber County, September 1871, and Merriam (1872:684, 708) collected eight skins and three sets of eggs in the same locality in June 1872. Henshaw (1875:303–304) reported taking specimens at Provo, Utah County, and in Washington County in July, August, late October, and November 1872. The field notes of Bailey, Preble, Osgood, and Birdseye also contain records of this bird from many localities in Utah. Numerous records from all of the counties of the state are available for more recent years.

SUBSPECIES: The breeding and common migrating and wintering subspecies in Utah is *P. e. montanus*. There was some confusion in the early literature on Utah birds, and many of the migrants were regarded as *P. e. arcticus* (Ridgway 1901:416). The only confirmed record of this latter race known to us is that of a specimen in the U.S. National Museum of Natural History taken by Yarrow and Henshaw at Provo, 30 November 1872 (Woodbury et al. 1949:32). This identification was made by J. W. Aldrich and A. R. Phillips.

Pipilo aberti aberti Baird
Abert's Towhee

STATUS: A resident of the Virgin River Valley in extreme southwestern Utah. It inhabits tall leafy shrubbery of streamsides.

RECORDS: Henshaw (1875:307) reported specimens from Washington and St. George, Washington County. Bailey took a specimen in Santa Clara Canyon, Washington County, 15 January 1889 (U.S. National Museum of Natural History). Fisher (1893:105) noted that Merriam found it

"breeding commonly" near St. George in May 1891. Birdseye (field notes) found it common in brushy areas at Washington, Washington County, and collected a specimen in early November 1909 (U.S. National Museum of Natural History). Wauer and Carter (1965:82) considered it common at Washington and St. George.

Spiza americana (Gmelin)
Dickcissel

STATUS: A casual or possibly accidental visitor to Utah.

RECORDS: The only collection record of this species known to us was taken at Provo, Utah County, 25 May 1964 (Frost 1966:126). One was seen at the Jordan Narrows, Utah County, 12 June 1955 (Kashin 1955:39) and five were observed in the Salt Lake Cemetery, Salt Lake County, 1 October 1959 (Scott 1960:60).

Pheucticus ludovicianus (Linnaeus)
Rose-breasted Grosbeak

STATUS: This species is of rare and rather irregular occurrence in Utah, found particularly in the southern and western parts of the state.

RECORDS: Behle (1973b:245) has summarized the collection and well-verified sight records known for this species to the present time: Kanab, Kane County, 26 April 1935 (sight, Behle et al. 1958:79); Salt Lake City, Salt Lake County, 4 August 1955 (not heretofore recorded, collected but not saved); Springdale Ponds, Washington County, 3 May 1965 (collected, Wauer and Carter 1965:78); Kanab, 7 June 1965 (sight, oral report from Wauer); Arches National Park, Grand County, 26 May 1965 (collected, Behle 1966:396–397); Fish Springs National Wildlife Refuge, Juab County, 2 June 1965 (collected) and 4 June 1965 (sight); Terry Ranch, Beaver Dam Wash, Washington County, 19 May 1972 (collected, Behle 1973b:245). Kingery (1975:889) reported one at Zion National Park, Washington County, in the spring of 1975.

Pheucticus melanocephalus melanocephalus (Swainson)
Black-headed Grosbeak

STATUS: A common summer resident throughout the state where it occurs from late April to September. It lives primarily in deciduous woodlands of the mountains and streamsides of the valleys. It adapts rather well to human populations and is frequently found in ornamental trees of towns and parks.

RECORDS: McCarthy, a collector of Simpson's expedition, took specimens in Skull and Rush valleys, Tooele County, about 1859 (Baird 1876:379). Ridgway (1877:489) took specimens near Salt Lake City, Salt Lake County in 1869. Henshaw in 1872 (1874:6; 1875:298) regarded it as common in Utah, but found it particularly numerous at Provo, Utah County, where he collected 11 specimens. Fisher (1893:106) reported that Merriam found it plentiful along Santa Clara River, Washington County, in May 1891. In more recent times there have been numerous observations and collections from all the counties of the state.

Passerina caerulea interfusa (Dwight and Griscom)
Blue Grosbeak

STATUS: A summer resident of shrubs and thickets usually near water from April to September. Early records indicate that it is primarily a bird of southern Utah, but more recent observations show that it is well distributed in lower valleys of more northern counties although it is less common northward.

RECORDS: A specimen in the U.S. National Museum of Natural History was collected by Vernon Bailey near St. George, Washington County, 14 May 1891. Fisher (1893:106) reported that Merriam found it to be common in the lower Santa Clara Valley, Washington County, 11–15 May 1891. More northern records have appeared in recent years: Behle and Selander (1952:31) report records for Vernal, Uintah

County, June 1950 and 4 August 1951. A specimen at Brigham Young University was taken at Myton, Duchesne County, 8 June 1957 (Killpack and Hayward 1958:24). Behle et al. (1964:455) recorded specimens from Lehi, Utah County, 29 June 1961. Roger Tory Peterson observed it at Farmington Bay Refuge, Davis County, 22 August 1962 (Behle et al. 1964:455). Geoghegan (1959:41; 1963:40–42) observed a single bird on 14 June 1959 and a pair on 9 June 1963 at Jordan Narrows, Utah County. Two pairs were seen at Grantsville, Tooele County, 31 May 1964 (Utah Audubon News 1964:42). A pair was observed by Frost at Provo Airport, Utah County, on several occasions during the summer of 1968.

Passerina amoena (Say)
Lazuli Bunting

STATUS: A summer resident from early May to early September occupying streamside shrubbery and mountain brush lands up to 9,000 feet.

RECORDS: Ridgway (1875:490–491) found it in Utah in 1869, where he noted it most frequently in streamside shrubs and found it nesting at Parley's Park, Summit County. Allen (1872b:168) found it not common near Ogden, Weber County, in September 1871. Henshaw (1875:300–301) reported it to be common in streamside vegetation near Provo, Utah County, in 1872 and recorded it from several other localities in the state. Later, field observers recorded the Lazuli Bunting in their field books: Powell at Gunnison, Sanpete County, in 1873; Bailey at many places from 1890 to 1893; Loring near Bear Lake, Rich County, in 1893. Merriam found it in the lower Santa Clara Valley, Washington County, where it was found nesting in May 1891 (Fisher 1893:107). Many specimens and observations have been made more recently, and there are numerous specimens in the several institutions of the state and elsewhere.

Passerina cyanea (Linnaeus)
Indigo Bunting

STATUS: A sparse breeding species in the Virgin River Valley of southwestern Utah and appearing elsewhere rarely during migration.

RECORDS: Hardy (1939:86) reported a specimen taken at St. George, Washington County, 11 July 1937. Behle (1943a:70) mentioned a sight record for St. George, 14 May 1940. Cottam (1941:122) observed a specimen at the mouth of Zion Canyon, Washington County, 21 July 1940. Wells (1958:223) observed a pair of Indigo Buntings along Leeds Creek in Pine Valley Mountains, Washington County, 6 June to 1 August 1957. Wauer and Carter (1965:79) listed a number of records from the Zion Park area, including several from Springdale, Washington County. One male was banded at Oak Creek Canyon by Wauer on 1 July 1963. Records from outside the Virgin River Valley are all sight observations. Scott (1957:368; 1966:537; 1968:633) reported specimens from Saratoga Springs, Utah County, 30 May 1957; near Provo, Utah County, 8 May 1966; and Cedar Valley, Iron County, 7 June 1968. Carl Wadsworth (field notes) observed a single male with a flock of Lazuli Buntings at Sheep Creek watershed, Sevier County, 22 August 1968. Worthen (1972b:220) collected one on the University of Utah campus, Salt Lake City, Salt Lake County, 20 May 1966. Whitmore (1975:509) has summarized the more recent records of the species.

Piranga rubra cooperi (Ridgway)
Summer Tanager

STATUS: Not reported in the state prior to 1962 (Zimmerman 1962:498). This species seems to have become fairly well established as a breeder in streamside cottonwoods and willows at Beaver Dam Wash and in the Virgin River Valley in Washington County. It has been reported as far north as Eureka, Juab County (Behle and Perry 1975:40).

RECORDS: Carter (Zimmerman 1962:498) observed the first specimen at Beaver Dam Wash, 3 August 1962. A few weeks later Murie (1963:45) reported one from near Parowan, Iron County, 21 August 1962. In 1963 three birds were observed by Wauer near Santa Clara, Washington County, one on 30 July and two on 19 September (Monson 1964:63). Easterla (1966:210) in 1964 reported the following sightings at the Terry Ranch, Beaver Dam Wash: one singing male, 20 May; two pairs, 10 June; one immature, 3 September; one adult male, 24 September. He also reported seeing a female about one mile west of Santa Clara on 22 July. On the following day at the same locality he saw another female and found a dead female which was made into a study skin and is now in the University of Utah collection, no. 18458. This was the first collection record for the state. Wauer and Russell (1967:422) observed a female and immature at the Terry Ranch on 25 August 1965 and two females at Santa Clara on 7 September 1965. Wauer (1969:334) collected a male at Berry Spring near Hurricane, Washington County, 11 May 1966. This specimen extended the range another 20 miles north along the Virgin River, indicating that in the future it may be found further north into Utah where suitable habitat is available. A specimen in Brigham Young University was collected near Santa Clara, 18 May 1974. Kingery (1975:889) reported one at Zion National Park, Washington County, during the spring of 1975.

Piranga ludoviciana (Wilson)
Western Tanager

STATUS: A common summer resident of mountains throughout the state where it inhabits coniferous and aspen forests. In May and early June and again in late August and September it often appears as a migrant in lower valleys where it is commonly seen in streamside woodlands and in ornamental trees.

RECORDS: Early naturalists who visited Utah reported the Western Tanager to be a common species. Ridgway (1877:455) found it breeding in the Wasatch and Uinta mountains during the summer of 1869. Allen (1872b:167) considered it frequent near Ogden, Weber County, in September 1871. Henshaw (1875:235–236) found it at Provo, Utah County, where he took an adult male on 29 July 1872. Many records from most of the counties of the state indicate that it is still a common species in the area.

FAMILY PARULIDAE

Mniotilta varia (Linnaeus)
Black and White Warbler

STATUS: This warbler is an accidental or casual visitor in Utah.

RECORDS: Behle and Selander (1952:30) reported a specimen found dead in Salt Lake City, Salt Lake County, 10 December 1951. Lockerbie (1953:79) recorded one seen at Centerville, Davis County, between 25 May and 6 June 1953. Kingery (1976: 105) reported one at Santa Clara, Washington County, 5 July 1975.

Vermivora celata (Say)
Orange-crowned Warbler

STATUS: A common breeding species and migrant throughout the state. Its summer habitat is principally the brush-covered slopes of the mountains at mid-elevations, but during spring and fall migration it may be found in streamside woodlands of the lower valleys. A small number winter in the Virgin River Valley, Washington County (Wauer 1969:333).

RECORDS: Early records include those of Ridgway (1877:429–430), who found this warbler at Parley's Park, Summit County, where he took specimens on 17 July and

12, 16 August 1869. He also noted numerous fall migrants in streamside shrubbery in the lower canyons. Stevenson (1872:463) reported specimens taken by the Hayden expedition at several localities in the Uinta Mountains in September and October 1870. Allen (1872b:166) found it near Ogden, Weber County, in September and October 1871. Numerous more recently collected specimens are in the several institutions of the state. Hayward picked up a fresh specimen found dead on a sidewalk in St. George, Washington County, 28 December 1972.

SUBSPECIES: The common breeding and migrating race found in Utah is *V. c. orestera*. The more northerly breeding race, *V. c. celata*, appears in the state during migration and may be more common at this time than is usually supposed. Cottam (1942b:255) reported the following specimens of *celata*: Parley's Park, Summit County, 16 August 1869; north slope of Uinta Mountains, 16 September 1870; Green River, south of mouth of Henry's Fork, Daggett County, 6 October 1870. A specimen in Brigham Young University was taken at Lyndyl, Millard County, 18 September 1926. Twomey (1942:438) collected two specimens of *celata*, one at Green Lake, Daggett County, 13 September 1937, and one south of Jensen, Uintah County, 29 September 1937. It has also been recorded in Raft River Canyon, Box Elder County, 18 September 1941. (Behle 1958:29), and south of Kanab, Kane County, 16 September 1946 (Behle et al. 1958:74). Behle and Selander (1952:30) reported specimens of *celata* from Lake Solitude, Salt Lake County, 4 September 1945, and from Arcadia, Duchesne County, 3 September 1949. A specimen of the Pacific Coast race, *V. c. lutescens*, in the Carnegie Museum was taken by Twomey (1944a:89) at St. George, Washington County, 12 October 1937. Wauer (1969:333) reported two races in Washington County: *lutescens* at Washington on 6 January 1966 and *orestera* at Springdale on 13 May 1965.

County, 16 September 1946 (Behle et al. 1958:74). Behle and Selander (1952:30) reported specimens of *celata* from Lake Solitude, Salt Lake County, 4 September 1945, and from Arcadia, Duchesne County, 3 September 1949. A specimen of the Pacific Coast race, *V. c. lutescans,* in the Carnegie Museum was taken by Twomey (1944a:89) at St. George, Washington County, 12 October 1937. Wauer (1969: 333) reported two races in Washington County: *lutescens* at Washington on 6 January 1966 and *orestera* at Springdale on 13 May 1965.

Vermivora ruficapilla ridgwayi van Rossem
Nashville Warbler

STATUS: An uncommon migrant through Utah where it appears in April and September along streamside woodlands in canyons and valleys. It has been reported to breed in the Northern Wasatch Mountains (AOU Check-list 1957:484), but Johnson (1976:224–225) conclusively showed that the Check-list is in error.

RECORDS: The earliest record of this species in the state appears to be that of Ridgway in 1869 (1873b:177). Allen (1872b: 166) collected one at Ogden, Weber County, 20 September 1871, and more recently it has been observed and collected consistently. Behle et al. (1958:74) recorded a sight record for Kanab, Kane County, 21 April 1935. Woodbury and Russell (1945: 119) listed specimens from Navajo Mountain, San Juan County, 11 August 1935, and East Gypsum Drainage, Monument Valley, 17 August 1936. Brigham Young University has specimens from Kamas, Summit County, 21 August 1930, and from Soapstone, Uinta Mountains, Wasatch County, 30 August 1940. Lockerbie (1948:21) reported a sight record for the Salt Lake area on 14 September 1947 and another sight record for near Salt Lake City, Salt Lake County, 26 December 1955 (Lockerbie 1956:208). One at Bear River, Box Elder County, 15 August 1974, and one at Springdale, Washington County, 15 September 1974 (Kingery 1975:97), have been recorded.

Vermivora virginiae (Baird)
Virginia's Warbler

STATUS: A common summer resident and breeding species throughout the state where it inhabits dense mountain brush and streamside thickets at mid-elevations and in lower valleys. Migration occurs in April and May and again in September.

RECORDS: Ridgway (1877:429) found Virginia's Warbler in City Creek Canyon, Salt Lake County, and near Salt Lake City, where he collected four specimens on 24 and 26 May and 21 June 1869. He also found a nest containing four eggs under an oak on 19 June. In July of that year he reported it from Pack's Canyon, Summit County (1877:376). It was apparently missed by other early ornithologists. Specimens have more recently been observed and collected in most of the counties of the state.

Vermivora luciae (Cooper)
Lucy's Warbler

STATUS: A fairly common summer resident and breeding species of southern Utah where it inhabits streamside vegetation along the lower San Juan, Colorado, and Virgin rivers and their tributaries.

RECORDS: Merriam, of the Death Valley expedition (Fisher 1893:117), took specimens at Santa Clara, Washington County, 11 May 1891, and at St. George, Washington County, 16 May 1891. A specimen in the American Museum was taken by Rowley at Riverview near Four Corners, San Juan County, 27 April 1892. Numerous records have since been obtained from Garfield, San Juan, Kane, and Washington counties.

Dendroica petechia (Linnaeus)
Yellow Warbler
Fig. 57, p. 148

STATUS: A common summer resident throughout Utah from late April to October. It lives mainly in the woodlands along streams in the lower valleys or in ornamental trees of farms and cities. It occurs less commonly in aspen forests and tall shrubbery in the mountains.

RECORDS: The Yellow Warbler was noted by several of the early ornithologists. Ridgway (1877:432) reported it for Salt Lake Valley and other localities in 1869. Allen (1872a: 396) also reported it for Salt Lake Valley in 1871. Henshaw (1875:192) collected six specimens at Provo, Utah County, in 1872. Several hundred observations and collections have been made more recently.

SUBSPECIES: The race *D. p. morcomi* is conceded to be the common migrant and breeding subspecies in the state and is identical with the West Coast population formerly known as *D. p. brewsteri* (Behle 1948a:77–78). Migrants of other races may occasionally appear in Utah. Specimens in the American Museum taken at Uncompahgre Indian Reservation, Uintah County, 3 May 1895, and from Riverview, San Juan County, 4 May 1892, were identified by A. R. Phillips as *D. p. aestiva* (Woodbury and Russell 1945:121). Another specimen from Strawberry Valley, Wasatch County, 17 May 1941, now in the Carnegie Museum, was identified as the same race by J. S. Aldrich. Cottam (1942b:255) reported a specimen collected by Henshaw in Provo, Utah County, 30 July 1872, as being of the race *amnicola*. Specimens in Brigham Young University collected near Provo on 27 May 1936 and 17 May 1945 were identified by J. W. Aldrich as *D. p. amnicola*. Wauer (1969:333) reported a specimen of the race *amnicola* collected at Springdale, Washington County, 6 May 1965. Woodbury et al. (1949:28) listed the race *rubiginosa* from Utah, Wasatch, and Washington

counties, 10, 27 May and 7, 30 July (no years given). Worthen (1968:487) also mentioned this race apparently on the basis of the Woodbury report.

Dendroica caerulescens (Gmelin)
Black-throated Blue Warbler

STATUS: A rare or accidental visitor to Utah only recently reported.

RECORDS: A male specimen of the Black-throated Blue Warbler in immature plumage was taken at the headquarters of the Desert Range Experiment Station, Millard County, 27 September 1974 (Porter and Pritchett 1975:31). These authors have also referred to additional sight records by Lockerbie and Emerson at Salt Lake City, 24 October 1953 (Scott 1954:33) and by Behle (letter 24 May 1973) in the Stansbury Mountains, Tooele County, 16 October 1955. Behle and Perry (1975:36) reported that Stewart Murie saw this species near Cedar City, Iron County, 16 October 1955. Behle and Perry (1975:36) reported that Stewart Murie saw this species near Cedar City, Iron County, 20 May, 19 August, 10 September, all in 1963.

SUBSPECIES: The above mentioned specimen was examined by Roxie C. Laybourne of the Bird and Mammal Laboratory, U.S. National Museum, and assigned to the race *D. c. caerulescens*.

Dendroica graciae graciae Baird
Grace's Warbler

STATUS: An uncommon summer resident in southern Utah where it inhabits ponderosa pine forests. Wauer and Carter (1965:75) regarded it as common in the higher country around Zion National Park. They stated that the bird arrives in late April and remains through August. It may rarely occur as far north as central Utah.

RECORDS: Benson (1935:445) included it in his list for Navajo Mountain, San Juan County, mid-June 1933. Woodbury and Russell (1945:125) collected a specimen at

Navajo Mountain, 15 June 1938. Behle (1960a:45) recorded a specimen taken at Kigalia Ranger Station, Elk Ridge, Garfield County, 27 August 1956. Wauer (1966b:352) reported that a bird was observed at Zion Park, Washington County, visiting a feeder for a week beginning 21 December 1965; it was considered by the Audubon Field Notes editor as a possible first winter record for this species in the United States. Kashin (Scott 1970:630) reported seeing Grace's Warbler at Provo, Utah County, 13 April 1970.

Dendroica nigrescens nigrescens (Townsend)
Black-throated Gray Warbler

STATUS: A common summer resident throughout the state from late April into September. During the nesting season it is most likely to be seen in pinyon-juniper forests.

RECORDS: Ridgway (1875:32) made reference to this species breeding in the Wasatch Mountains of Utah. He also referred to it breeding in the Uinta Mountains (1877:433). Most of the other early ornithologists seemed to have missed it possibly because of its restricted habitat. Still a common species in pinyon-juniper woodlands, the Black-throated Gray Warbler has numerous observations and specimens on record.

Dendroica townsendi (Townsend)
Townsend's Warbler

STATUS: A seemingly regular but uncommon migrant through Utah in spring and fall.

RECORDS: All of the published records for this species appear to be of more recent date. It was reported first by Stanford (1931:8), who took a specimen in the Henry Mountains, Garfield County, 12 September 1929. Behle (1960a:45) summarized a number of records from southeastern Utah, and later several additional records were published by Hayward (1967:50). Brigham Young University has the following specimens from Utah: Bennion Park, Duchesne County, 24 August 1957; Provo Boat Harbor, Utah County, 24 September 1960; Bluff, San Juan County, 13 September 1966.

Dendroica occidentalis (Townsend)
Hermit Warbler

STATUS: An uncommon summer resident and migrant of southern Utah.

RECORDS: Woodbury and Russell (1945: 125) referred to specimens from Navajo Mountain, San Juan County, 11 August 1935. Woodbury et al. (1949:29) reported a specimen from Navajo Mountain, 13 August 1936. Behle (1960a:45) mentioned a specimen taken on the slope of Mount Ellen, Henry Mountains, Garfield County, 13 August 1956. Wauer and Russell (1967: 422) reported a specimen from Beaver Dam, Mohave County, Arizona, 17 August 1965. Since Beaver Dam is about seven miles south of the Arizona-Utah border, this warbler could be looked for in the Virgin River drainage of Utah.

Dendroica magnolia (Wilson)
Magnolia Warbler

STATUS: An uncommon spring and fall migrant through Utah to be looked for in company with other more common species of warblers.

RECORDS: This species has been reported only in recent years. Sight records are as follows: Scott (1963:54), two at Salt Lake City, Salt Lake County, 14 October 1962; Scott (1968:561), one at Green River, Emery County, 30 May 1968; Kingery (1972:98), several at Bear River, Box Elder County, 26 September 1971. Behle (1973b:244) collected a specimen at Terry Ranch, Beaver Dam Wash, southwestern Washington County, 19 May 1972.

Dendroica coronata (Linnaeus)
Yellow-rumped Warbler
Fig. 58, p. 149

STATUS: The Yellow-rumped Warbler, a variety of which has been commonly known as Audubon's Warbler, is a common summer resident of montane forests throughout the state and is frequently seen in lower valleys during migration. A few may remain in warmer sections of the state throughout the winter.

RECORDS: A few references to this species were made by early ornithologists. Ridgway (1877:433–434) included the subspecies *auduboni* (see subspecies account below) in his Utah list and stated that it bred in the pine belt of the mountains and wintered in the valleys in 1869. Cottam (1942b:254) listed a specimen of the race *coronata*, which was collected by the Hayden Survey of 1870 on the Green River south of the mouth of Henry's Fork in what is now Daggett County on 9 October 1870. A second record of *coronata* was listed by Gunther and Van den Akker (1946:285) for Bear River Migratory Bird Refuge, Box Elder County, 7 May 1946. Henshaw (1875:194–195) mentioned collecting specimens of *auduboni* in 1872 from half a dozen localities in Utah. Brigham Young University has several wintering specimens of *auduboni* as follows: St. George, Washington County, 27 December 1926 and 5 January 1934; Provo, Utah County, 4 January 1937 and 17 January 1955. There are also abundant sight and collection records for other months of the year.

SUBSPECIES: According to the account in Check-list of Birds of the World (1968 [14]: 29–31), the yellow-throated form previously given full species status as *D. auduboni* is now considered to be a subspecies under *D. coronata*, since the two are known to interbreed (Hubbard 1969:393–432). This taxonomic decision is also accepted by the AOU Check-list (1973:417). Furthermore, the intermountain breeding race, known for many years as *D. a. memorabilis*

(Oberholser 1921:243), is now considered to be in synonymy with *D. c. auduboni*. There are, therefore, two kinds of warblers in the Utah population: *D. c. coronata*, which appears as an uncommon spring and fall migrant, and the common *D. c. auduboni*, which is the breeding, migrating, and wintering race.

Dendroica striata (Forster)
Blackpoll Warbler

STATUS: A species of rare occurrence in Utah known presently only as a spring and fall migrant.

RECORDS: One specimen found dead on the Brigham Young University campus, Provo, Utah County, 3 October 1973. The specimen was a fall bird of uncertain sex. It was found by M. Vanhille and is now in the university collection (museum number 5364). Sight records were reported by Behle and Perry (1975:37) for Bear River Migratory Bird Refuge, Box Elder County, 15 June 1970, and at the same locality, 19 September 1974.

Dendroica castanea (Wilson)
Bay-breasted Warbler

STATUS: A rare and possibly accidental or casual migrant in Utah.

RECORDS: A male specimen (number 22249 in University of Utah) was taken along the floodplain of White River near Bonanza, Uintah County, 25 May 1974 (Behle and Perry 1975:37). This appears to be the only record known for Utah.

Setophaga ruticilla tricolora (Müller)
American Redstart

STATUS: A sparse breeder in deciduous trees of valleys and low canyons in northern Utah. Apparently more common formerly than at present.

RECORDS: Ridgway (1877:367; 372–373; 376–377; 438–439) found it from 20 May to 16 August 1869 along City Creek, near Salt

Lake City, Salt Lake County, in Parley's Park, Summit County, and Provo Canyon, Utah County. Henshaw (1875:209) regarded it as common in wooded lowlands and collected a specimen at Provo on 29 July 1872. Hayward (field notes) found it to be of regular occurrence in streamside woodlands near Provo in the early 1930s, took specimens, and found it nesting. Other earlier collection localities include Riverdale, Weber River, 10 June 1942 (University of Utah), and Jensen, Uintah County, 20 August 1935 (Royal Ontario Museum). Porter (1954:363) reported making collections at Warburton Ranch, Pilot Mountain, Box Elder County, 31 August and 1 September 1935, and Cedar Mountains, Tooele County, 22 September 1953. Behle and Selander (1952:30–31) took specimens near Vernal, Uintah County, 12 June 1949, near Duchesne, Duchesne County, 3 September 1949, and on the north side of the Uinta Mountains at Hideout Canyon along the Green River, Daggett County, 12 September 1950. Behle et al. (1964:454) published an additional record for Camel Back Mountain, Tooele County, 30 August 1961. Wauer (Snider 1966:538) saw several Redstarts in Washington County on 18 May 1966.

Seiurus noveboracensis (Gmelin)
Northern Waterthrush

STATUS: A sparse but apparently regular migrant along water courses in the state in May and again in August and September. Possibly occurs rarely in winter (Bader 1948:109).

RECORDS: Most of the early-day ornithologists did not record this species for Utah perhaps because of its scattered occurrence during migration. A specimen in the U.S. National Museum of Natural History was taken by Merriam and Bailey at Santa Clara, Washington County, 11 May 1891 (Fisher 1893:122). Two other specimens in the same museum were collected by Wetmore at Bear River, 12 and 21

August 1915, and several others were observed by him. Cottam (1942b:255) mentioned a sight record of one on 20 May and three on 22 May 1917 at Linwood, Daggett County. The Royal Ontario Museum contains three specimens collected by Lloyd near Jensen, Uintah County, 8 May and 11 August 1935 (Twomey 1942:445). Woodbury took one near Bluff, San Juan County, 11 May 1933 (Woodbury and Russell 1945:125). The following more recent collection records have been published: Behle and Selander (1952:30), Farmington Bay Refuge, Davis County, 10 May 1949; near Snyderville, Summit County, 14 May 1949; and Benjamin, Utah County, 15 May 1949; Behle et al. (1964:454), near Natural Bridges National Monument, San Juan County, 13 May 1960, and Dugway, Tooele County, 21 May 1961. There are also numerous sight records.

SUBSPECIES: Formerly it was thought that both the races S. n. notabilis and S. n. limnaeus occurred in the migratory population, but the species is now considered to be without subspecific differentiation (Check-list of Birds of the World 1968 [14]: 35–36).

Geothlypis trichas (Linnaeus)
Common Yellowthroat

STATUS: A rather common summer resident and migrant throughout the state wherever there are suitable habitats. It inhabits sedge and cattail vegetation around the borders of lakes and ponds and is also found in willow thickets near water especially during migration.

RECORDS: Ridgway (1877:366–367) found this warbler at Deep Creek, Box Elder County, 5 October 1868, and near Salt Lake City, Salt Lake County, through August 1869. Allen (1872a:396) took specimens near Ogden, Weber County, in September 1871 and considered it common. Merriam (1873:674, 705) collected it near Ogden, 17 June 1872, and found it nesting. Henshaw (1874:10) considered it common and

(1875:205) found it in various parts of Utah. He collected it at Panguitch, Garfield County, 17 September 1872. Such early naturalist visitors as Vernon Bailey, Osgood, and others made references to it in their field notes. Merriam (Fisher 1893:123) observed it along the lower Santa Clara River, Washington County, 11–15 May 1891. Numerous additional records have been published in recent years.

SUBSPECIES: The most widespread breeding Yellowthroat in Utah is *G. t. occidentalis,* which also includes *G. t. utahicola* described by Oberholser (1948:3). *G. t. scirpicola* occurs only in the extreme southwestern part of the state (Behle 1950a:210). Recently, Wauer (1969:333) reported the race *occidentalis* as also breeding in southwestern Utah. The race *G. t. campicola* is known to migrate through the state (Behle 1948a:78).

Geothlypis agilis (Wilson)
Connecticut Warbler

STATUS: Known only as an accidental visitor to the state.

RECORDS: The only collection record of this warbler known to us is that published by Porter and Bushman (1956:153). A specimen was obtained by them at the mouth of South Willow Canyon, 10 miles south of Grantsville, Tooele County, 22 September 1954. A sight record by Kashin in City Creek Canyon, Salt Lake City, Salt Lake County, 26 August 1972 (Behle and Perry 1975:37) has been published.

Geothlypis tolmiei (Townsend)
MacGillivray's Warbler

STATUS: A common breeding species and migrant throughout the state with two races being represented in the Utah population. The breeding birds live at midelevations where they nest and forage in rather dense shrubby vegetation in canyons or under aspens.

RECORDS: Ridgway (1877:435–436) found this warbler in "all the fertile canyons from the Sierra Nevada to the Uintahs [*sic*]. It inhabited the rank herbage near the streams, or the undergrowth of the thickets and aspen copses." He took nests and eggs at Parley's Park, Summit County, in June and July 1869. Allen (1872a:396) obtained specimens near Ogden, Weber County, in September 1871. Henshaw (1875:205–206) referred to its presence in Utah but apparently took no specimens. There have since been many records from most of the counties of the state.

SUBSPECIES: The subspecies *G. t. monticola* is the breeding form found in Utah and throughout most of the intermountain area. The more northern breeding race *G. t. tolmiei,* including *G. t. austinsmithi* described by Phillips (1974:298), is a regular migrant through the state (Behle et al. 1958:76; Behle 1958:31, 1960a:46). The spring migration occurs mainly in May and the fall migration takes place from mid-August into October.

Wilsonia pusilla (Wilson)
Wilson's Warbler

STATUS: A common migrant especially along the streams in the lower valleys during May and again in August and September. Known also to breed in small numbers in the high mountain forests.

RECORDS: Most, if not all, of the specimens taken by early-day ornithologists were probably migrants. Ridgway (1877:438) collected one on Antelope Island, Great Salt Lake, 24 May 1869. Stevenson (1872:463) reported specimens from the northern slope of the Uinta Mountains on 16 September 1870. Allen (1872b:167) found it common and took specimens near Ogden, Weber County, 11–30 September 1871 (1872a:396). Nesting records are scarce, but Higgins (field notes) reported seeing several dozen birds around his camp on Boulder Mountain, Sevier County, 27 July to 2 August 1941. Twomey (1942:448–449) found young birds and family groups on Bald Mountain, Summit County, 19

July 1937, and at Moon Lake, Duchesne County, 21 August 1937. Many records of migrant birds are available for more recent years.

SUBSPECIES: The breeding and migrant race found in the state is *W. p. pileolata;* however, Cottam (1942a:127) reported the collection of a specimen of *W. p. pusilla* at the west base of Pilot Peak, Elko County, Nevada, 20 September 1941. This collection site is only two miles west of the Utah-Nevada border, so it appears that this race probably migrates through Utah, although not in any great numbers.

Wilsonia canadensis (Linnaeus)
Canada Warbler

STATUS: A rare migrant in the state.

RECORDS: A partially decomposed body of a bird of this species was found at Callao, Juab County, 31 May 1975. It is in the Brigham Young University Life Sciences Museum (museum number 5390).

Myioborus pictus pictus (Swainson)
Painted Redstart

STATUS: An uncommon and perhaps accidental visitor to the Virgin River area in southwestern Utah.

RECORDS: Presnell (1935b:207) first published a record of this species based on an observation by V. M. Tanner at Zion National Park, Washington County, 26 April 1930. Dixon Joyner saw one at the Terry Ranch, Beaver Dam Wash, Washington County, 22 May 1965 (Behle and Perry 1975:38). Wauer (1969:333–334) summarized several other sight records, all from Zion National Park in 1966. These are as follows: 22 April, three individuals; 24 April, two seen and one heard; 30 April, one observed. The 1930 sighting and the 1966 observations were within a quarter mile of each other. Kingery (1975:88) reported a Painted Redstart at Zion National Park during the period 28 April to 2 May 1975.

Icteria virens auricollis (Deppe)
Yellow-breasted Chat

STATUS: A common summer resident and breeding species in suitable habitats throughout the state. The Yellow-breasted Chat is an inhabitant of dense thickets along natural waterways and canal banks in the lower valleys and canyons.

RECORDS: Henshaw (1875:206–207) referred to the Yellow-breasted Chat from several localities in Utah, and Allen (1872b:166) found it moderately common in the vicinity of Ogden, Weber County. Ridgway (1875:24) considered it to be a common breeder in the Salt Lake Valley in 1869. Merriam (Fisher 1893:124) indicated it as a "tolerably common breeder," 11-15 May 1891, in the Santa Clara Valley, Washington County. Many more recent occurrences are on record.

FAMILY VIREONIDAE

Vireo griseus noveboracensis (Gmelin)
White-eyed Vireo

STATUS: An accidental or casual visitor to Utah.

RECORDS: This species was reported by Porter and Bushman (1956:153), who recorded a specimen taken by Heber H. Hall eight miles west of Boulder, Garfield County, 11 May 1953. It was found in a fruit orchard in a mixed flock of other species of birds.

Vireo bellii arizonae Ridgway
Bell's Vireo

STATUS: This vireo is an uncommon but regular summer resident in the Virgin River Valley of southwestern Utah.

RECORDS: Two males were collected by Ross Hardy three miles south of St. George, Washington County, 19 and 20 April 1940. These records were reported by Hardy and Higgins (1940:105) as being of the race *V. b. pusillus.* Later, Hardy (1941a:125) corrected the subspecies name to *arizonae.*

Wauer and Carter (1965:73) published a sight record from Parunuweap Canyon, Zion National Park, Washington County, 17 August 1962 and 26 August 1962. In the latter case an immature bird was seen with adults.

Vireo vicinior Coues
Gray Vireo

STATUS: A fairly common summer resident, particularly of the more southern counties where it inhabits principally the arid pinyon-juniper forests and dry brushlands.

RECORDS: The University of Utah has several specimens from Washington County, including Beaver Dam Mountains, 22 April 1930 and 4–6 May 1941 and a locality near Leeds, 30 April–4 May 1939 (Behle 1943:62). A specimen in the Dixie Junior College collection was taken on Beaver Dam Mountains, 29 June 1940 (Hardy and Higgins 1940:105). More recent published records (Behle et al. 1958:73) are from Cave Lakes Canyon, Kane County, 15 May 1946 and 23 May 1947, and from confluence of Calf Creek and Escalante River, Garfield County, 7 May 1954. Wauer (1969:333) considered it a common resident from 2 April to 30 June in the mountains near Zion National Park, Washington County. Sight records include that of Webster (1947:40), who reported seeing two in a pinyon-juniper forest near Salina, Sevier County, 22 August 1945. Scott (1965:567–568) reported that Carter saw the Gray Vireo at Arches National Park, Grand County, and in the nearby La Sal Mountains and that it was found nesting in both localities in June 1965. The following year it was again recorded all during the summer at Arches National Monument (Scott 1966:589).

Vireo solitarius (Wilson)
Solitary Vireo
Fig. 59, p. 150

STATUS: A rather common summer resi-

dent throughout the state where it inhabits streamside woodlands, pinyon-juniper forests, and yellow pine forests.

RECORDS: Ridgway (1875:321, 367, 374) observed it in scrub oak and pinyon-juniper habitats of City Creek Canyon, Salt Lake County, in July and August 1869, and also at Parley's Park, Summit County. Allen (1872:167) collected it at Ogden, Weber County, 8 September 1871, and considered it to be "rather frequent." Henshaw (1875:225) found it in the Wasatch Mountains. In addition, many recent occurrences are on record.

SUBSPECIES: The common breeding subspecies in the state is *V. s. plumbeus.* The race *V. s. cassinii* may also appear as a spring and fall migrant. Some recent published records of this race include those of Stanford (1938:142), Logan, Cache County, 27 September 1930; Behle (1943:62), Beaver Dam Wash, Washington County, 18 April 1932; Behle (1958:29), Clear Creek, Box Elder County, 3 September 1932; Behle (1955:27), Queen of Sheba Mine, Deep Creek Mountains, Juab County, 16 September 1947; Behle (1960a:43), La Sal Mountains, San Juan County, 14 September 1955; Hayward (1967:48), White River near Bonanza, Uintah County, 20 September 1966.

Vireo olivaceus olivaceus (Linnaeus)
Red-eyed Vireo

STATUS: A sparse migrant through the state in late May and early June and again in September. It usually appears as a migrant in streamside vegetation of the lower valleys, although an observation by Cottam and Kalmbach (field notes) for Aspen Grove, Mt. Timpanogos, Utah County, 7 July 1938, indicated that it might rarely nest in the state.

RECORDS: The only records from the early naturalists were those of Allen (1872b:167), who collected it near Ogden, Weber County, 8 September 1871. He regarded it as more or less common in that area in

September and early October. More recent collection records for the state include the following: four miles south of Jensen, Uintah County, May and June 1937 (Twomey 1942:437); near Logan, Cache County, 30 May 1941 (Stanford 1944:151); Iosepa, Skull Valley, Tooele County, 11 September 1953 (Porter 1954:363); Salt Lake City, Salt Lake County, June 1962, and Dugway, Tooele County, 6 September 1962 (Behle et al. 1964:454). A number of sight records have also been reported.

Vireo gilvus (Vieillot)
Warbling Vireo
Fig. 60, p. 151

STATUS: A common summer resident and breeding species in the state from late March through September. It inhabits deciduous woods along valley and mountain streams but is especially abundant in aspen forests.

RECORDS: Most of the early-day ornithologists either collected or observed this species in various sections of the state. Ridgway (1875:449) took a specimen at Antelope Island, Davis County, 5 June 1869. He also found nests and eggs at Parley's Park, Summit County, 23–24 June 1869. Stevenson (1872:464) found it along Green River, Daggett County, in October 1870. Allen (1872b:167) regarded it as "rather common" around Ogden, Weber County, in September and early October 1871. Henshaw (1875:221) found it to be a widespread and common vireo in several localities he visited. Two specimens collected by Granger in Uintah County on 31 May 1895 are in the American Museum. Numerous collection and sight records have been made more recently.

SUBSPECIES: The common breeding and migrating race in the state is V. g. leucopolius. V. g. swainsonii appears as an uncommon migrant. The University of Utah collection contains specimens of the latter from King's Ranch, Henry Mountains, Garfield County, 10 September 1929, and from

Deep Creek Mountains, Tooele County, 16 September 1947 (Woodbury et al. 1949: 217; Behle 1948a:77). A specimen at Brigham Young University from Henrieville, Garfield County, 7 September 1937, also appears to be V. g. swainsonii (Hayward 1967:49). There are four specimens of this race taken at Clear Creek and along the slope of the Raft River Mountains, Box Elder County, 18 May 1948 and 25 August 1949 (Behle 1958:29). However, on the basis of a study of some 200 specimens, Worthen (1968:367–368) doubted that swainsonii occurs in the Utah population at all.

FAMILY ICTERIDAE

Icterus cucullatus nelsoni Ridgway
Hooded Oriole

STATUS: This oriole is an uncommon summer resident in extreme southwestern Utah.

RECORDS: Behle (1943a:68) reported a specimen at Terry Ranch, Beaver Dam Wash, Washington County, 22 April 1930. Hardy and Higgins (1940:107) obtained a specimen on 23 April 1940 at St. George, Washington County, which they indicated was of the race sennetti. Later Hardy (1941a:125) reported that the specimen had been misidentified and belonged to the race nelsoni. Behle et al. (1964:455) also recorded a male specimen with enlarged testes taken at Lytle Ranch, Beaver Dam Wash, 25 June 1961, and mentioned that this was the third specimen known for the state. Wauer (1969:334) collected a male at the Lytle Ranch, Beaver Dam Wash, 27 April 1966. He observed this species from 8 April to 25 August in the Virgin River Valley of Utah, Arizona, and Nevada.

Icterus galbula (Linnaeus)
Northern Oriole
Fig. 61, p. 154

STATUS: A common summer resident and

breeding species throughout the state from early May through August. Its natural habitat appears to be woodlands along the streams of the lower valleys, but it has also adapted rather well to ornamental trees in towns and parks.

RECORDS: Ridgway (1877:509) collected specimens, nests, and eggs in the Salt Lake Valley and Wasatch Mountains in 1869. Henshaw (1875:320) referred to finding this species in several localities in Utah during his fieldwork in 1872. All the other early naturalists to visit the state recorded its occurrence in their reports and field notes. The species is still common in the state, and many specimens are in local collections.

SUBSPECIES: The subspecies *I. g. bullockii*, known as Bullock's Oriole for many years, is by far the most common and widespread, if not the only, morphologically distinct form occurring in Utah. It was formerly given full species status but is now considered as a subspecies of the ubiquitous *I. galbula* (AOU Check-list 1973:417). Worthen (1968:385; 1973b:677–678) reported a specimen of *I. g. galbula* in the University of Utah collection from Milford, Millard County, 27 June 1964.

Icterus parisorum Bonaparte
Scott's Oriole

STATUS: An uncommon summer resident more frequently found in the southern part of the state, but in recent years reported in a number of locations in the north. It inhabits pinyon-juniper woodlands and semidesert country where there are tall shrubs.

RECORDS: There seem to be few references to this oriole in the early reports on Utah birds. Fisher (1893:77) mentioned its occurrence in the Beaver Dam Mountains of southwestern Utah. Behle et al. (1964:455) collected several specimens at Lytle Ranch, Washington County, 25 June 1961. Behle and Selander (1952:31) collected it 25 miles east of Hanksville, Wayne County, 20 May 1951. Carter (1967a:5) included it

for Arches National Park, Grand County, 30 May and 29 June 1965; it was also reported to have nested there. Long (1943:39) reported seeing it at Nephi, Juab County, 17 May 1942. Porter (1954:363) reported a sight record for Cedar Mountains, Tooele County, 7 May 1953. Hayward and Frost (field notes) saw a male near Fish Springs, Juab County, 19 May 1966. Some additional sight records have appeared as follows: Scott (1959:391; 1962:436; 1965:568) near Eureka, Juab County, 30 May 1959; Salt Lake City, Salt Lake County, 30 April 1962; nest with young, Arches National Park, 29 June 1965; and Kingery (1971:887), Topaz Mountain, Juab County, summer 1971. Hayward (field notes) found it nesting near Topaz Mountain, Juab County, 29 May 1973.

Xanthocephalus xanthocephalus
(Bonaparte)
Yellow-headed Blackbird

STATUS: A common summer resident throughout the state in lower valleys where there are swamplands or lake borders with ample rushes or other emergent vegetation suitable for nesting colonies. It may occasionally remain all winter as witnessed by Cottam et al. (1942:53), who observed one at Bear River Marshes, Box Elder County, 16 December 1941. In addition, Wauer (1969:334) saw five at Washington, Washington County, 28 December 1965.

RECORDS: This conspicuous bird was noted by all of the early investigators to visit the state. Ridgway (1877:502–503) found it plentiful at the mouth of Jordan River, Davis County, in 1869, as well as at other localities. Allen (1872b:168) found it in the marshes near Ogden, Weber County, and Henshaw (1874:7) reported it as being very numerous in the state. Many colonies of this species may still be found throughout the state. The abundance of this species may, in part, be attributed to the creation of new water storage reservoirs wherein emergent vegetation is able to grow around

Fig. 64. Gray Jay. Paradise Park, Uinta Mountains, Uintah County, Utah, 30 July 1953. Photo by R. J. Erwin.

the borders. This has apparently increased their numbers and extended their distribution.

Agelaius phoeniceus (Linnaeus)
Red-winged Blackbird

STATUS: A common resident of valley marshlands and meadows where it nests. In winter large flocks remain in the warmer valleys.

RECORDS: A number of references to this species for Utah were found in the early records of Allen (1872b:168), Henshaw (1874:7; 1875:314–315), and Ridgway (1877: 505). Since this is one of the more common birds in the state, hundreds of records have been made in recent years.

SUBSPECIES: The breeding and wintering population found throughout Utah appears to be A. p. fortis. A race named A. p. utahensis was proposed by Bishop (1938:2), and Behle (1940b:234–240) supported this view principally on the basis of the de-

cidedly pinkish color found on the throat in many females. However, Blake (Checklist of Birds of the World 1968 [14] :168) has placed *utahensis* in synonymy with *fortis*. Behle (1948a:78–79) indicated that there is some evidence of intergradation of *fortis* with *A. p. nevadensis* on the western border of the state, where he considered collected birds to be atypical breeding *A. P. nevadensis* individuals. Twomey (1942:453) collected three specimens, which he considered to be migrants of the race *nevadensis*, two miles south of Jensen, Uintah County, in late September 1937. Behle (1976b:44) reported a specimen in the Zion National Park collection as being of the race *A. p. sonoriensis*.

Sturnella neglecta Audubon
Western Meadowlark

STATUS: A permanent resident throughout the valleys of the state especially in grasslands or cultivated fields and pasturelands. It also sometimes occurs in sage-brush or other low growing shrubs. In winter it tends to congregate in small flocks especially around cattle feed lots.

RECORDS: Baird (1852:316), in Stansbury's report on his explorations of Great Salt Lake, found the meadowlark in that area in 1850. Ridgway (1875:30, 33) indicated it as a breeding species in the Salt Lake Valley and at Parley's Park, Summit County, in 1869, and Henshaw (1875:318) also reported it from Panguitch, Garfield County, and from Washington County in September and October 1872. Bailey and Loring (field notes), during their travels throughout much of the state in 1888–89 and 1893, recorded it frequently. The meadowlark still maintains itself well in the state and seems to adapt to the expanding human population.

Quiscalus quiscula (Linnaeus)
Common Grackle

STATUS: An accidental visitor to Utah.

RECORDS: Talley (1957:400) reported a specimen collected near Provo, Utah County, 21 March 1957. Lockerbie and Behle (1952b:53) recorded a specimen seen at Salt Lake City, Salt Lake County, 20 November 1952. Behle and Perry (1975: 39) reported the following sight records: eight at Bear River Marshes, Box Elder County, 13 September 1941; Salt Lake City, Salt Lake County, 26 November 1952, late fall 1958, and 17 May 1969; Farmington Bay, Davis County, 8 August 1954; Jordan Narrows, Salt Lake County, 30 November 1957. Kashin (1974:489) reported two at Salt Lake City on 16 December 1973.

Euphagus carolinus carolinus (Müller)
Rusty Blackbird

STATUS: A casual and rare visitor in Utah.

RECORDS: Porter (1954:363) reported collecting a male Rusty Blackbird near Camel Back Mountain, Tooele County, 24 November 1952. Two were seen at Trial Lake,

Summit County, in early August 1956 by Kashin (Behle and Perry 1975:39). A male specimen at Brigham Young University was taken by Merlin L. Killpack near Soldier's Summit, Utah County, 18 October 1963. Wauer and Carter (1965:77) also recorded a sight record for Zion National Park, Washington County, 1 June 1965.

Euphagus cyanocephalus (Wagler)
Brewer's Blackbird
Fig. 62, p. 155

STATUS: A common resident in the lower valleys throughout the state. It frequently nests in willow thickets or trees along natural streams and irrigation canals. It is often seen feeding on lawns and in pastures and commonly occurs in small flocks along roadways.

RECORDS: Early records in the state include those of Henshaw (1875:323), who found it at several localities in the state during his fieldwork in 1872. Ridgway (1877:368, 374) recorded it from localities in Utah in 1869. Bailey (field notes) made reference to this species from many localities through the state in 1888–89. Many observations have been made in more recent times, indicating that the species is still common although there is some evidence of a decline in population in the last five years.

Molothrus ater (Boddaert)
Brown-headed Cowbird

STATUS: A rather common summer resident throughout the lower valleys of the state where it inhabits streamside woodlands and ornamental trees in parks and towns. It may also sometimes be seen in small flocks in open country or pastures where cattle are feeding.

RECORDS: During his fieldwork in Utah, Ridgway (1877:501) found a few cowbirds at Parley's Park, Summit County, and in Bear River Valley in June 1869. Henshaw (1875:312) collected specimens near Provo,

Utah County, in 1872. There have since been many collections and observations made in the state.

SUBSPECIES: *M. a. artemisiae* is the race occupying most of the state, with *M. a. obscurus* occurring in southwestern Utah (Blake in Check-list of Birds of the World 1968[14]:199–200). Hardy (1941a:125) reported four specimens of *obscurus* from St. George, Washington County, 7 May 1939, 26 April 1940, and 15–16 May 1940.

Dolichonyx oryzivorus (Linnaeus)
Bobolink

STATUS: An uncommon summer resident seemingly confined mainly to the valleys west of the Wasatch Front. Its habitat is restricted almost entirely to wet, short grass fields and pastures. Its numbers seem to have declined somewhat over the past 10 years.

RECORDS: All of the early investigators visiting Utah prior to the turn of the century found this bird present and in considerable numbers. Allen (1872b:168) and others considered it to be a common breeder in Salt Lake Valley in 1871 and 1872. Henshaw (1875:311) collected it near Provo, Utah County, where he found it feeding young on 25 June 1872. Occasionally it has been found in irrigated land in the very arid areas of western Utah. Behle (1955:28) collected one at Ibapah, Tooele County, 25 July 1950, and Frost (field notes) saw two in an alfalfa field at Callao, Juab County, 31 May 1975.

FAMILY FRINGILLIDAE

Carduelis pinus pinus (Wilson)
Pine Siskin

STATUS: An abundant resident species found throughout the state where it nests primarily in conifer trees from the lower valleys to timberline. In winter it occurs in large flocks especially in the valleys and on foothills where weed seeds are exposed.

RECORDS: Ridgway (1877:464) collected a nest with one egg from a fir tree in Parley's Park, Summit County, 23 June 1869. Henshaw took a specimen at Provo, Utah County, in 1872 (U.S. National Museum of Natural History). Osgood and Birdseye (field notes) found it in the Beaver Mountains, Beaver and Piute counties, and the Henry Mountains, Garfield County, in 1908, and in the Pine Valley Mountains, Washington County, in 1909. There have since been many reports of its occurrence in the state.

Carduelis tristis pallida (Mearns)
American Goldfinch

STATUS: A common resident throughout the state where it breeds in lower valleys and lower canyons. It nests primarily in deciduous trees growing along valley streams or in ornamental trees of towns and parks. In winter it may appear in the valleys in large flocks especially where sunflower seeds are available.

RECORDS: Ridgway (1877:461) found this finch nesting in Pack's Canyon on the west slope of the Uinta Mountains in 1869. Stevenson (1872:464) reported taking five specimens along the Green River in Daggett County in northeastern Utah, and Allen (1872b:167) recorded it as abundant near Ogden, Weber County, in September 1871. Henshaw (1875:244) thought it to be common in Utah where it appeared to live and nest in cottonwood trees. Bailey (field notes) found it common from one end of the state to the other during his travels from 1888 to 1893. Loring in 1893 and Osgood in 1908 (field notes) also noted it on many occasions. This species is still common in Utah, and many records have been made in recent years.

Carduelis psaltria hesperophila
(Oberholser)
Lesser Goldfinch

STATUS: A common resident throughout the state but more abundant southward especially in the Virgin River Valley. It inhabits deciduous trees along the valley streams and in the parks and settlements. In winter it is especially fond of the seeds of several kinds of native and ornamental birches.

RECORDS: Most of the early investigators in the state reported this finch as being common. Allen (1872b:167) found it at Ogden, Weber County, in September 1871. Henshaw (1875:246) recorded it from St. George, Washington County, in October 1872, and Ridgway (1875:33;1877:462–463) found it breeding in the lower canyons of the Wasatch and Uinta mountains in the summer of 1869. Numerous more recent accounts from most of the counties of the state are on record.

Carduelis flammea flammea (Linnaeus)
Common Redpoll

STATUS: An uncommon and irregular visitor to Utah. It should be looked for along streams where birch and alder are growing and in birch trees of settlements and parks.

RECORDS: Stevenson (1872:464) and Cottam (1942b:254) referred to two specimens taken by the Hayden expedition on the north slope of the Uinta Mountains, 10 October 1870. Killpack (Killpack and Hayward 1958:24) collected a female from a flock of 40 birds 11 miles west of Roosevelt, Duchesne County, 1 January 1958. A number of sight records have been reported in more recent years. Webster (1947:40) saw flocks near Perry, Box Elder County, 20 February 1944. In the Uinta Basin one was observed near Roosevelt, Duchesne County, 27 or 28 December 1956 (Killpack 1957:215; Scott 1957:285). Murie (1963:45) observed several at close range at Parowan, Iron County, 19 and 23 November 1962. Kashin (1964a:37) stated that 25–30 Common Redpolls were seen in City Creek Canyon, near Salt Lake City, Salt Lake County, 7 March 1964. Hayward (field notes) saw three feeding in a birch tree at his home in Provo, Utah County, 1 February 1969.

Leucosticte arctoa (Pallas)
Rosy Finch

STATUS: A common summer and wintering species throughout the state, being restricted in breeding to the higher mountain ranges where it is found mainly in alpine areas. In winter it is found in large restless flocks of several subspecies in valleys and on low hills.

RECORDS: The occurrence of this bird in Utah was not reported by most of the early naturalists who visited the area, presumably because they did not visit alpine areas where these birds breed nor did they encounter the large but irregular wintering flocks. The second specimen known of the race *L. a. tephrocotis* and the first specimen located in the United States is now in the U.S. National Museum of Natural History and was taken at Salt Lake City, Salt Lake County, by R. J. Pollard of the Stansbury Expedition on 21 March 1850. It was described by Baird (1852:317–318) and reported again by Remy (1860[2]:450). Stevenson (1872:464) reported a specimen taken by Schmidt on the north slope of the Uinta Mountains on 20 September 1870. This specimen proved to be a juvenile of the breeding race *L. a. atrata*. In recent years it has been observed and collected in many localities throughout the state.

SUBSPECIES: Three races of *L. arctoa* are known to occur in the state. *L. a. atrata* is the breeding subspecies found in the Wasatch and Uinta mountains. *L. a. littoralis* and *L. a. tephrocotis* are widespread in winter, with *tephrocotis* being the more common. All three races may appear together in wintering flocks. *L. a. tephrocotis* and *L. a. atrata* were formerly considered to be separate species, but are now known to be conspecific with *L. arctoa* (Howell in Check-list of Birds of the World 1968 [14]:261–262; Mayr and Short 1970:80).

Carpodacus cassinii Baird
Cassin's Finch

STATUS: A common summer resident of

the mountains throughout the state where it inhabits montane forests and nests in conifers and aspens. The species winters in lesser numbers in lower valleys where it is sometimes seen in small flocks feeding on the buds of deciduous trees in early spring.

RECORDS: Most of the early naturalists reported Cassin's Finch as being common in the mountains. Ridgway (1877:457–458) found it at Parley's Park, Summit County, and in City Creek Canyon near Salt Lake, Salt Lake County, in 1869; he also collected nests and eggs from aspens and cottonwoods. Allen (1872b:167) found it near Ogden, Weber County, in September 1871. Henshaw (1875:240) considered it to be abundant in 1872. Bailey, Cary, and Osgood all refer to it in their field notes from 1890 to 1908. Many recent accounts attest to the species' abundance in the mountains.

Carpodacus mexicanus frontalis (Say)
House Finch
Fig. 63, p. 167

STATUS: A common year-round resident in lower valleys throughout the state. Its natural habitat appears to have been desert brush, streamside woodlands, and pinyon-juniper forests, but it has readily adapted to human communities where it may at times live in orchards and feed to some extent on ripened fruits.

RECORDS: Judging from the earliest writings on Utah birds, this finch was common in the state when the pioneer settlers arrived. Henshaw (1874:5; 1875:241–243), Ridgway (1877:458–461), Fisher (1893:81), and several others made frequent reference to it as being abundant in all areas of the state visited by them. The species is still common, and numerous accounts of its occurrence are on record.

SUBSPECIES: The subspecies *C. m. solitudinus*, *C. m. grinnelli*, and *C. m. sordidus* have recently been consolidated under *C. m. frontalis* (Howell in Check-list of Birds of the World 1968 [14] :272).

Pinicola enucleator montanus Ridgway
Pine Grosbeak

STATUS: An uncommon resident of coniferous forests in most of the mountain ranges of the state. In severe winters the birds tend to drift downward along the canyon streams and may even appear in the higher valleys.

RECORDS: Some of the early-day naturalists failed to report this species in the state, undoubtedly because they did not work extensively in the higher elevations where Pine Grosbeaks are found. Stevenson (1872:464) reported a juvenile specimen taken on the north slopes of the Uinta Mountains on 20 September 1870, and Nelson (1875:344) found it common in about the same locality between 22 June and 24 July 1872. Osgood (field notes) found it in the Beaver Mountains, Beaver County, and at Brian Head, Iron County, September 1908. More recent records are numerous from all the major mountain ranges and high plateaus of the state.

Loxia curvirostra Linnaeus
Red Crossbill

STATUS: An irregular but sometimes common summer resident of coniferous forests in the high mountain ranges and plateaus of the state. Known to nest in the Uinta Mountains and in the vicinity of Navajo Lake, Kane County. Crossbills normally appear in restless flocks flying from tree to tree and remaining only a few minutes in one place.

RECORDS: Records of crossbills in the early literature on Utah birds are scarce. Stevenson (1872:464) reported a specimen taken by the Hayden expedition on the Green River in early October 1870. Nelson (1875:344) saw flocks on the north slope of the Uinta Mountains and noted that nearly full-grown young were present. Specimens in the U.S. National Museum of Natural History were taken by Osgood in the Beaver Mountains, Beaver County, 17 August 1907. He also found them in the Parowan Mountains, Iron County, and

Henry Mountains, Garfield County, in September and October of the same year. Many additional records have been established more recently. Papers summarizing much of this information have been published by Hayward (1943:276–277), Selander (1953:158–160), and Behle and Ghiselin (1958:18).

SUBSPECIES: Several authors have discussed the subspecific status of the Red Crossbill population in Utah (Woodbury 1939:162; Behle 1944a:84; Selander 1953: 158–160). It appears that there are several races within the area with considerable overlapping of racial characteristics. *L. c. benti* seems to be the most common nesting subspecies especially in the Uinta Mountains. Typical *L. c. bendirei* appears less commonly, and *L. c. grinnelli* is the least common of the three. The southern race *L. c. stricklandi* may appear as a wanderer in southern Utah (Howell in Check-list of Birds of the World 1968 [14] :292; Woodbury 1939:162; Woodbury and Russell 1945:140–141; Behle et al. 1958:83).

Loxia leucoptera leucoptera Gmelin
White-winged Crossbill

STATUS: A rare and presumably accidental visitor to Utah.

RECORDS: Worthen (1968:431; 1972a:243–244) reported three specimens in the University of Utah collection (nos. 19577–19579) from Pioneer Ranger Station, one mile north of Mount Catherine, Pavant Mountains, Millard County, 2 August 1965. Kashin (1970:416) saw three White-winged Crossbills at Salt Lake City, Salt Lake County, on several occasions prior to 21 December 1969, and another one at Salt Lake City, 16 December 1973 (Kashin 1974: 489). One was reported at Salt Lake City in January 1974 (Kingery 1974:671).

Coccothraustes vespertinus brooksi
(Grinnell)
Evening Grosbeak

STATUS: A common but erratic winter resident in lower valleys throughout the

state where it is found in small flocks feeding on buds and fruits of native and ornamental trees. It has been reported as nesting in small numbers in conifer and deciduous trees in higher mountains.

RECORDS: Early ornithologists visiting Utah, such as Henshaw, Ridgway, and Allen, seem not to have encountered this species, probably because of its erratic distribution. All major reports of more recent years, however, indicate its widespread and rather common occurrence, especially in winter and early spring.

FAMILY PLOCEIDAE

Passer domesticus domesticus (Linnaeus)
House Sparrow

STATUS: The House Sparrow, also called English Sparrow, was introduced in Utah sometime prior to 1870 and has since spread throughout the state wherever there are settlements or ranches.

RECORDS: Allen (1872a:395; 1872b:167) reported this species from Ogden, Weber County, and Salt Lake Valley during his visit to the area in the fall of 1871. Numerous reports have been made since that time.

FAMILY STURNIDAE

Sturnus vulgaris vulgaris Linnaeus
Starling

STATUS: A common introduced resident species throughout the state principally in and near human habitations and livestock feeding areas. Occasionally found in woodlands along the streams of the lower valleys.

RECORDS: Although the Starling was introduced into eastern United States many years ago, it did not appear in Utah until the late 1930s. Lockerbie (1939:170) reported a specimen in the University of Utah collection taken by Thayer Evans near Salt Lake City on 26 February 1939. Behle (1954a:49–50) reviewed the history of the bird in Utah. Cottam (1945b:172) reported a dead starling at the Desert Range Experimental Station in southwestern Millard County on 1 September 1942. The first records were for wintering birds, and nesting was not reported before 1949 (Utah Audubon News 1949:1). Killpack and Crittenden (1952:338–344) have given an account of the Starling in the Uinta Basin from 1947 to 1951 and indicate that it might have appeared in that area at least 10 years prior to that time. At present the species nests commonly in the state and winters in flocks of hundreds wherever it can obtain food.

Family Corvidae

Gymnorhinus cyanocephala Wied
Piñon Jay

Status: A common resident species living primarily in pinyon-juniper forests wherever such forests are to be found in the state. It usually appears as family groups or small, loosely organized flocks that wander restlessly over large areas of their habitat.

Records: Ridgway (1877:517) did not specifically mention its occurrence in Utah; he did, however, refer to its presence throughout the West. Henshaw (1875:331–333) collected specimens near Beaver, Beaver County, in 1872, and considered it to be common in that area. Merriam (Fisher 1893:73) reported it to be present on the east slope of the Beaver Dam Mountains, Washington County, in southern Utah. Because of the state's extensive and relatively undisturbed areas of pinyon-juniper, the Piñon Jay is still frequently reported.

Cyanocitta cristata cyanotephra Sutton
Blue Jay

Status: A species common to eastern North America and of accidental occurrence in Utah.

Records: A Blue Jay specimen collected by John Bushman at Holladay, Salt Lake County, 30 April 1970, was reported by Behle (1973b:244). In the same account Behle also included sight records from the vicinity of Holladay where one had been seen for some time prior to 5 January 1969; another was observed in the same area during the winter of 1970–1971; one was reported on the Markagunt Plateau, Iron County, beside state highway 143, 25 June 1950. One was seen by Stewart Murie on Cedar Mountain, Iron County, 29 October 1966 (Scott 1967:63).

Cyanocitta stelleri (Gmelin)
Steller's Jay

Status: A fairly common although irregular resident of coniferous forests and adjacent mountain shrub areas throughout the mountains of the state. In winter a few birds may descend to lower valleys where they appear in streamside woodlands or ornamental trees.

Records: The earliest reports of Steller's Jay in Utah referred to it under the name Cyanura stelleri var. macrolophus (Henshaw 1874:7). Ridgway (1877:525–526) considered it comparatively plentiful in the Uinta Mountains in 1869. Allen (1872b:178) reported it from near Ogden, Weber County, and Henshaw (1875:336) collected specimens in Provo Canyon, Utah County, 31 July 1872 and 30 November 1872. Since that time numerous specimens have been collected.

Subspecies: Various subspecific names have, at one time or another, been applied to the Utah population. Behle (1943a:48–51) and Phillips (1950:252–254) have reviewed the races found in Utah and adjacent areas. Blake and Vaurie (Check-list of Birds of the World 1962[15]:209) refer all Utah birds to the race C. s. macrolopha. The subspecies C. s. percontatrix, C. s. cottami, and C. s. browni have been placed in synonymy with the above race. There is evidence that the northern breeding subspecies C. s. annectens may wander into northern Utah (Stanford 1938:140).

Aphelocoma coerulescens (Bosc)
Scrub Jay
Fig. 65, p. 197

STATUS: A common jay throughout the state occurring usually in shrubby vegetation or pinyon-juniper forests along the foothills.

RECORDS: This widespread and common jay was reported by all the early-day naturalists who worked in Utah. Ridgway (1877:526–527) recorded it from the Wasatch Mountains in 1869. Merriam (1873: 688) reported it from near Ogden, Weber County, Utah, in 1872. Henshaw (1875: 338) referred to this species from several locations in Utah in 1872, and Fisher (1893: 69) recorded it from the Beaver Dam Mountains of Washington County in 1891. More recent references in the literature are abundant.

SUBSPECIES: While there appears to be considerable intergradation between them, two rather distinct subspecies of Scrub Jay have been recognized in the Utah population (Behle 1948a:74). A race described by Pitelka (1945:24), known as *A c. nevadae*, occupies western Utah, especially the Great Basin, while *A. c. woodhouseii* occurs in the eastern part of the state in the Upper Colorado River Basin (Hayward 1967:42).

Perisoreus canadensis capitalis Ridgway
Gray Jay
Fig. 64, 182

STATUS: The Gray Jay, also sometimes called the "Camp Robber," is a rather common resident of spruce-fir forests in the higher mountain ranges and plateaus of central and southern Utah. In winter this jay may drift to lower elevations in yellow pine forests, but it is rarely seen in lower valleys.

RECORDS: Some of the early workers in the state, such as Allen (1872b), Merriam (1873), and Henshaw (1875), missed this species probably because they did relatively little fieldwork in the high spruce-fir

forests where the species lives. It was reported by Stevenson (1872:465) from the Uinta Mountains, 20 September and 2 October 1870 (U.S. National Museum of Natural History). Nelson (1875:344) also found it on the north slope of the Uinta Mountains in July 1872. Specimens were taken by the Stansbury Expedition in 1849–50 and by the Simpson Expedition (Baird 1876:380); exact localities are unknown. Many other occurrences have been recorded more recently.

Pica pica hudsonia (Sabine)
Black-billed Magpie

STATUS: A common resident throughout the state living in shrubby and wooded areas along the lower foothills and in the valleys. It is more abundant in the northern part of the state and occurs more sparingly in the south. Judging from early reports, it may have increased somewhat as the area became populated with white settlers.

RECORDS: Captain J. C. Fremont (1845: 156) reported that on 9 September 1843 a Magpie visited his camp on Fremont Island in Great Salt Lake. Ridgway (1877: 521) found it abundant in Nevada in 1869 but noted that it was absent from many favorable localities on the east side of the Great Basin in Utah; however, in his report of traveling down Provo Canyon, Utah County, 10–11 July 1869 (1877:377), he recorded several different species of birds and stated, "And the Magpie again numerous." In an earlier preliminary report (1875:35) he recorded Magpies in Provo Canyon and stated that this species "in other localities in Utah was found to be rare or entirely wanting." Stevenson (1872: 465) noted that it was abundant in northeastern Utah (now Daggett County) in October 1870. Allen (1872b:169) found it common around Ogden, Weber County, during September-October 1872. In the summer and fall of 1872, Henshaw (1875: 334) found it a common resident of the lower portions of the mountains, the valleys, and the plains where the streams issue out upon them. Many hundreds of records have been made for all of the counties of the state in recent years.

Nucifraga columbiana (Wilson)
Clark's Nutcracker

STATUS: A resident of coniferous forests of the higher mountains and plateaus throughout the state. In winter it tends to drift to lower elevations where it may be found in pinyon-juniper forests of the Wasatch and Uinta mountains.

RECORDS: Ridgway (1877:515) called it common in the high coniferous forests of the Wasatch and Uinta mountains in the summer of 1869. Henshaw (1875:329) found it in more open coniferous forests and first saw it at Otter Creek, Piute County, 8 September 1872. Bailey (field notes) found it at the divide between the Sevier and Virgin rivers, Kane County, 18 December 1888. Osgood (field notes) also reported it from Fishlake Plateau, Henry Mountain, and other localities in September and October 1908. Birdseye (field notes) recorded it from Pine Valley Mountain, Washington County, 1909. Recent recordings include nearly every county in the state.

Corvus brachyrhynchos Brehm
Common Crow

STATUS: A common wintering bird in the central valleys of the state especially in Salt Lake and Utah valleys and a sparse breeder in wooded areas along the streams. Along the Bear River in Rich County it nests rather commonly in colonies.

RECORDS: Ridgway (1877:514–515) did not report the presence of crows in Utah in 1869, and Henshaw (1875:327) called it rather rare in the state in 1872. He saw a few at Provo, Utah County, during his fieldwork in Utah Valley. Other early workers, such as Allen, Merriam, and Nelson, apparently did not find it. Most of the records

for more recent years have been for the large wintering flocks. Richards and White (1963:530–531) have summarized the nesting records that are available.

SUBSPECIES: For many years it has been assumed that the breeding and wintering crows of Utah were of the race *C. b. hesperis*. However, Richards (1971:116–118), who studied a large series of residents as well as wintering specimens from Utah localities, has concluded that the Utah birds are in most respects more closely related to *C. b. brachyrhynchos*.

Corvus corax sinuatus Wagler
Raven

STATUS: A common resident of widespread habitats, living usually at lower elevations but sometimes moving to higher elevations, even alpine, for feeding. It is more commonly seen in desert country where it feeds on animals killed along the highways. It nests in cliffs or trees or sometimes on deserted buildings.

RECORDS: Captain Bonneville (Irving 1868:491) reported an abundance of Ravens in Bear River Valley, Rich County, in 1835. Gunnison and Beckwith (Baird 1854:14) obtained a Raven between White River and San Rafael, Utah. This is in present-day Emery County. Simpson (1876:380) reported two specimens from Fairfield, Utah County, May 1859. Ridgway (1877: 368, 374) found it common in the Great Basin in 1869. Allen (1872b:169) reported it common around Ogden, Weber County, in the fall of 1872. Bailey (field notes) during his fieldwork in Utah from 1888 to 1890 recorded it from many localities. Numerous records have been added in more recent years.

SPECIES OF UNCERTAIN STATUS

The following species have been reported as sight records from the state. They have not been documented by specimens, photographs, or by several detailed descriptions.

Thus, for the present, we prefer to separate them from the main body of the annotated list. Wherever possible, observations from adjacent states are given to help substantiate the records from Utah. Where there are several records from neighboring states or from within a single state, we have used that report closest to Utah.

Podiceps grisegena (Boddaert)
Red-necked Grebe

RECORDS: The Red-necked Grebe was reported at Farmington Bay, Davis County, 20 May 1963, by Kashin and Webb (Utah Audubon News 1963:38), and by Behle and Perry (1975:7) along the causeway from Syracuse to the north end of Antelope Island, Davis County, 3 December 1970. Has been found at Lake Coeur d'Alene, Kootenai County, Idaho, 11 October 1950 (Burleigh 1972:3). Recently it was recorded from Lake Mead, Clark County, Nevada, 15 December 1973 (Mowbray 1974:496; Kingery 1974:669).

Dichromanassa rufescens (Gmelin)
Reddish Egret

RECORDS: A single sight record at Farmington Bay, Davis County, 15 April 1949, seen by Calvin D. Wilson and Boyd Shaffer of the Tracy Aviary (Behle and Perry 1975:8). The AOU Check-list indicated it as accidental in Arizona and Colorado (1957:46). Phillips et al. (1964:6) recorded several sightings from southern Arizona. The most northern report was one across the state line on the San Bernardino County, California, side of Lake Havasu on 9 September 1954.

Hydranassa tricolor (Müller)
Louisiana Heron

RECORDS: Two sight records in Utah, one seen at Farmington Bay Refuge, Davis County, by Calvin Wilson, 15 May 1947, and another at the same locality, 15 June

1973, observed by Dorothy Platt (Behle and Perry 1975:8). In Arizona it has been reported north to Camp Verde, Yavapai County, 27 August 1886 (Phillips et al. 1964: 6). The AOU Check-list (1957:49) listed it as wandering north to southern Nevada.

Anas fulvigula Ridgway
Mottled Duck

RECORDS: W. E. Ritter reported a flock of 21 seen near Hurricane, Washington County, 25 September 1965 (Behle and Perry 1975:11). Mottled Ducks have been designated as being of casual occurrence in Colorado (AOU Check-list 1957:73). We have no other records of this species in adjacent states.

Melanitta nigra (Linnaeus)
Black Scoter

RECORDS: One seen at Bear River Migratory Bird Refuge, Box Elder County, by Lloyd F. Gunther in the fall of 1966 (Scott 1967:63). Behle and Perry (1975:12) dated this record as 9 September 1966. This northern species is reported in the AOU Check-list (1957:94) as being found irregularly in Wyoming and Colorado. We have not found it reported in the literature from any of the other states adjacent to Utah.

Buteo platypterus (Vieillot)
Broad-winged Hawk

RECORDS: Observed in Big Cottonwood Canyon, Salt Lake County, 25 September 1970 by Vernon Kousky (Behle and Perry 1975:14). Kingery (1975:886) reported one seen at Provo, Utah County, 25 April 1975. A Broad-winged Hawk was banded and remained in a woodlot at Pocatello, Bannock County, Idaho, 30 April 1973 (Kingery 1973:800). One was seen at Cheyenne, Laramie County, 19 May 1968, and was considered to be a new record for Wyoming (Scott 1968:561). The AOU Check-list (1957:108) listed it as casual in Colorado.

In Arizona this species has been collected once, on 22 September 1956, in the Chiricahua Mountains, Cochise County, in the southeastern area of the state (Phillips et al. 1964:22). The first record for Nevada was at Corn Creek, Desert National Wildlife Range, Clark County, 7 May 1973 (Monson 1973:804).

Buteo albicaudatus Vieillot
White-tailed Hawk

RECORDS: There have been a number of sight records of this species in the state. Behle and Perry (1975:14) reported the following: near Vernon, Tooele County, 27 February 1957, observed by John B. Bushman and D. Elmer Johnson; near Eureka, Juab County, in 1942, 1953, and 1956, seen by Clyde Ward; one at Hell's Backbone, near Boulder, Garfield County, early August 1960, observed by Gleb Kashin. Kashin and Albert Webb reported one near Tooele, Tooele County, 10 April 1960 (Scott 1960:410). It has been reported in Arizona around Phoenix, Maricopa County, from 1899 to the winter of 1955 (Phillips et al. 1962:22–23).

Parabuteo unicinctus (Temminck)
Harris' Hawk

RECORDS: A bird of this species has been reported at Parowan, Iron County, 1 or 11 April 1963. Murie (1963:46), who saw the bird, reported it as 1 April 1963, while Scott (1963:422) reported it for 11 April. Behle and Perry (1975:14) indicated that the correct date is 1 April 1963. This widespread species over the southern tier of western states is reported as far north in Arizona as Topock in southern Mohave County (Phillips et al. 1964:23–24).

Falco rusticolus Linnaeus
Gyrfalcon

RECORDS: Clayton White (pers. comm.) has furnished us with the following sight

records in Utah. In December 1946–48 Boyd Shaffer saw one at Red Butte Canyon, Salt Lake County. Gary Lloyd, Robert Ford, and Clayton White were flying trained Prairie Falcons west of Salt Lake City, Salt Lake County, in November 1954, when a large falcon was attracted to them. It was about twice the size of the female Prairie they were flying. Ford had a close look at it and thought it was a Gyrfalcon. Lee Camp of Logan reported the occurrence of one in Logan, Cache County, in the winter of 1970. During the winter of 1970 or 1971 Terry Roundy saw one near Sandy, Salt Lake County. Behle and Perry (1975:15) reported one seen by Jim Hatchett, a falconer, at Riverton, Salt Lake County, December 1969. Kingery (1972:635) reported sight records at Pocatello, Bannock County, Idaho, 4 March 1972, and at Curlew Valley, Oneida County, Idaho, 11 March 1972. He also reported it being sighted at Sheridan, Sheridan County, Wyoming, 5 January 1972. Rogers (1974: 80) saw another bird in southeastern Idaho, 21 November 1973.

Lagopus leucurus (Richardson)
White-tailed Ptarmigan

RECORDS: Woodbury et al. (1949:36) listed it as hypothetical. They stated: "Reported by stockmen, sportsmen and others from mountain tops above timberline in Raft River, Uinta and Tusher Mountains, but no authentic record is available." Worthern (1968:470) did not find White-tailed Ptarmigans in the Tusher Mountains, Beaver and Piute counties, during his study of the area, although he indicated suitable habitat was available. White-tailed Ptarmigans have been released by the Utah State Division of Wildlife Resources at the head of Painter Basin near Gilbert Peak in the Uinta Mountains, Duchesne County. The first release of 23 birds was made on 3 June 1976, and an additional release of 32 birds occurred on 3 September 1976. These birds were obtained from Colorado and are of the race *L. l. altipetens* (personal communication Darrell H. Nish and LaVar A. Ware, Utah State Division of Wildlife Resources). Ptarmigans are found in the mountains of Wyoming and Colorado southward to northern New Mexico (AOU Check-list 1957:136).

Coturnicops noveboracensis (Gmelin)
Yellow Rail

RECORDS: Woodbury et al. (1949:37) reported it under the hypothetical list for Utah. The AOU Check-list (1931:98) reported it as casual in Utah. This statement was dropped in the 1957 (157–158) edition. The original record for this rail is Ridgway (1877:613), who reported seeing it at Parley's Park, Summit County, and several other localities. Stewart Murie reported two sight records for Cedar Valley, Iron County, one about 1947, the other on 14 July 1969 (Behle and Perry 1975:17). There is a summer report for Barr Lake, Adams County, in eastern Colorado (AOU Check-list 1957:157–158), and one caught alive at Sacaton, Pineal County (southeast of Phoenix, Arizona), 28 March 1909 (Phillips et al. 1964:31).

Haematopus bachmani Audubon
Black Oystercatcher

RECORDS: Wilson and Norr (1949:246) reported that C. L. Lockerbie observed a Black Oystercatcher at Farmington Bay Refuge, Davis County, 5 August 1949. It was observed in company with Willets. This West Coast species occurs as far south as Baja California but has not been reported inland (AOU Check-list 1957:165).

Bartramia longicauda (Beckstein)
Upland Sandpiper "Plover"

RECORDS: This species has been reported sporadically over the past century in Utah. Ridgway (1877:611) considered it common in the Kamas Prairie area of Summit County

in July 1869. One was seen by Stanford (1931:4), probably in Sevier County, 16 April 1929, and Webster (1947:40) reported one at Perry, Box Elder County, 6 May 1945. Murie observed one at Cedar City, Iron County, 28–29 August 1965 (Scott 1966:77). Burleigh (1972:13) has reported it from Kootenai County in Idaho's panhandle, and Snider (1970:631) listed one near Las Vegas, Clark County, Nevada, 19 April 1970. Phillips et al. (1964:34) reported one on the San Bernardino County, California, side of Lake Havasu on 11 September 1952.

Heteroscelus incanum (Gmelin)
Wandering Tattler

RECORDS: Behle and Perry (1975:18) reported the following sight records of the Wandering Tattler: two birds seen at Farmington Bay, Davis County, 13 August 1961, by Gleb Kashin. In 1974 Vernon Kousky saw one at Farmington Bay, 2 September, and later this one was observed by Paul Adamus on 4 and 11 September. Kingery (1976:102) reported a Wandering Tattler at Farmington Bay in the fall of 1975 in the same locality as the one reported in 1974. One was reported at Phoenix, Maricopa County, Arizona, between 18 September and 9 October 1971 (Monson 1972:101).

Calidris fusciollis (Vieillot)
White-rumped Sandpiper

RECORDS: A single bird was observed feeding and in flight at Fish Springs National Wildlife Refuge, Juab County, 29 March 1974, by Clyde L. Pritchett. Burleigh (1972:123–124) reported one collected at Hauser, Kootenai County, Idaho, 26 May 1960. In Colorado, Kingery (1971:884) reported one from Antero Reservoir, Park County, during the summer of 1971. Monson (1973:804) recorded 35 at Bosque del Apache National Wildlife Refuge, Socorro County, New Mexico, 6 May 1973, and

Snider (1970:76) reported two at Tuscon, Pima County, Arizona, 5 October 1969.

Limosa lapponica (Linnaeus)
Bar-tailed Godwit

RECORDS: One observed at Bear River Migratory Bird Refuge, Box Elder County, 24 August 1973 by Mark Collie (Behle and Perry 1975:20). There are no records from adjacent states. There were several reports of this species on the Pacific Coast in 1973 and 1974. Two reports are listed for California: one at Bolinas Lagoon, Marin County, 26 October 1973, where it was photographed (Remsen and Gaines 1974: 101), and another at Arcata, Humboldt County, 17–31 July 1974 (Stallcup and Greenberg 1974:944).

Limosa haemastica (Linnaeus)
Hudsonian Godwit

RECORDS: Six Hudsonian Godwits were observed by Stewart Murie at Cedar City, Iron County, 28 April 1968 (Scott 1968:561). Burleigh (1972:133) reported one in south central Idaho (Minidoka County), 7 July 1919, and Scott (1968:561) reported one near Cheyenne, Laramie County, Wyoming, 19 May 1968.

Cyclorrhynchus psittacula (Pallas)
Parakeet Auklet

RECORDS: One bird was seen at Farmington Bay Refuge, Davis County, 19 August 1962, by Gleb Kashin and Bert Webb (Behle and Perry 1975:22). It has not been reported inland in any of the adjacent states.

Columbina passerina (Linnaeus)
Ground Dove

RECORDS: A Ground Dove was seen at Cedar City, Iron County, 4 September 1963, by Stewart Murie (Behle and Perry

1975:22). Two were observed in Wyoming in 1972, one at Green River and the other at Seedskadee National Wildlife Refuge, Sweetwater County, 20 October. This species has been found at Grand Canyon Village, Coconino County, Arizona, 22–23 October 1930 (Phillip et al. 1964:43). It has been collected at two localities in Nevada. Wauer (1969:332) obtained one at Overton, Clark County, 20 July 1966, and Monson (1972:639) reported a collection at Mormon Farm, Clark County (near Las Vegas), 25 December 1971.

Caprimulgus vociferus Wilson
Whip-poor-will

RECORDS: The Hardens heard this species calling in Oak Creek Canyon, Zion National Park, Washington County, on two consecutive nights in early May 1965 (Wauer and Carter 1965:56). Richard W. Russell reported hearing it calling at Pine Lake, northeast of Bryce Canyon National Park, Garfield County, 7 and 9 July 1965 (Scott 1966:77). It is considered as casual at Fort Collins, Larimer County, Colorado (AOU Check-list 1957:291), and in Arizona it has been found as far north as Kingman, Mohave County (Phillips et al. 1964:55–56).

Lampornis clemenciae (Lesson)
Blue-throated Hummingbird

RECORDS: Reported at Springdale, Washington County. The bird was described as "a large hummingbird with white rectal and postocular stripes, white tail feathers, and an aggressive behavior contrasting markedly with the docile Rivoli's" (Kingery 1973:94). The date of this quoted observation was not given; however, in corresponding with Kingery we found that the bird was first observed 3 August 1972 and was seen 12 times in the following few days by Jerome Gifford and one other competent observer. This species, which is found in southern Arizona, southern New Mexico, and western Texas, has been reported twice from Colorado in the past few years. In 1970 it was found at Evergreen, Jefferson County (in mountains west of Denver), 7 September (Scott 1971:85). Two years later Kingery (1972:885) reported one at Rock Creek Canyon, El Paso County, south of Colorado Springs, 30 July 1972.

Melanerpes formicivorus (Swainson)
Acorn Woodpecker

RECORDS: There have been three observations of this species in southern Utah. Stewart Murie saw one seven miles north of Cedar City, Iron County, 25 May 1963, and one near Cedar City, 20 October 1971 (Behle and Perry 1975:26). Phillip Sollins saw a woodpecker of this species near Springdale, Washington County, 25 August 1970 (Scott 1971:85). It has been reported at the south rim of the Grand Canyon, Coconino County, Arizona, by Phillips et al. (1964:70–71) and at Tsegi Canyon, Navajo County, Arizona, 23 July 1936, by Woodbury and Russell (1945:66). Recently it has been seen twice in Nevada: at Boulder City, Clark County, 23–31 October 1971 (Monson 1972:102), and east of Las Vegas, Clark County, 27 October 1972 (specimen collected, Monson 1973:99).

Anthus spragueii (Audubon)
Sprague's Pipit

RECORDS: Behle and Perry (1975:33) reported this species in the Salt Lake City, Salt Lake County, and Cedar City, Iron County, areas. Observations are 3 and 23 January, 11 March, 27 August, 16 October, 14 November, 22–23 December. It has been found in north central Wyoming at Lake DeSmet, Johnson County, November 1967 (Scott 1968:74), and near Durango, La Plata County, Colorado, 28 February 1969 (Scott 1969:504). In New Mexico one was sighted at Bitter Lake Refuge, Chaves County, 29 April 1972 (Monson 1972:794). It has been found as far north in Arizona as Wikieup, Mohave County (Phillips et al. 1964.138).

Catharus minimus (Lafresnaye)
Gray-cheeked Thrush

RECORDS: There are two sight records of this species in Utah, both reported by Kashin. He observed one in south Willow Canyon, Stansbury Mountains, Tooele County, 18 October 1972, and the other in Salt Lake City, Salt Lake County, 7 November 1972 (Kingery 1973:94). It has been reported from Fort Collins, Larimer County, Colorado, 15 May 1973, where a specimen was collected (Kingery 1974:85), and again on 13 May 1974 (Kingery 1974:834). Monson (1972:794) reported one at Tule Springs Park, Las Vegas, Clark County, Nevada, 13 May 1972, and Kingery (1974:834) gave a sight record for the spring of 1974 at the same locality.

Popioptila melanura Lawrence
Black-tailed Gnatcatcher

RECORDS: The Christmas Bird Count of the National Audubon Society at St. George, Washington County, 29 December 1969, recorded this species (Lund 1970:416). It has been seen a number of times in Nevada. At an earlier date (Fisher 1893: 110) took one at Bunkerville, Clark County, Nevada, 9 May 1891. Lawson and Mowbray (1970:423; 1971:469; 1972:487) found it at Henderson, Clark County, Nevada, 21 December 1969, 2 January 1971, and 18 December 1971. Austin (1968:366; 1969:396) and Mowbray (1973:487) found it at the Desert Game Range, Clark and Lincoln counties, 28 December 1967, 22 December 1968, and 30 December 1972. Wauer (1969:333) obtained a specimen at Overton, Clark County, Nevada, 12 May 1966.

Calcarius mccowanii (Lawrence)
McCowan's Longspur

RECORDS: McCowan's Longspurs have been reported from west of Ogden, Weber County, 22 October 1953 (Scott 1954:33);

at Logan, Cache County, 27 December 1956, by Ronald Ryder (1957:215); and in Cedar Valley, Iron County, 24 November 1966 (Scott 1967:64). Burleigh (1972:440) reported one from Butte County in southeastern Idaho, 6 August 1890. Woodbury and Russell (1945:154) reported observations from the following northeastern Arizona locations: Cameron and Tuba City, Coconino County, 17 February 1937, 19 February 1937; Ganado, Apache County, 10 February 1938; Polacca, Navajo County, 30 September 1938.

Ammodramus bairdii (Audubon)
Baird's Sparrow

RECORDS: This species has been reported at Farmington Bay, Davis County, 12 March 1961, by Kashin (Scott 1961:348). Behle and Perry (1975:42) reported the following dates in northern Utah without any definite localities: in the spring (24, 30 April; 10 May); in the fall (14, 19 September; 12 October). It breeds in southern Canada and usually migrates east of the Rockies to southern New Mexico and Arizona (AOU Check-list 1957:592). Phillips et al. (1964:193, 194) recorded it in Arizona northward to the vicinity of Maverick in the southern part of Apache County.

Spizella pusilla (Wilson)
Field Sparrow

RECORDS: Several were seen at Salt Lake City, Salt Lake County, in late September and early October 1972 by Kashin (Behle and Perry 1975:44). It breeds in the Boulder, Boulder County, and Fort Morgan, Morgan County, Colorado, areas (AOU Check-list 1957:616).

Aimophila cassinii (Woodhouse)
Cassin's Sparrow

RECORDS: Woodbury et al. (1949:39) reported that A. O. Treganza saw one in April (no year given) near Low, Tooele County. Murie (1963:45) reported Cassin's Sparrows "in groups of 3–4, among Brewers, lark, chipping and white-crowned sparrows" at Parowan, Iron County, 18 September 1962. A Cassin's Sparrow was found at Evergreen, Jefferson County, Colorado, 9 November 1970. It was seen by many observers and banded (Scott 1971:86). It remained all winter in Evergreen at a feeder (Scott 1971:608) and was last seen on 13 May 1971 (Kingery 1971:779). It has been found in central Arizona near Camp Verde, Yavapai County (Phillips et al. 1964:200–201). In 1891 Merriam obtained a specimen at Timpahute Valley, Lincoln County, Nevada, on 26 May (Fisher 1893: 98).

Piranga olivacea (Gmelin)
Scarlet Tanager

RECORDS: Behle and Perry (1975:39) reported that A. Dean Stock obtained a specimen at St. George, Washington County, 17 June 1950. The skin was later destroyed. A nest with four eggs was found during the same summer in this area. A sight record in Salt Lake City, Salt Lake County, 29 June 1963, was given by Mrs. Gleb Kashin to Behle and Perry (1975:39). The AOU Check-list (1957:543–544) indicated it as being accidental in Cheyenne, Laramie County, Wyoming. Kingery (1973: 95) reported a sight record at Gunnison, Gunnison County, Colorado, 3 September 1972. A male was seen in Farmington, San Juan County, New Mexico, 19 and 28 May 1970 (Snider 1970:632). Phillips et al. (1964:175) gave three records for Tucson, Pima County, Arizona, for 18 May 1884, and Scott (1968:633) stated that Fritz Ryser found one at Genoa, Douglas County, Nevada, 8 June 1968.

Piranga flava (Vieillot)
Hepatic Tanager

RECORDS: A male Hepatic Tanager was observed at a feeder at the headquarters of

Bryce Canyon National Park, Garfield County, for almost a month commencing in late August 1964 (Scott 1965:64). One was reported by D. Elmer Johnson at Three Lakes near Kanab, Kane County, 4 June 1965 (Behle and Perry 1975:39). Phillips et al. (1964:175) reported it as far north as the south rim of the Grand Canyon, Coconino County, Arizona. Mowbray (1974:496) has found it at the Desert Game Range, Clark and Lincoln counties, Nevada, 29 December 1973.

Vermivora peregrina (Wilson)
Tenessee Warbler

RECORDS: Observed several times by Stewart Murie in the Cedar City area, Iron County, between 9 August and 16 October 1963; six or seven were seen in South Willow Canyon, Stansbury Mountains, Tooele County, 26 September 1972 by Kashin (Behle and Perry 1975:35). One collected at Potlatch, Latah County, Idaho, 13 September 1949 (Burleigh 1972:328). In Colorado it has been found at Durango,

La Plata County, 12 October 1970 (Scott 1971:86), and in New Mexico near Questa, Taos County, 21 May 1970 (Snider 1970: 632). One was collected in the Chiricahua Mountains, Cochise County, Arizona, 7 April 1925. (Phillips et al. 1964:146). Several have been reported from Corn Creek, Desert Game Range, Clark County, Nevada, 9 and 18 October 1972 and 8 May 1973 (Monson 1973:100, 805).

Parula americana (Linnaeus)
Northern Parula Warbler

RECORDS: One observed at Farmington Bay, Davis County, 5 September 1968, by Kashin (Scott 1969:87). This northern and eastern species has been recorded as casual at Cheyenne, Laramie County, Wyoming, and at Clear Creek, Jefferson County, Colorado (AOU Check-list 1957:485–486). Mowbray has reported this species at the Desert Game Range, Clark and Lincoln counties, Nevada, 4 May 1969 (Snider 1969:614) and 16 and 19 May 1971 (Snider 1971:784).

Fig. 65. Scrub Jay. Ogden, Weber County, Utah, 10 May 1959. Photo by R. J. Erwin.

Dendroica dominica (Linnaeus)
Yellow-throated Warbler

RECORDS: One seen by Robert Sundell and William H. Behle at East Canyon, Wasatch County, 19 May 1962 (Behle and Perry 1975:37). There are two recent records for southern Arizona, one at Guadalupe Canyon, Cochise County, 19 May 1972 (Monson 1972:794), and the other at Patagonia, Santa Cruz County, 2 June 1972 (Monson 1972:889).

Dendroica virens (Gmelin)
Black-throated Green Warbler

RECORDS: Murie (1966:8–9) reported two sight records of this species at Parowan, Iron County, 5 September 1963 and 10 September 1963. Kashin found one at Salt Lake City, Salt Lake County, 2 October 1971 (Kingery 1972:98). It has been reported as casual at Barr, Adams County, Colorado (AOU Check-list 1957:496). Snider (1970:632) reported one at Farmington, San Juan County, New Mexico, 8–9 May 1970.

Dendroica fusca (Müller)
Blackburnian Warbler

RECORDS: Reported early from the Ogden area by Allen (1872:166, 175). Jules Dreyfous saw one at the Old Mill, near the mouth of Big Cottonwood Canyon, Salt Lake County, 4 June 1974 (Behle and Perry 1975:36). It has been found at Fort Collins, Larimer County, Colorado, 13–17 October 1973 (Kingery 1974:86); Fort Bayard, Grant County, New Mexico (AOU Check-list 1957:497); Arizona-Sonora Desert Museum, near Tucson, Pima County, Arizona, 8 October 1973 (Parker 1974:90); and in Nevada (no locality given), 19 September 1973 (Kingery 1974:86).

Dendroica palmarum (Gmelin)
Palm Warbler

RECORDS: Palm Warblers have been recorded at Zion National Park, Washington County, 20 October 1963 (Scott 1964: 60); Fish Springs National Wildlife Refuge, Juab County, 25 May 1968 (Scott 1968:561); Bear River Migratory Bird Refuge, Box Elder County, 19 September 1974, by Bruce Webb (Behle and Perry 1975:37). One was seen at Salt Lake City, Salt Lake County, 27 October 1974, by Gleb Kashin (Kingery 1975:97). The AOU Check-list (1957:504) recorded it as casual at Tarrington, Goshen County, and Laramie, Albany County, Wyoming. Scott (1968:74) reported one from Lookout Mountain, Jefferson County, Colorado, 30 September 1967. One was identified near Farmington, San Juan County, New Mexico, 13 May 1972 (Monson 1972:794). Phillips et al. (1964:155) reported sight records from central Arizona (Walnut Grove, Yavapai County), 29 April 1956.

Seiurus aurocapillus (Linnaeus)
Ovenbird

RECORDS: One was seen in South Willow Canyon, Stansbury Range, Tooele County, 14 October 1953 (Scott 1954:33), and another was observed near Salt Lake City, Salt Lake County, 20 May 1961, by Kashin (Behle and Perry 1975:37). Kingery (1971: 886) reported one at Rupert, Minidoka County, Idaho, 29 May 1971, and a bird was found breeding at Storey, Sheridan County, Wyoming, during the late spring of 1971. It also breeds at Colorado Springs, El Paso County, Colorado (AOU Check-list 1957:506). Snider (1968:76) recorded a bird near Tucson, Pima County, Arizona, 3 October 1967. Monson (1973:805) found one at Corn Creek, Desert National Wildlife Range, Clark County, Nevada, 27 May 1973.

Vireo flavifrons Vieillot
Yellow-throated Vireo

RECORDS: Keith Dixon reported one "singing steadily in cottonwoods along a river near Logan," Cache County, 11 June 1974 (Kingery 1975:96). Two have been reported from Phoenix, Maricopa County, Arizona, 29 August 1969 (Snider 1970:78) and 18 August 1971 (Monson 1972:103). Mowbray saw one at Las Vegas, Clark County, Nevada, 27 October 1974 (Kingery 1975:96).

Vireo philadelphicus (Cassin)
Philadelphia Vireo

RECORDS: First reported at Salt Lake City, Salt Lake County, 15 September 1964 (Scott 1965:64), and again at the same locality on 22 September 1968 by Kashin (Scott 1969:87). There are two reports for Durango, La Plata County, southwestern Colorado, one on 16 September 1967 (Scott 1968:74), and the other on 10 July 1969 (Scott 1969:680). One was collected south of Phoenix, Maricopa County, Arizona, 12 October 1963 (Phillips et al. 1964:145).

Carduelis lawrencei Cassin
Lawrence's Goldfinch

RECORDS: A flock of 24 was reported by Lois and Clyde Harden at Kanab, Kane County, 29 December 1966 (Lund 1967: 346). A specimen was taken at Wickenburg, northern Maricopa County, Arizona, 12 May 1953 (Phillips et al. 1964:188). Johnson and Banks (1959:303) collected one in the extreme southern part of Clark County, Nevada, 4 April 1958. One was photographed at Corn Creek, Desert Game Range, Clark County, Nevada, 1 October 1972, and erroneously reported as the first record for Nevada (Monson 1973:101).

Carpodacus purpureus (Gmelin)
Purple Finch

RECORDS: There have been several sightings of this species but no collection records. Behle and Perry (1975:40) reported the following: a few seen at Bountiful, Davis County, 26 November 1949, by Rex Snow; several at Tracy Aviary, Salt Lake City, Salt Lake County, winter 1949–50, by Calvin Wilson; many females at Holladay, Salt Lake County, winter 1972–73, by Steve Carr. Fifty-nine were reported at Kanab, Kane County, 20 December 1972, by Richard and Georgina Stuart, who indicated they had been there "all fall" (1973:479). Three were reported at Zion National Park, Washington County, 19 December 1972 (Foster 1973:480). Kingery (1973:645–646) indicated that not only were there the above mentioned sightings in southern Utah, but there had been one sighting somewhere in the northern part of the state. No details were available. Wilt (1973:484) reported nine at Pipe Springs National Monument, Mohave County, Arizona, 26 December 1972. Two were collected at the Nevada Test Site, Nye County, Nevada, 24–25 October 1961 (Hayward et al. 1963:23).

Aphelocoma ultramarina (Bonaparte)
Mexican Jay

RECORDS: One was seen at the Cactus Mine, about two miles south of Frisco Peak, San Francisco Mountains, Beaver County, 17 August 1949 (Taylor 1949:3). In Arizona, Mexican Jays have been reported as far north as the Mogollon Rim in northwestern Gila County (Phillips et al. 1964:105).

SUBSPECIES OF UNCERTAIN STATUS

Oberholser (1974) proposed changing the names of several species and described a number of new subspecies, 12 of which have ranges extending into or through Utah. Since neither the species nor the subspecies have been critically reviewed, we have listed the subspecies with Utah affinities below. Thus, we recognize their presence in the literature but do not accept them as valid changes at the present time.

Leucophoyx thula arileuca Oberholser: Utah Snowy Egret.

Type specimen Bear River, Box Elder County, 6 June 1916. U.S. National Museum No. 261042.

Anas platyrhyncha neoboria Oberholser: American Mallard.

Chordeiles minor divisus Oberholser: Wyoming Common Nighthawk.

Solivireo solitarius jacksoni Oberholser: Jackson's Solitary Vireo.

Melodivireo gilvus petrorus Oberholser: Wyoming Warbling Vireo.

Dendroica petechia hypochlora Oberholser: Arizona Yellow Warbler.

Passer domesticus plecticus Oberholser: Pale House Sparrow.

Agelaius phoeniceus stereus Oberholser: Colorado Red-winged Blackbird.

Agelaius phoeniceus zastereus Oberholser: Idaho Red-winged Blackbird.

Piranga ludoviciana zephyrica Oberholser: Rocky Mountain Western Tanager.

Junco oreganus eumesus Oberholser: Coues' Oregon Junco.

Zonotrichia leucophrys aphaea Oberholser: Idaho White-crowned Sparrow.

LITERATURE CITED

ABLE, K. W. 1974. The changing seasons. American Birds 28:22–27.

ALDRICH, J. W. 1968. Population characteristics and nomenclature of the Hermit Thrush. Proceedings U.S. National Museum 124:1–33.

ALDRICH, J. W., AND H. FRIEDMANN. 1943. A revision of the Ruffed Grouse. Condor 45:85–103.

ALLEN, J. 1972. Christmas bird count, Bear River Migratory Bird Refuge, Utah. American Birds 26:478.

ALLEN, J. A. 1872a. Ornithological notes from the west. American Naturalist Part I, 6:263–275; Part II, 6:342–351; Part III, 6:394–404.

———. 1872b. Notes of an ornithological reconnaissance of portions of Kansas, Colorado, Wyoming, and Utah. Bulletin Museum Comparative Zoology 3:113–183.

AMERICAN ORNITHOLOGISTS' UNION. 1931. Checklist of North American birds, 4th ed. Lancaster, Pennsylvania. 526 pp.

———. 1957. Check-list of North American birds, 5th ed. Lord Baltimore Press, Baltimore, Maryland. 691 pp.

———. 1973. Thirty-second supplement to the American Ornithologists' Union check-list of North American birds. Auk 90:411–419.

———. 1976. Thirty-third supplement to the American Ornithologists' Union check-list of North American birds. Auk 93:875–879.

ARVEY, M. D. 1941. A new race of Bushtit from southeastern California. Condor 43:74–75.

AUERBACH, H. S. 1943. Father Escalante's journal with related documents and maps. Utah State Historical Quarterly 11:1–142.

AUSTIN, G. 1968. Christmas bird count, Desert Game Range, Nevada. Audubon Field Notes 22:366.

———. 1969. Christmas bird count, Desert Game Range, Nevada. Audubon Field Notes 23:396.

BADER, W. 1947. Christmas bird count, Salt Lake City, Utah. Audubon Field Notes 1:107–108.

BADER, W. A. 1948. Christmas bird count, Salt Lake City, Utah. Audubon Field Notes 2:109–110.

BAILEY, V. 1888, 1893. Field notes. U.S. Bureau of Biological Survey. Copy located in Brigham Young University Life Sciences Museum.

———. 1905. A correction. Condor 7:82.

BAIRD, S. F. 1852. Birds. Appendix C. Pages 314–335 in Howard Stansbury, Exploration and survey of the valley of the Great Salt Lake of Utah, including a reconnaissance of a new route through the Rocky Mountains. Senate Special Session, March 1851. Executive No. 3. Lippincott, Grambo and Co., Philadelphia.

———. 1854. Report on birds collected on the survey. Pages 11–16 in Report of Lieut. E. Beckwith, Third Artillery, upon exploration for a railroad route, near the 38th and 39th parallels of North Latitude by Capt. J. W. Gunnison, Corps of Topographical Engineers and near the Forty-first parallel of North Latitude by Lieut. E. G. Beckwith. Volume X. Zoological Report. No. 2.

———. 1858. Birds, Volume IX, Part II. General report upon the zoology of the several railroad routes. Pages 1–1005 in Reports of explorations and surveys, to ascertain the most practicable and economical route for a railroad from the Mississippi River to the Pacific Ocean made under the direction of the Secretary of War, in 1853–6, according to acts of Congress of March 3, 1853, May 31, 1854 and August 5, 1854. House of Representatives 33rd Congress, 2nd Session. Ex.

Doc. No. 91. A. O. P. Nicholson, Washington, D.C.

——. 1876. Ornithology. A list of birds. Appendix K. List of birds collected by Charles S. McCarthy, taxidermist. Pages 375–381 *in* J. H. Simpson, Report of explorations across the Great Basin of the territory of Utah for a direct wagon-route from Camp Floyd to Genoa, in Carson Valley, in 1859. Engineer Department U.S. Army. Government Printing Office, Washington, D.C.

BALPH, M. H. 1976. Golden-crowned Sparrows in northern Utah. North American Bird Bander 1:67.

BANKS, R. C. 1964. Geographic variation in the White-crowned Sparrow *Zonotrichia leucophrys*. University of California Publications Zoology 70:1–123.

BARNES, C. T. 1919. Roseate Spoonbill in Utah. Auk 36:565–566.

——. 1943. Spring migration on Farmington Bay, Utah. Auk 60:102–103.

——. 1946. Rare Utah birds. Auk 63:258–259.

BARTONEK, J. C. 1966. Trumpeter Swan in Utah. Condor 68:521.

BEALL, D. 1974. Christmas bird count, Bear River Migratory Bird Refuge, Utah. American Birds 28:487.

BECK, D. E. 1942. Notes on the occurrence of gulls at Utah Lake. Great Basin Naturalist 3:54.

BECKWITH, E. G. 1854–1855. Report of exploration for the Pacific Railroad, on the line of the Forty-first parallel of North Latitude. *In* Report of the Secretary of War communicating the several Pacific Railroad explorations. 33rd Congress, 1st Session. House of Representatives. Ex. Doc. No. 129. A. O. P. Nicholson, Washington, D.C. 136 pp.

BEE, R. G., AND J. HUTCHINGS. 1942. Breeding records of Utah Birds. Great Basin Naturalist 3:61–90.

BEHLE, W. H. 1935. A history of the bird colonies of Great Salt Lake. Condor 37:24–35.

——. 1936a. Status of the Cormorants of Great Salt Lake. Condor 38:76–79.

——. 1936b. The present status of the Great Salt Lake bird colonies. Condor 38:220–221.

——. 1938. Highlights of ornithological work in Utah. Condor 40:165–173.

——. 1940a. Extension of range of the Black-chinned Sparrow into Utah. Condor 42:224.

——. 1940b. Distribution and characters of the Utah Red-wing. Wilson Bulletin, 52:234–240.

——. 1941a. Barn Owls nesting at Kanab, Utah. Condor 43:160.

——. 1941b. A collection of birds from La Sal Mountain region of southeastern Utah. Wilson Bulletin 53:181–184.

——. 1942a. Distribution and variation of the Horned Larks (*Otocoris alpestris*) of western North America. University of California Publications Zoology 46:205–316.

——. 1942b. Records of the Herring Gull, Sanderling, and Lark Bunting in Utah. Condor 44:230–231.

——. 1943a. Birds of Pine Valley Mountain region, southwestern Utah. Bulletin of University of Utah, 34, Biological Series 7:1–85.

——. 1943b. Notes on the synonymy and distribution of the Horned Larks of Utah. Proceeding Utah Academy Sciences, Arts, and Letters 19–20:153–156.

——. 1944a. Check-list of the birds of Utah. Condor 46:67–87.

——. 1944b. The pelican colony at Gunnison Island, Great Salt Lake, in 1943. Condor 46:198–200.

——. 1948a. Systematic comment on some geographically variable birds occurring in Utah. Condor 50:71–80.

——. 1948b. Birds observed in April along the Colorado River from Hite to Lee's Ferry. Auk 65:303–306.

——. 1949a. Second record of the Sabine Gull from Utah. Condor 51:98.

——. 1949b. Report on the colonial nesting birds of Great Salt Lake 1947–49. Condor 51:268–270.

——. 1950a. Clines in the Yellow-throats of Western North America. Condor 52:193–219.

——. 1950b. A new race of Mountain Chickadee from the Utah-Idaho area. Condor 52:273–274.

——. 1951. A new race of the Black-capped Chickadee from the Rocky Mountain Region. Auk 68:75–79.

——. 1954a. Changing status of the Starling in Utah. Condor 56:49–50.

——. 1954b. Second records of the Swamp Sparrow and Brown Thrasher in Utah. Condor 56:312–313.

——. 1955. The birds of the Deep Creek Mountains of central western Utah. University of Utah Biological Series 11:1–34.

——. 1956. Field observations. Utah Audubon News 8:72.

——. 1958. The birds of the Raft River Mountains, northwestern Utah. University of Utah Biological Series 11:1–40.

——. 1960a. The birds of southeastern Utah. University of Utah Biological Series 12:1–56.

——. 1960b. Problems of distribution and speciation in Utah birds. Proceedings Utah Academy of Sciences, Arts, and Letters 37:13–36.

——. 1966. Noteworthy records of Utah birds. Condor 68:396-397.

——. 1967. Migrant races of Western Wood Pewee in Utah. Auk 84:133-134.

——. 1968a. A new race of the Purple Martin from Utah. Condor 70:166-169.

——. 1968b. Records of the Snowy Owl for Utah. Wilson Bulletin 80:231-232.

——. 1971. Check-list of the birds of Utah. Mimeographed. 8 pp.

——. 1973a. Clinal variation in White-throated Swifts from Utah and the Rocky Mountain Region. Auk 90:299-306.

——. 1973b. Significant bird records from Utah. Great Basin Naturalist 33:243-245.

——. 1976a. Systematic review, intergradation, and clinal variation in Cliff Swallows. Auk 93:66-67.

——. 1976b. Mohave desert avifauna in the Virgin River Valley of Utah, Nevada, and Arizona. Condor 78:40-48.

BEHLE, W. H., AND J. GHISELIN. 1958. Additional data on the birds of the Uinta Mountains and Basin of northeastern Utah. Great Basin Naturalist 18:1-22.

BEHLE, W. H., AND H. HIGGINS. 1942. Winter records of the Slate-colored Junco and Harris Sparrow in Utah. Wilson Bulletin 54:54-55.

BEHLE, W. H., AND M. L. PERRY. 1975. Utah birds: guide, check-list and occurrence charts. Utah Museum of Natural History, University of Utah, Salt Lake City. 144 pp.

BEHLE, W. H., AND A. ROSS. 1945. Miscellaneous records of birds uncommon in Utah. Condor 47:168-170.

BEHLE, W. H., AND R. K. SELANDER. 1951a. The systematic relationships of the Fox Sparrows (Passerella iliaca) of the Wasatch Mountains, Utah, and the Great Basin. Journal Washington Academy of Science 41:364-367.

——. 1951b. A new race of Dusky Grouse (Dendragapus obscurus) from the Great Basin. Proceedings Biological Society of Washington 64:125-128.

——. 1952. New and additional records of Utah birds. Wilson Bulletin 64:26-32.

BEHLE, W. H., J. B. BUSHMAN, AND C. M. GREENHALGH. 1958. Birds of the Kanab area and adjacent high plateaus of southern Utah. University of Utah Biological Series 11:1-92.

BEHLE, W. H., J. B. BUSHMAN, AND C. M. WHITE. 1964. Distributional data on uncommon birds in Utah and adjacent states. Wilson Bulletin 75:450-456.

BENSON, S. B. 1935. A biological reconnaissance of Navajo Mountain, Utah. University of California Publications Zoology 40: 439-456.

BENT, A. C. 1925. Life histories of North American Wildfowl. Bulletin U.S. National Museum 130. 316 pp.

——. 1926. Life histories of North American marsh birds. Bulletin U.S. National Museum 135. 490 pp.

——. 1932. Life histories of North American gallinaceous birds. Bulletin U.S. National Museum 162. 477 pp.

——. 1938. Life histories of North American birds of prey. Part 2. Bulletin U.S. National Museum 170. 482 pp.

BIENNIAL REPORT of the Board of Trustees of the Agricultural College of Utah for the years 1901-1902 accompanied by the report of the President and the Secretary's report of the receipts and disbursements. Star Printing Company. 71 pp.

BIRDSEYE, C. 1909. Field notes. U.S. Bureau of Biological Survey. Copy located in Brigham Young University Life Sciences Museum.

BISHOP, L. B. 1938. An apparently unrecognized race of Redwing from Utah. Transactions San Diego Society of Natural History 9:1-4.

BOND, G. M. 1963. Geographic variations in the thrush Hylocichla ustulata. Proceedings of the U.S. National Museum 114:373-387.

BURLEIGH, T. D. 1960. Geographic variation in the Western Wood Pewee (Contopus sordidulus). Proceedings of Biological Society of Washington 73:141-146.

——. 1972. Birds of Idaho. Caxton Printers, Caldwell, Idaho. 467 pp.

CARTER, D. L. 1967a. Birds of Arches National Monument. Mimeographed. 6 pp.

——. 1967b. Christmas bird count, Arches National Monument, Utah. Audubon Field Notes 21:344-345.

CARTER, D. L., AND R. H. WAUER. 1965. Black Hawk nesting in Utah. Condor 67:82-83.

CARY, M. 1907. Field notes. U.S. Bureau of Biological Survey. Copy located in Brigham Young University Life Sciences Museum.

CHECK-LIST OF BIRDS OF THE WORLD. 1931-1951. Vols. 1-7. J. L. Peters. Harvard University Press, Cambridge, Mass. 345 pp., 401 pp., 311 pp., 291 pp., 306 pp., 259 pp., 318 pp.

——. 1960. Vol. 9. Edited by E. Mayr and J. C. Greenway, Jr. Museum of Comparative Zoology, Cambridge, Mass. 506 pp.

——. 1962. Vol. 15. Edited by E. Mayr and J. C. Greenway, Jr. Museum of Comparative Zoology, Cambridge, Mass. 315 pp.

——. 1964. Vol. 10. Edited by E. Mayr and R. A. Paynter, Jr. Museum of Comparative Zoology, Cambridge, Mass. 502 pp.

——. 1967. Vol. 12. Edited by R. A. Paynter, Jr. Museum of Comparative Zoology, Cambridge, Mass. 495 pp.

——. 1968. Vol. 14. Edited by R. A. Paynter, Jr. Museum of Comparative Zoology, Cambridge, Mass. 443 pp.

——. 1970. Vol. 13. Edited by R. A. Paynter, Jr. Museum of Comparative Zoology, Cambridge, Mass. 443 pp.

CLAYTON, W. 1921. William Clayton's journal. A daily record of the journey of the original company of "Mormon" pioneers from Nauvoo, Illinois, to the valley of the Great Salt Lake. Deseret News Press, Salt Lake City. 376 pp.

COALE, H. K. 1915. The present status of the Trumpeter Swan (*Olor buccinator*). Auk 32: 82-90.

CONOVER, B. 1944. The races of the Solitary Sandpiper. Auk 61:537-544.

COTTAM, C. 1927. Distributional list of the birds of Utah. Unpublished thesis. Brigham Young University, Department of Zoology and Entomology. 164 pp.

——. 1929. A shower of grebes. Condor 31: 80-81.

——. 1941a. Leconte Sparrow in Utah. Condor 43:116-117.

——. 1941b. Indigo Bunting and Band-tailed Pigeon in Utah. Condor 43:122.

——. 1942a. Records from extreme northeastern Nevada. Condor 44:127-128.

——. 1942b. New or uncommon Utah bird records. Wilson Bulletin 54:254-255.

——. 1945a. The Ruddy Turnstone in Utah. Condor 47:79.

——. 1945b. Some records of birds in Utah. Condor 47:172-173.

——. 1946. Late nesting of the Caspian Tern in Utah. Condor 48:94-95.

COTTAM, C., AND J. B. LOW. 1948. Florida Gallinule in Utah. Auk 65:459.

COTTAM, C., AND F. M. UHLER. 1937. Birds in relation to fishes. U.S. Department of Agriculture Bureau of Biological Survey. Wildlife Research and Management Leaflet BS-83. 16 pp.

COTTAM, C., AND C. S. WILLIAMS. 1939. Food and habits of some birds nesting on islands in Great Salt Lake. Wilson Bulletin 51:150-155.

COTTAM, C., C. S. WILLIAMS, AND C. A. SOOTER. 1942. Some unusual winter visitors or late migrants to the Bear River Marshes, Utah. Great Basin Naturalist 3:51-53.

COUES, E. 1874. Birds of the northwest. A handbook of the ornithology of the region drained by the Missouri River and its tributaries. U.S. Geological Survey of the Territories. Miscellaneous publications No. 3. Government Printing Office, Washington, D.C. 791 pp.

——. 1899. Very early record of the Cliff Swallow. Auk 16:359.

COURT, E. J. 1908. Treganza Blue Heron. Auk 25:291-296.

CRACRAFT, J. 1972. The relationships of the higher taxa of birds: problems in phylogenetic reasoning. Condor 74:379-392.

CROFT, G. Y. 1932. Cedar Waxwing (*Bombycilla cedrorum*) breeding in Utah. Auk 49: 91.

DELACOUR, J. 1954. The waterfowl of the world. Country Life Limited, London. 284 pp.

DESERET EVENING NEWS. 1869. Salt Lake City, Utah. Local and other matters. 10 November: 3.

EASTERLA, D. A. 1966. First specimen of the Summer Tanager in Utah. Condor 68:210.

EDWARDS, C. C. 1969. Winter behavior and population dynamics of American Eagles in western Utah. Unpublished Ph.D. dissertation. Brigham Young University. 142 pp.

ELLIS, D. H., D. G. SMITH, AND J. R. MURPHY. 1969. Studies on raptor mortality in western Utah. Great Basin Naturalist 29:165-167.

EVENING HERALD. 1936. Provo, Utah. Drainage of Mud Lake is protested. 15 April:1, 8.

FERRIS, R. 1963. Jordan Narrows field trip, Sunday, October 13, 1963. Utah Audubon News 15:62-63.

FISHER, A. K. 1893. Report on the ornithology of the Death Valley expedition of 1891, comprising notes on the birds observed in southern California, southern Nevada and parts of Arizona and Utah. North American Fauna No. 7. Part 2. 158 pp.

——. 1937. Long-tailed Jaeger observed on the Bear River Marshes, Utah. Auk 54:389-390.

FOLLETT, R. F. 1960. Christmas bird count, Hyde Park, Utah. Audubon Field Notes 14: 253.

FOSTER, R. 1971. Christmas bird count, Zion National Park. American Birds 25:463.

——. 1973. Christmas bird count, Zion National Park, Utah. American Birds 27:480.

FREMONT, J. C. 1845. Report of the exploring expedition to the Rocky Mountains in the year 1842, and to Oregon and North California in the years 1843-44. Printed by order of the Senate of the United States. Public Documents 2nd Session, 28th Congress. Vol. 11. No. 174. Gales and Seaton, Washington, D.C. 693 pp.

FRIEDMANN, H. 1950. The birds of North and Middle America. Bulletin U.S. National Museum No. 50. Part 11. 793 pp.

FROST, H. H. 1966. Dickcissel in Utah. Wilson Bulletin 78:126.

FROST, H. H., AND J. R. MURPHY. 1905. Observations on birds along the Colorado in the vicinity of Moab, Utah. Proceedings of the

Utah Academy of Sciences, Arts, and Letters 42:180–185.

GEOGHEGAN, E. 1959. Jordan Narrows fieldtrip. Utah Audubon News 11:41.

———. 1963. Fieldtrip to Jordan Narrows. Utah Audubon News 15:40–41.

GOODWIN, S. H. 1904a. About the Utah gull. Condor 6:99–100.

———. 1904b. Pelicans nesting at Utah Lake. Condor 6:126–129.

———. 1905. Bohemian Waxwings in Utah — range of Cliff Swallows. Condor 7:52.

GRANTHAM, H. 1936. The Brown Thrasher in Utah. Condor 38:85.

GRATER, R. K. 1937. Check-list of birds of Grand Canyon National Park. Natural History Bulletin No. 8. Grand Canyon, Natural History Association. 55 pp.

———. 1943. Bird notes from southwestern Utah. Condor 45:75–76.

GREENHALGH, C. M. 1948. Second record of the Golden-crowned Sparrow in Utah. Condor 50:46.

GUNTHER, L. F., AND J. B. VAN DEN AKKER. 1946. A record of the Myrtle Warbler for Box Elder County, Utah. Condor 48:285.

HAIGHT, I. C. 1936. Diary of Isaac C. Haight, 7 June 1842 to 12 February 1862. Historical Records Survey Project of the Work Progress Administration of St. George, Utah. Microfilm copy located in Brigham Young University Library.

HARDY, R. 1939. Two new bird records for Utah. Condor 41:86.

———. 1941a. Utah bird records. Wilson Bulletin 53:124–125.

———. 1941b. Records of the Nevada Nuthatch in Utah. Wilson Bulletin 53:236.

HARDY, R., AND H. G. HIGGINS. 1940. An annotated check-list of the birds of Washington County, Utah. Proceedings Utah Academy of Sciences, Arts, and Letters 17:95–111.

HARGRAVE, L. L. 1939. Bird bones from abandoned Indian dwellings in Arizona and Utah. Condor 41:206–210.

HAYWARD, C. L. 1931. A preliminary list of the birds of the subalpine and alpine zones of the Uintah [sic] Mountains. Proceedings Utah Academy of Science 8:151–152.

———. 1935a. Breeding status and migration of the Caspian Tern in Utah. Condor 37:140–144.

———. 1935b. A study of the winter bird life in Bear Lake and Utah Lake valleys. Wilson Bulletin 47:278–284.

———. 1936-1968. Field notes. Located in Brigham Young University Life Sciences Museum.

———. 1937. Some new and unusual bird rec-

ords from Utah. Wilson Bulletin 49:303–305.

———. 1940. Notes on the distribution of nighthawks in Utah. Great Basin Naturalist 1:93–96.

———. 1941. Notes on the nesting habits of some mountain-dwelling birds in Utah. Great Basin Naturalist 2:1–8.

———. 1943. Notes on the status of the Red Crossbill in Utah. Auk 60:276–277.

———. 1944. Additional records of uncommon birds in Utah. Condor 46:204–205.

———. 1958. Additional notes on the Purple Martin in Utah. Condor 60:406.

———. 1966. New and unusual bird records from Utah. Condor 68:305–306.

———. 1967. Birds of the upper Colorado River basin. Brigham Young University Science Bulletin, Biological Series 9:1–64.

HAYWARD, C. L., M. L. KILLPACK, AND G. L. RICHARDS. 1963. Birds of the Nevada Test Site. Brigham Young University Science Bulletin, Biological Series 3:1–27.

HENSHAW, H. W. 1874. Annotated list of birds of Utah. Annals New York Lyceum Natural History 11:1–14.

———. 1875. Report upon the ornithological collections made in portions of Nevada, Utah, California, Colorado, New Mexico, and Arizona, during the years 1871, 1872, 1873, and 1874. Chapter 3. Pages 131–508, 977–989 in Vol. 5 (Zoology) in Report upon geographical and geological explorations and surveys west of the one-hundredth meridian in charge of First Lieut. Geo. M. Wheeler, Corps of Engineers, U.S. Army, under the direction of Brig. Gen. A. A. Humphreys, Chief of Engineers, U.S. Army.

HUBBARD, J. P. 1969. The relationships and evolution of the Dendroica coronata complex. Auk 86:393–432.

IRVING, W. 1868. The adventures of Captain Bonneville, USA, in the Rocky Mountains and the Far West digested from his journal and illustrated from various other sources. G. P. Putnam's Sons, New York. 524 pp.

JOHNSON, D. E. 1935a. Some bird notes from Utah. Wilson Bulletin 47:160.

———. 1935b. Another Snow Bunting record for Utah. Wilson Bulletin 47:294.

JOHNSON, H. C. 1899a. Nesting of the Wilson's Snipe in Utah. Bulletin of the Cooper Ornithological Club 1:26.

———. 1899b. A successful day with the Duck Hawks. Bulletin of the Cooper Ornithological Club 1:45–46.

———. 1899c. Ravens nesting on a railroad bridge. Bulletin of the Cooper Ornithological Club 1:71–72.

———. 1900. In the breeding home of Clark's Nutcracker (*Nucifraga columbianus*). Condor 2:49-52.

———. 1902a. The Piñon Jay. Condor 4:14.

———. 1902b. An unusual set of eggs of Clarke [*sic*] Nutcracker. Condor 4:87-88.

———. 1903. Pygmy Owl in town. Condor 5:81.

JOHNSON, N. K. 1966. Morphological stability versus adaptive variation in the Hammond's Flycatcher. Auk 83:179-299.

JOHNSON, N. K., AND R. C. BANKS. 1959. Pine Grosbeak and Lawrence Goldfinch in Nevada. Condor 61:303.

———. 1976. Breeding distribution of Nashville and Virginia's Warblers. Auk 93:219-230.

JOURNAL HISTORY. 1848. Microfilm copy 22 July 1847-8 October 1848. Brigham Young University Library, Provo, Utah. n.p.

KASHIN, G. 1955. The June trip to Jordan Narrows. Utah Audubon News 7:39-40.

———. 1963a. Trip to Fairmont Park and lower Parley's Canyon, February 10, 1963. Utah Audubon News 15:16, 60-61.

———. 1963b. Christmas bird count, Salt Lake City, Utah. Audubon Field Notes 17:263-264.

———. 1964a. Field notes. Utah Audubon News 16:3-4, 37, 50, 55.

———. 1964b. Christmas bird count, Salt Lake City, Utah. Audubon Field Notes 18:293.

———. 1966. Christmas bird count, Salt Lake City, Utah. Audubon Field Notes 20:351-352.

———. 1967. Christmas bird count, Salt Lake City, Utah. Audubon Field Notes 21:347.

———. 1968. Christmas bird count, Salt Lake City, Utah. Audubon Field Notes 22:361.

———. 1970. Christmas bird count, Salt Lake City, Utah. Audubon Field Notes 24:416.

———. 1974. Christmas bird count, Salt Lake City, Utah. American Birds 28:488-489.

KEITH, A. R. 1968. A summary of the extra-limital records of the Varied Thrush, 1848 to 1966. Bird Banding 34:245-276.

KILLPACK, M. L. 1951. Lark Bunting in Uintah [*sic*] Basin, Utah. Condor 53:99.

———. 1953. Lapland Longspur and Snow Bunting recorded in Utah. Condor 55:152.

———. 1957. Christmas bird count, Roosevelt, Utah. Audubon Field Notes 10:215.

———. 1959. Christmas bird count, Roosevelt, Utah. Audubon Field Notes 13:238.

KILLPACK, M. L., AND D. N. CRITTENDEN. 1952. Starlings as winter residents in the Uinta Basin, Utah. Condor 54:338-344.

KILLPACK, M. L., AND C. L. HAYWARD. 1958. New and unusual records of birds from the Uinta Basin. Great Basin Naturalist 18:23-25.

KINGERY, H. E. 1971. Great Basin-central Rocky Mountain region. American Birds 25:774-780, 882-888.

———. 1972. Great Basin-central Rocky Mountain region. American Birds 26:92-99, 634-638, 882-887.

———. 1973. Great Basin-central Rocky Mountain region. American Birds 27:91-96, 643-646, 799-803.

———. 1974. Mountain West. American Birds 28:83-86, 668-672, 832-836.

———. 1975. Mountain West. American Birds 29:93-98, 720-724, 885-890.

———. 1976. Mountain West. American Birds 30:101-105.

KNOPF, F. L., AND J. C. STREET. 1974. Insecticide residues in White Pelican eggs from Utah. Wilson Bulletin 84:428-433.

KNORR, O. A. 1962. Black Swift breeds in Utah. Condor 64:79.

KNOWLTON, G. F. 1937. Utah birds in the control of certain insect pests. Proceedings of Utah Academy of Sciences, Arts, and Letters 14:159-166.

KNOWLTON, G. F., AND F. C. HARMSTON. 1943. Grasshoppers and crickets eaten by Utah birds. Auk 60:589-591.

LAWSON, C. S., AND M. V. MOWBRAY. 1970. Christmas bird count, Henderson, Nevada. Audubon Field Notes 24:423-424.

———. 1971. Christmas bird count, Henderson, Nevada. American Birds 25:469.

———. 1972. Christmas bird count, Henderson, Nevada. American Birds 26:486-487.

LEWIS, H. F. 1929. The natural history of the Double-crested Cormorant (*Phalacrocorax auritus auritus* [Lesson]). Ru-Mi-Lou, O'Hara, Canada. 94 pp.

LIES, M. F., AND W. H. BEHLE. 1966. Status of the White Pelican in the United States and Canada through 1964. Condor 68:279-292.

LOCKERBIE, C. W. 1939. Starlings arrive in Utah. Condor 41:170.

———. 1947. Utah Region. Audubon Field Notes 1:14-17, 161-162.

———. 1948. Utah Region. Audubon Field Notes 2:20-22.

———. 1951. Report on October fieldtrip to Lower City Creek Canyon. Utah Audubon News 3:53-54.

———. 1952. Christmas bird count, Salt Lake City, Utah. Audubon Field Notes 6:159-160.

———. 1953. Field notes. Utah Audubon News 5:79.

———. 1956. Christmas bird count, Salt Lake City, Utah. Audubon Field Notes 10:208-209.

LOCKERBIE, C. W., AND W. H. BEHLE. 1952.

Field notes. Utah Audubon News 4:17, 52–53.

LONG, W. S. 1936. Golden-crowned Sparrow in Zion National Park. Condor 38:89–90.

———. 1940. Lesser Loon and Wood Ibis in Utah. Condor 42:122.

———. 1943. Scott Oriole and Harris Sparrow in central Utah. Condor 45:39.

LORING, J. A. 1893. Field notes. U.S. Bureau of Biological Survey. Copy located in Brigham Young University Life Sciences Museum.

LOW, J. B., AND D. M. GAUFIN. 1946. An unusual flight of Sharp-tailed Grouse. Condor 48:180.

LOW, J. B., AND M. NELSON. 1945. Recent records of breeding waterfowl in Utah and southern Idaho. Condor 47:131–132.

LUND, B. 1967. Christmas bird count, Kanab, Utah. Audubon Field Notes 21:346.

———. 1968a. Christmas bird count, Kanab, Utah. Audubon Field Notes 22:360.

———. 1968b. Christmas bird count, Zion National Park, Utah. Audubon Field Notes 22:361.

———. 1970. Christmas bird count, St. George, Utah. Audubon Field Notes 24:415–416.

MARSHALL, J. T., AND W. H. BEHLE. 1942. The Song Sparrows of the Virgin River Valley, Utah. Condor 44:122–124.

MARSHALL, W. H. 1937a. A Blue Goose record from Utah. Condor 39:128.

———. 1937b. A Herring Gull record for Utah. Condor 39:258.

MAYR, E., AND L. L. SHORT. 1970. Species taxa of North American birds. Publication of the Nuttall Ornithological Club No. 9. 322 pp.

MERRIAM, C. H. 1873. Report on the mammals and birds of the expedition. Part 3. Pages 670–715 in F. V. Hayden, Sixth annual report of the United States Geological Survey of the territories embracing portions of Montana, Idaho, Wyoming, and Utah; being a report of progress of the expeditions for the year 1872. Washington, D.C.

MERRILL, J. C. 1888. Notes on the birds of Fort Klamath, Oregon. Auk 5:251–262.

MILLER, A. H. 1930. Two new races of the Loggerhead Shrike from western North America. Condor 32:155–156.

———. 1934. Field experiences with mountain-dwelling birds of southern Utah. Wilson Bulletin 46:156–168.

———. 1941. A review of centers of differentiation for birds in the western Great Basin region. Condor 43:257–267.

MILLER, A. H., AND T. T. MCCABE. 1935. Racial differentiation in Passerella (Melospiza) lincolnii. Condor 37:144–160.

MITCHELL, R. M. 1975. The current status of the Double-crested Cormorant in Utah: a plea for protection. American Birds 29:927–930.

MONSON, G. 1963. Southwest region. Audubon Field Notes 17:423–425.

———. 1964. Southwest region. Audubon Field Notes 18:61–64.

———. 1972. Southwest region. American Birds 26:100–104, 638–642, 791–794, 887–890.

———. 1973. Southwest region. American Birds 27:96–102, 803–806.

MOWBRAY, V. 1973. Christmas bird count, Desert Game Range, Nevada. American Birds 27:487.

———. 1974. Christmas bird count, Desert Game Range, Nevada. American Birds 28:495–496.

MURIE, S. 1963. Birding in Parowan, Utah. Utah Audubon News 15:45–46.

———. 1966. Birding in Parowan, Utah. Utah Audubon News 18:6–9.

MURPHY, J. R., F. J. CAMENZIND, D. G. SMITH, AND J. B. WESTON. 1969. Nesting ecology of raptorial birds in central Utah. Brigham Young University Science Bulletin, Biological Series 10:1–36.

MUSHBACK, G. E. 1932. The new home of our waterfowl. Utah Juniper 3:7–9, 39–40.

NELSON, E. W. 1875. Notes on birds observed in portions of Utah, Nevada, and California. Proceedings Boston Society of Natural History 17:338–365.

OATES, E. W. 1902. Catalogue of the collection of bird's eggs in the British Museum (Natural History) 2:338.

OBERHOLSER, H. C. 1899. The Flammulated Screech Owls, Megascops flammeolus (Kaup) and Megascops flammeolus idahoensis Merriam. Ornis 10(1):23–38.

———. 1911. A revision of the forms of the Hairy Woodpecker (Dryobates villosas [Linnaeus]). Proceedings U.S. National Museum 40:595–622.

———. 1918a. New light on the status of Empidonax traillii (Audubon). Ohio Journal of Science 18:85–98.

———. 1918b. Notes on the subspecies of Numenius americanus Beckstein. Auk 35:188–195.

———. 1921. A revision of the races of Dendroica auduboni. Ohio Journal of Science 21:240–248.

———. 1932. Descriptions of new birds from Oregon, chiefly from the Warner Valley region. Scientific Publications Cleveland Museum Natural History 4:1–12.

———. 1948. Descriptions of new races of

Geothlypis trichas (Linnaeus). Privately printed, Cleveland, Ohio. 4 pp.

——. 1974. The bird life of Texas. E. B. Kincaid, Jr., ed., with paintings by L. A. Fuertes, University of Texas Press, Austin and London. Vol. 1:1–530; 2:531–1069.

OSGOOD, W. 1908. Field notes. U.S. Bureau of Biological Survey. Copy located in Brigham Young University Life Sciences Museum.

PALMER, R. S., ed. 1962. Handbook of North American birds. Yale University Press, New Haven and London. 567 pp.

PARKER, T. 1974. Southwest region. American Birds 28:87–90.

PARKER, W. H., AND H. C. JOHNSON. 1899. Checklist of Utah bird eggs. Privately published. 2 pp.

PARKES, K. C. 1955. Systematic notes on North American birds. The herons and ibises (Ciconiiformes). Annals Carnegie Museum 33:287–293.

PEARSON, T. G. 1927. A-birding in Utah. Bird Lore 29:379–383.

PEDERSON, J. C., AND D. H. NISH. 1975. The Band-tailed Pigeon in Utah. Utah State Department of Natural Resources. Division of Wildlife Resources Publication No. 75-1. 75 pp.

PETERSON, R. T. 1961. A field guide to western birds, 2nd ed. Houghton Mifflin Company, Boston. 366 pp.

PHILLIPS, A. R. 1947. The races of MacGillivray's Warbler. Auk 64:296–300.

——. 1950. The pale races of the Steller Jay. Condor 52:252–254.

——. 1958. Las especies de la Codorniz de Gambel y el problema de las cambios climaticos en Sonora. Anales del Instituto de Biologia Universidad de Mexico 29:361–374.

PHILLIPS, A. R., J. MARSHALL, AND G. MONSON. 1964. The birds of Arizona. University of Arizona Press, Tucson. 212 pp.

PITELKA, F. A. 1945. Differentiation of the Scrub Jay, *Aphelocoma coerulescens*, in the Great Basin and Arizona. Condor 47:23–26.

——. 1950. Geographic variation and the species problem in the shore-bird genus *Limnodramus*. University of California Publications Zoology 50:1–108.

PLATT, J. B. 1976. Sharp-shinned Hawk nesting and nest selection in Utah. Condor 178:102–103.

POPOV, B. H. 1949. The introduced fishes, game birds, and game and fur-bearing mammals of Utah. Unpublished M.S. thesis, Utah State Agricultural College. Department of Zoology. 197 pp.

PORTER, R. D. 1954. Additional and new bird records for Utah. Condor 56:362–364.

——. 1955. The Hungarian Partr. Journal of Wildlife Management 19.

PORTER, R. D., AND J. B. BUSHMAN. 195. records for Utah. Wilson Bulletin 68:15.

——. 1957. Characteristics and status of Solitary Sandpiper in Utah. Condor 59:203–206.

PORTER, R. D., AND H. J. EGOSCUE. 1954. The Lark Bunting in Utah. Wilson Bulletin 66:219–221.

PORTER, R. D., AND H. KNIGHT. 1952. Records of the Black Pigeon Hawk, *Falco columbarius suckleyi*, in Utah. Auk 69:84–85.

PORTER, R. D., AND L. C. PRITCHETT. 1975. Black-throated Blue Warbler in Utah. Western Birds 6:31.

PORTER, R. D., AND C. M. WHITE in collaboration with R. J. ERWIN. 1973. The Peregrine Falcon in Utah, emphasizing ecology and competition with Prairie Falcon. Brigham Young University Science Bulletin, Biological Series 18:1–74.

PRATT, O. 1926. Extracts from the private journal of Orson Pratt. Utah Genealogical and Historical Magazine (July) 209–214.

PRESNELL, C. C. 1935a. Four new records from Zion National Park, Utah. Condor 37:82.

——. 1935b. The birds of Zion National Park. Proceedings Utah Academy of Sciences, Arts, and Letters 12:197–210.

——. 1937. Three new records from Bryce Canyon, Utah. Condor 39:259.

REMSEN, V., AND D. A. GAINES. 1974. Mid-Pacific coast region. American Birds 28:98–106.

REMY, J. 1860. Voyage au pays des Mormons. E. Dentu, Paris. Vol. 1:154; 2:222; 449–450.

REMY, J., AND J. BRENCHLEY. 1861. A journey to Great Salt Lake City with a sketch of the history, religion, and customs of the Mormons, and an introduction on the religious movement in the United States. W. Jeffs, London. Vol. 1, 501 pp.; Vol. 2, 605 pp.

RICH, W. J. T. 1967. The woodpeckers of Utah. Unpublished M.S. thesis, University of Utah. 130 pp.

RICHARDS, G. L. 1971. The common crow, *Corvus brachyrhynchos*, in the Great Basin. Condor 73:116–118.

RICHARDS, G. L., AND C. M. WHITE. 1963. Common crow nesting in Utah. Condor 65:530–531.

RICHMOND, C. W. 1902. *Parus inornatus griseus* renamed. Proceeding Biological Society of Washington 15:155.

RIDGWAY, R. 1873a. Notes on the bird-fauna of the Salt Lake Valley and the adjacent portions of the Wahsatch [sic] Mountains. Bulletin of the Essex Institute 5:168–173.

——. 1873b. The birds of Colorado. Bulletin of Essex Institute 5:174-195.

——. 1875. List of birds observed at various localities contiguous to the Central Pacific Railroad from Sacramento City, California, to Salt Lake Valley, Utah. Bulletin of the Essex Institute 7:10-24, 30-40.

——. 1877. Ornithology. Pages 303-643, 652-669 in Vol. 4, Part 3, in Report of the geological exploration of the fortieth parallel made by order of the Secretary of War according to acts of Congress of March 2, 1867 and March 3, 1869, under the direction of Brig. and Bvt. Major General A. A. Humphreys, Chief of Engineers by Clarence King. Professional papers of the Engineer Department, U.S. Army No. 18.

——. 1901. The birds of North and Middle America. Bulletin U.S. National Museum No. 50. Part 1. 715 pp.

ROGERS, T. H. 1974. Northern Rocky Mountains-Intermountain Region. American Birds 28:78-83.

RYDER, R. A. 1957. Christmas bird count Logan, Utah. Audubon Field Notes 11:215.

SCHROEDER, A. H. 1955. Archeology of Zion Park. University of Utah Anthropological Papers No. 22:1-212.

SCIPLE, G. W. 1953. Red Phalarope in Utah. Wilson Bulletin 65:205.

SCOTT, O. K. 1954. Great Basin, central Rocky Mountain region. Audubon Field Notes 8: 32-33, 322-323, 354-355.

——. 1957. Great Basin, central Rocky Mountain region. Audubon Field Notes 11:283-285, 367-368.

——. 1958. Great Basin, central Rocky Mountain region. Audubon Field Notes 12:47-49.

——. 1959. Great Basin, central Rocky Mountain region. Audubon Field Notes 13:51-53, 311-312, 390-391.

——. 1960. Great Basin, central Rocky Mountain region. Audubon Field Notes 14:58-60, 328-329, 409-410.

——. 1961. Great Basin, central Rocky Mountain region. Audubon Field Notes 15:346-348.

——. 1962. Great Basin, central Rocky Mountain region. Audubon Field Notes 16: 435-436.

——. 1963. Great Basin, central Rocky Mountain region. Audubon Field Notes 17: 53-54, 345-347, 422-423.

——. 1964. Great Basin, central Rocky Mountain region. Audubon Field Notes 18:60-61, 374-376.

——. 1965. Great Basin, Central Rocky Mountain Region. Audubon Field Notes 19: 63-64, 404-406, 500-501, 567-568.

——. 1966. Great Basin, central Rocky Mountain region. Audubon Field Notes 20:76-77, 535-537, 588-589.

——. 1967. Great Basin, central Rocky Mountain region. Audubon Field Notes 21: 62-64, 443-444, 527-528, 590-592.

——. 1968. Great Basin, central Rocky Mountain region. Audubon Field Notes 22:73-74, 560-562, 632-634.

——. 1969. Great Basin, central Rocky Mountain region. Audubon Field Notes 23:86-87, 503-504, 611-612, 679-680.

——. 1970. Great Basin, central Rocky Mountain region. Audubon Field Notes 24:74-75, 628-630.

——. 1971. Great Basin, central Rocky Mountain region. American Birds 25:84-86, 606-608.

SCOTT, P. 1974. Christmas bird count, Zion National Park, Utah. American Birds 28: 489.

SELANDER, R. K. 1953. Notes on the Red Crossbills of the Uinta and Wasatch Mountains. Condor 55:158-160.

——. 1954. A systematic review of the booming nighthawks of western North America. Condor 56:57-82.

SHARROCK, F. W. 1966. An archeological survey of Canyonlands National Park. Pages 49-84 in Miscellaneous Collected Papers 11-14, University of Utah Anthropological Papers No. 83.

SHARROCK, F. W., AND E. G. KEANE. 1962. Carnegie Museum collection from southeast Utah. University of Utah Anthropological Papers No. 57. 71 pp.

SHERWOOD, G. A. 1960. The Whistling Swan in the west with particular reference to Great Salt Lake Valley, Utah. Condor 62:370-377.

SIMPSON, J. H. 1876. Report of explorations across the Great Basin of the territory of Utah for a direct wagon-route from Camp Floyd to Genoa, in Carson Valley, in 1859. Engineer Department, U.S. Army. Government Printing Office, Washington, D.C. 518 pp.

SMITH, D. G., C. R. WILSON, AND H. H. FROST. 1970. Fall nesting Barn Owls in Utah. Condor 72:492.

——. 1972a. The biology of the American Kestrel in central Utah. Southwestern Naturalist 17:73-83.

——. 1972b. Seasonal food habits of Barn Owls in Utah. Great Basin Naturalist 32:229-234.

——. 1974. History and ecology of a colony of Barn Owls in Utah. Condor 76:131-136.

SNIDER, P. R. 1964. Southwest region. Audubon Field Notes 18:376-378, 526-528.

———. 1965. Southwest region. Audubon Field Notes 19:64-66, 501-503.

———. 1966. Southwest region. Audubon Field Notes 20:78-80, 446-448, 537-539, 589-591.

———. 1968. Southwest region. Audubon Field Notes 22:75-77.

———. 1969. Southwest region. Audubon Field Notes 24:612-615.

———. 1970. Southwest region. Audubon Field Notes 24:75-79, 526-528, 630-633.

———. 1971. Southwest region. American Birds 25:780-784.

SNOW, E. R. 1846-1849. Eliza R. Snow's journal. Microfilm of original located in Brigham Young University Library, Provo, Utah.

SNYDER, L. L. 1953. On eastern empidonaces with particular references to variation in *E. traillii*. Contributions Royal Ontario Museum of Zoology and Palaeontology No. 35:1-26.

SPRINGER, C. E. 1931. Wood Ibis in Utah. Bird Lore 33:120.

STALLCUP, R., AND R. GREENBERG. 1974. Mid-Pacific coast region. American Birds 28: 943-947.

STANFORD, J. S. 1931. Records of birds in central and southeastern Utah. Bulletin University of Utah 21, Biological Series 1:1-10.

———. 1937. Cormorant and heron colonies in Cache Valley, Utah. Proceedings Utah Academy of Sciences, Arts, and Letters 14: 195.

———. 1938. An annotated list of the birds in the USAC Zoological Museum. Proceedings of Utah Academy of Sciences, Arts, and Letters 15:135-146.

———. 1944. New records of birds collected for the USAC Zoological Museum. Proceedings Utah Academy of Sciences, Arts, and Letters 19-20:151.

———. 1969. An annotated check list of birds of Cache Valley, Utah-Idaho. Utah Academy of Sciences, Arts, and Letters 46:134-141.

STANSBURY, H. 1852. Explorations and survey of the valley of the Great Salt Lake of Utah, including a reconnoissance [sic] of a new route through the Rocky Mountains. Senate Special Session, March 1851. Executive No. 3. Lippincott, Grambo and Co., Philadelphia. 487 pp.

STATE FISH AND GAME COMMISSIONER. 1929. Utah Fish and Game Laws: Revision of 1929. Salt Lake City, Utah.

STATE OF UTAH DIVISION OF WILDLIFE RESOURCES. 1972. 40th biennial report July 1970 to July 1972. 48 pp.

STEVENSON, J. 1872. A list of mammals and birds collected in Wyoming Territory, by Mr. H. D. Smith and Mr. James Stevenson, during the expeditions of 1870. Pages 461-466 in F. V. Hayden, preliminary report of the United States Geological Survey of Wyoming, and portions of contiguous territories (being a second annual report of progress), conducted under the authority of the Secretary of the Interior, 42nd Congress, Second Session. House of Representatives Ex. Doc. No. 325. Government Printing Office, Washington, D.C.

STORER, R. W. 1971. Classification of birds. Pages 1-18 in D. S. Farner, J. R. King, and K. C. Parkes, Avian biology. Academic Press, New York.

STUART, R., AND G. STUART. 1973. Christmas bird count, Kanab, Utah. American Birds 27: 479.

SUGDEN, J. W. 1925. Purple Gallinule in Utah. Condor 27:210.

———. 1938. The status of the Sandhill Crane in Utah and southern Idaho. Condor 40: 18-22.

TALLEY, G. M. 1957. Common Grackle in Utah. Condor 59:400.

TANNER, V. M. 1927. Notes on birds collected in the Virgin River Valley of Utah. Condor 29:198-202.

———. 1936. The Western Mocking Bird [sic] in Utah. Proceedings Utah Academy of Sciences, Arts, and Letters 13:185-187.

———. 1941. Lesser Yellow Legs [sic] new record for Washington County, Utah. Great Basin Naturalist 2:86.

TANNER, V. M., AND C. L. HAYWARD. 1934. A biological study of the La Sal Mountains, Utah Report No. 1 (Ecology). Proceedings Utah Academy of Sciences, Arts, and Letters 11:209-235.

TAYLOR, H. G. 1949. Bird observations July 25 to August 25. Utah Audubon News 1:2-3.

TODD, W. E. C. 1963. Birds of the Labrador Peninsula and adjacent areas. University of Toronto Press, Toronto. 819 pp.

TREGANZA, A., E. TREGANZA, AND A. O. TREGANZA. 1914. A forty-five-year history of the Snowy Heron in Utah. Condor 16:245-250.

TWOMEY, A. C. 1942. The birds of the Uinta Basin, Utah. Annals of the Carnegie Museum 28:341-490.

———. 1944a. Notes on some birds taken in Utah. Condor 46:89.

———. 1944b. A correction of identification of sandpipers. Condor 46:90.

UTAH AUDUBON NEWS. 1949. Starling found nesting in Utah. 1:1.

———. 1952. Field notes. 4:52-53.

———. 1955. Field notes. 7:30.

——. 1962. The rare and unusual observations. 14:32.

——. 1963. Farmington Bay. 15:38.

——. 1964. The 1963 Christmas census. 16:2-3, 42.

VAN DEN AKKER, J. B. 1946. A Mountain Plover from Utah. Condor 48:246.

——. 1949. Great Basin, central Rocky Mountain region. Audubon Field Notes 3:23-26, 178-180.

VAN ROSSEM, A. J. 1945. The Golden-crowned Kinglet of Southern California. Condor 47:77-78.

VERBEEK, N. A. M. 1966. Wanderings of the Ancient Murrelet: some additional comments. Condor 68:510-511.

WARNER, T. J. 1975. The significance of the Domínguez-Velez de Escalante Expedition. Charles Redd Monographs in Western History 5:63-80.

WAUER, R. H. 1963. Christmas bird count, St. George, Utah. Audubon Field Notes 17:263.

——. 1964. Christmas bird count, St. George, Utah. Audubon Field Notes 18:292-293.

——. 1965a. Christmas bird count, Zion National Park. Audubon Field Notes 19:311.

——. 1965b. Wintering Rufous-crowned Sparrows found in Utah. Condor 67:447.

——. 1966a. Flammulated Owl records following May storms in Zion Canyon, Utah. Condor 68:211.

——. 1966b. Christmas bird count, St. George, Utah. Audubon Field Notes 20:351-352.

——. 1966c. Eastern Phoebe in Utah. Condor 68:519.

——. 1968. Northern range extension of Wied's Crested Flycatcher. Condor 70:88.

——. 1969. Recent bird records from the Virgin River Valley of Utah, Arizona, and Nevada. Condor 71:331-335.

WAUER, R. H., AND D. L. CARTER. 1965. Birds of Zion National Park and vicinity. Zion Natural History Association. Springdale, Utah. 92 pp.

WAUER, R. H., AND R. C. RUSSELL. 1967. New and additional records of birds in the Virgin River Valley. Condor 69:420-423.

WEBSTER, J. D. 1947. Notes on the birds of Utah. Condor 49:40-41.

WELLS, P. 1958. Indigo Buntings in Lazuli Bunting habitat in southwestern Utah. Auk 75:223-224.

WESTON, J. B., AND D. H. ELLIS. 1968. Ground nesting of the Ferruginous Hawk in west-central Utah. Great Basin Naturalist 28:111.

WETMORE, A. 1914-1916. Field notes. U.S. National Museum of Natural History, Washington, D.C.

——. 1960. A classification for the birds of the world. Smithsonian Miscellaneous Collection 139:1-37.

WHITE, C. M. 1968. Biosystematics of North American Peregrine Falcons. Unpublished Ph.D. dissertation, University of Utah. 195 pp.

WHITE, C. M., G. D. LLOYD, AND G. L. RICHARDS. 1965. Goshawk nesting in the upper Sonoran in Colorado and Utah. Condor 67:269.

WHITMORE, R. C. 1975. Indigo Buntings in Utah with special reference to interspecific relations with Lazuli Buntings. Condor 77:509-510.

WILLIAMS, C. S. 1942. Two new bird records for Utah. Auk 59:578.

WILLIAMS, C. S., G. H. JENSEN, AND C. COTTAM. 1943. Some birds not commonly observed in Utah. Condor 45:159-160.

WILSON, V. T. 1952. Christmas bird count. Bear River Migratory Bird Refuge, Utah. Audubon Field Notes 6:159.

——. 1965. Christmas bird count, Bear River Migratory Bird Refuge, Utah. Audubon Field Notes 19:309.

WILSON, V. T., AND R. H. NORR. 1949. Great Basin–central Rocky Mountain region. Audubon Field Notes 3:246-247.

——. 1950. Great Basin-central Rocky Mountain region. Audubon Field Notes 4:26-28.

——. 1951. Great Basin–central Rocky Mountain region. Audubon Field Notes 5:30-32.

WILSON, V. T., AND W. A. REID. 1958. First occurrence of Little Blue Heron in Utah. Auk 75:214.

WILSON, V. T., AND L. T. YOUNG. 1956. European Widgeon and Glaucous Gull in Utah. Condor 58:390.

WILT, R. 1973. Christmas bird count, Pipe Spring National Monument, Arizona. American Birds 27:483-484.

WOLFE, L. R. 1928. The breeding accipitres of Utah. Oologists' Record 8:90-102.

——. 1946. Pigeon Hawk breeding in Utah. Condor 48:97.

WOODBURY, A. M. 1937. A Brown Pelican record from Utah. Condor 29:225.

——. 1939. Bird records from Utah and Arizona. Condor 41:157-163.

WOODBURY, A. M., AND H. N. RUSSELL, JR. 1945. Birds of the Navajo country. Bulletin University of Utah 35, Biological Series 9:1-160.

WOODBURY, A. M., C. COTTAM, AND J. W. SUGDEN. 1949. Annotated check-list of the birds of Utah. Bulletin University of Utah 39, Biological Series 11:1-40.

WORTHEN, G. L. 1968. The taxonomy and distribution of the birds of the southeastern

Great Basin, Utah. Unpublished M.S. thesis, University of Utah. 588 pp.

———. 1972a. First-recorded specimens of the White-winged Crossbill from Utah. Wilson Bulletin 85:243–244.

———. 1972b. A record of an Indigo Bunting and a wintering Say's Phoebe for northern Utah. Great Basin Naturalist 32:220.

———. 1973a. Harlan's Hawk from Utah: first record for the Great Basin. Wilson Bulletin 85:79.

———. 1973b. First Utah record of the Baltimore Oriole. Auk 90:677–678.

WYMAN, G. H. 1889. Quail in Dixie. Forest and Stream 33:123.

YARROW, H. C. 1877. The Black Duck in the Rocky Mountains. Forest and Stream 8:4.

YARROW, H. C., AND H. W. HENSHAW. 1874. Report upon and list of birds collected by the expedition for explorations west of the one-hundredth meridian in 1872. Lieut. Geo. M. Wheeler, Corps of Engineers, in charge. Pages 5–33 in Report upon ornithological specimens collected in the years 1871, 1872, and 1873. Engineer Department, U.S. Army. Geographical and geological explorations and surveys, west of the one-hundredth meridian. Government Printing Office, Washington, D.C.

YOUNG, L. T. 1951. Christmas bird count, Bear River Migratory Bird Refuge, Utah. Audubon Field Notes 5:169.

ZIMMERMAN, D. A. 1962. Southwest region. Audubon Field Notes 16:496–498.

INDEX